TITUREL

❦ ❦ ❦

TITUREL

Wolfram of Eschenbach

❀ ❀ ❀

Translation and Studies by
CHARLES E. PASSAGE

Frederick Ungar Publishing Co.
New York

Copyright © 1984 by Frederick Ungar Publishing Co., Inc.
Printed in the United States of America

Library of Congress Cataloging in Publication Data

Wolfram, von Eschenbach, 12th cent.
  Titurel.

  I. Passage, Charles E.   II. Title.
PT1682.T6E56   1984   831'.2   84-28064
ISBN 0-8044-2181-1
ISBN 0-8044-6142-2 (pbk.)

Contents

❀ ❀ ❀

Preface
🎕 🎕 🎕

UNFINISHED WORKS by great authors have a special fascination, and so it is with the two discontinuous sections of a story-poem by Wolfram of Eschenbach that goes by the name of *Titurel*. The longer First Fragment, stately and stylized, prepares for a love story to follow and also sheds light upon Wolfram's masterpiece *Parzival* by reintroducing several characters from that poem. The shorter Second Fragment relates a single woodland episode of memorable beauty. The opening chapter of the present book, after a brief account of the manuscripts involved, offers the first complete translation of the two Fragments into English.*

Some decades after Wolfram's time a Bavarian poet named Albrecht—whether or not "of Scharfenberg" remains moot— "completed" this work as a novel-length romance known as "The Later Titurel" (*Der Jüngere Titurel*). Immensely admired *as a work by Wolfram of Eschenbach* both in the late medieval centuries and again upon its rediscovery in the Romantic period, this long romance, in rhymed quatrains, of fine passages and of admitted *longueurs*, has gravely declined in esteem since the 1840s or so, but its significance remains considerable for literary history, for

* Hitherto *Titurel* has been accessible to English-language readers only in the writings of Margaret F. Richey: a partial verse rendition of the First Fragment in 1926, reissued in 1960; then a partial prose rendition of the Second Fragment, with interconnecting summaries, in 1960; and finally a paraphrase of both Fragments in *Modern Language Review*, 56 (1961), pp. 180–193.
A line-by-line version of the First Fragment in French prose by Jean Fourquet appeared in *Lumière du Graal*, Paris, 1951, pp. 235–262. A complete rendition into modern German was published in 1971 by Walter Johannes Schröder and Gisela Hollandt; Darmstadt: *Wissenschaftliche Buchgesellschaft*. Previous modern German versions were made by Karl Simrock, 1842, and by Albert Rapp, 1925.

the spiritual history of central Europe, and for Grail studies. Conceived on a grand scale, it comprises two distinct stories, one about Titurel and the Grail and one about the young lovers Schionatulander and Sigune, this latter—running to nearly 22,000 lines—being encapsulated between the two halves of the former. Our second chapter is devoted to an account of the total work and to the principal scholarship about it,—the first such account, we believe, in English.

Into his long central romance about the young lovers and about the fateful dog Gardeviaz, Albrecht incorporated all 170 quatrains of Wolfram's two Fragments, rewording them stanza by stanza, bridging the gap between them, and carrying the story to conclusion. Since the 1830s the besetting question has been: to what extent—if any—does this full scenario represent Wolfram's original plan? Our third chapter proposes an answer to this troublesome question. First, by extracting the basic scenario from the mass of ornament imposed upon it by Albrecht, and then by tracing Keltic analogues of the characters and situation, we infer the main origins and nature of the source work. In our opinion, the same lost narrative poem, in Old French, served as the basis for both Wolfram's partial, and Albrecht's complete, scenarios.

Our fourth chapter explores the hero's claim to the title of *Dauphin* and to the territory of Grésivaudan—Wolfram's *Grâswaldân*—near Grenoble. We find the hero's mother, Mahaute, to have been a historical personage of that name, whose title in preserved Latin records of the region is "Queen of England."

By rights, our Chapter V should follow the "List of 57 Proper Names in Wolfram's *Titurel*," upon which it depends to some degree. Entitled "Angevins and Iberians," it collects historical data considerably more extensive than hitherto assembled and analyses the use of these data in the creation of both *Parzival* and *Titurel*. The process of gathering the information and of making literature from it must, we explain, have been the work of some person other than Wolfram, who then served as Wolfram's informant. We believe this person was "Kyot the Provençal."

The "List of 57 Proper Names in Wolfram's *Titurel*," placed last in the book, is a kind of dictionary. Each entry digests information about the character or place from both *Parzival* and *Titurel*, occasionally from *Willehalm* and elsewhere, reviews the principal explanations of the 57 terms by scholars since 1870, and then, in many cases, proposes new interpretations. The List seeks to be objective; the implications derived from it are the concern of Chapter V. In the onomasticon special attention is given to the hitherto neglected Keltic element.

In this book we have not sought to compose oracles, nor a facile popularization, nor a scholarly disputation. The subject is many-sided and fascinating, and we aim at that wider readership that is always pleased to discover an excellent story long obscured.

C. E. P.
Dansville, New York

·I·

ABOUT THE TEXT
OF WOLFRAM'S TITUREL

AMONG THE SEVENTEEN preserved manuscripts of the complete *Parzival*, Manuscript G is unique in that it also contains, along with two lyric poems of Sir Wolfram of Eschenbach, the text of an unfinished work, undoubtedly his, that goes by the name of *Titurel*. Marti (Introduction, p. LVIII) dates this Manuscript G, which is kept in Munich, "presumably between 1228 and 1236," which is to say within a decade of 1226, the probable year of the poet's death.

The subject of this unfinished work is the love story of two young people, Schionatulander and Sigune, whose destinies are known from *Parzival*. In Book III of that work (138,9 ff.) the youthful Parzival comes riding through uninhabited country to discover the lady Sigune in frantic lamentation over the corpse of Schionatulander which she is holding across her lap. He has just been slain in a joust with Duke Orilus de Lalander. Later portions of the poem will relate how Sigune lived out the years of her life in a hermitage, ever praying and mourning beside the embalmed body of her chaste lover. Necessarily, then, the love story of these young persons is antecedent to the death of Schionatulander a half-hour or so before the scene in *Parzival* 138,9 ff. As to the long-traditional title of *Titurel* for this love story, it is customarily explained from the occurrence of that name in the opening line of text.

In sharp contrast to the short tetrameter and trimeter couplets of both *Parzival* and *Willehalm*, the unfinished *Titurel* is narrated in long lines grouped in quatrains rhymed a—a—b—b. The metrical pattern resembles, but is not identical with, the long lines of the *Nibelungenlied* quatrains; *this* stanza pattern is Wolfram's own, invented no doubt for this particular work. Because of unpredictable up-beat syllables the cadence hovers between trochaic and iambic, and because of other unpredictable syllables the lines are sometimes difficult to scan. In each line except the third, a caesura or breath-pause divides the long line into two half-lines. The basic, but not invariable, pattern is as follows:

Line 1   3 (or 4) strong beats—caesura—3 strong beats
Line 2   3 (or 4) strong beats—caesura—5 strong beats
Line 3   5 strong beats (with no caesura)
Line 4   3 (or 4) strong beats—caesura—5 strong beats

The a—a—b—b rhymes are regularly feminine, i.e., they end with an unaccented syllable, e.g., in the opening stanza: *gerüeren/gefüeren* and *lerne/gerne*. Stanza 51 of our translation, even though it lacks the feminine endings, gives a fair impression of the *Titurel* verse form.

Manuscript G presents 164 such stanzas; but fragments of a second manuscript, M, also from Munich and also from the thirteenth century, contain 45 *Titurel* stanzas, while a sixteenth-century manuscript, H, contains 68 *Titurel* stanzas, with the result that a *Titurel* text is plagued with eleven stanzas which are not found in Manuscript G. For these extra stanzas no satisfactory explanation has been found. There are also discrepancies in wording and in stanza sequence. Since the 1830s, however, six of the dubious stanzas—30, 31, 33, 34, 36, and 53—have been admitted, under suspicion, so that *Titurel* texts have regularly counted 170, not 164, stanzas total. Marti relegates the six to Appendix I (p. 249) but keeps the now-traditional numbering; Leitzmann brackets them in their positions; our translation shows them, in their positions, in smaller typeface. Readers may judge for themselves as to their value.

The traditional "editors' text" of 170 stanzas divides into two unequal portions, a "First Fragment" of 131 stanzas and a "Second Fragment" of 39 stanzas (132–170), with an obvious time lapse and with breaking of the story line in between. The First Fragment begins with the aged and enfeebled Titurel's speech of abdication from the Grail kingship in favor of his son Frimutel. The five children of Frimutel—all significant characters in *Parzival*—are named by the resigning king, but attention soon passes to daughter Schoysiane (previously the Grail Bearer, 24,3–4), to Schoysiane's marriage to Duke Kyot of Katelangen, to her death in giving birth to Sigune, and to subsequent circumstances of her family. Stanzas 26–36 regard Frimutel's daughter Herzeloyde, the "virgin-widow" of King Kastis, from whom she inherited the two kingdoms of Waleis and Norgals. To her is brought the five-year-old Sigune, her niece, for rearing.

In stanza 37 the poet says he "will pass over in silence" Gahmuret's love relationships with the French queen Anphlise and with Belacane and the story of how he came to marry Herzeloyde, thus recalling in a mere four lines the subject matters of Books I and II of *Parzival*. Wolfram then proceeds to an account of Schionatulander's ancestry, remarking in 39,4 that Schionatulander "will be the lord of this adventure," i.e., the hero of the present story.

The contents of the First Fragment may be outlined as follows:

Stanzas
1—36   Ancestry and childhood of Sigune, heroine of the poem, offspring of the Grail dynasty, and great-granddaughter of Titurel.

37—   Allusion to Gahmuret's three love relationships in Books I and II of *Parzival*.

38—56   Ancestry and childhood of Schionatulander, hero of the poem.

57—72   Schionatulander's love suit to Sigune.

73—82   As Gahmuret's squire, Schionatulander departs with

The topical distribution reveals that the first 36 stanzas concerning Sigune are balanced by 36 stanzas concerning Schionatulander, i.e. 38–72 plus the obviously missing quatrain after stanza 63. Stanza 37, about Gahmuret's three loves, is a transition stanza. Without the six "dubious" stanzas, however, this neat symmetry is undone.

Ten stanzas, 73–82, explain how the lovers came to be separated, and then follow the two "colloquies" of 25 and 24 stanzas respectively. The one-stanza disparity is unexplained. In this First Fragment verbal stylization matches organizational stylization, and herein lies the modern reader's initial difficulty— and, on closer consideration, his greater delight.

Up to stanza 82 all events occur prior to Gahmuret's departure for the East in *Parzival* 101,21, though in that poem neither of the young lovers has been mentioned yet. The two colloquies, 83–107 and 108–131, take place during the period of the outward journey.

The present poem stresses the tender years of these two children in love but specifies no ages. Schionatulander has been a page to the French queen Anphlise and is now a squire to Gahmuret; traditionally such assignments were made at ages seven and fourteen, respectively, but our impression is that tradition has not been followed in this case. The modern reader craves to know the ages of these "children" who exchange statements about serious love in stanzas 57–72. The only clue, in 72,1, is to the effect that the lad is yet too young to use weapons. Age ten would leave some modern readers incredulous. Age twelve is possible. (It may be irrelevant to recall Gotfried of Strassburg's remark in *Tristan* 17,140–1 about having known love since age eleven.) Under "Schionatulander" in the List of Proper Names

(p. 192 below), "A Schionatulander Chronology" presents our considered estimate of the matter; for the moment we mention only that we take the *future* "lord of this adventure" to be fifteen as of the description of him in stanza 89 on the eve of his departure for the East. Sigune might "appropriately" be a year or so younger—at Juliet's age of fourteen. By our calculations the precocious love of these "children" has already gone on for about two years. Let us note here the author's insistence, at all stages of their story, upon the chasteness of their passion. A passion at once so intense and so chaste must, we feel, end in disaster. And so it proves.

What interval of time separates the two Fragments cannot be exactly determined. From *Parzival* 109,5 we must allow eighteen weeks between Gahmuret's (and Schionatulander's) departure for the East and the bringing of the news of Gahmuret's death "before Baldac," but there must be an indeterminate further interval before we find the young lovers encamped, with attendants, in a summer woodland. Schionatulander is likely to be sixteen now—the year which medievals considered the transition year from boyhood into young manhood. At most, he is seventeen. It is our impression that he is still a squire and not yet a knight.

"They had not long been thus encamped," begins the Second Fragment, when Schionatulander hears the barking of a hunting dog on the track of some prey through the forest. He outruns the animal, catches it, and carries it in his arms to Sigune. Tied to the dog's "Arabian" (*arâbensch*) collar is a seventy-foot length of leash composed of four silken strands of different colors, with pearl clasps at hand's-breadth intervals, and in between the clasps a message is spelled out in jewels that are fastened to the silks by golden nails. In the tent Sigune reads the beginning of the message while her *ami* is off fishing, bare-legged in a brook, for perch and trout. In order to disengage more of the jeweled message she unties the leash from the tentpole—and the dog gets away from her. Off he runs again, this dog named Gardeviaz, loud on the trail of some quarry and dragging the leash behind him. Sigune must have that dog and leash back, she declares, and she promises Schionatulander her love if he will get them for her. Rashly the youth vows to perform that task. There the 39 stanzas (132–170) of the Second Fragment break off. From *Parzival* 138–141 we know that Schionatulander perished in that quest: "It was a hound's leash that brought him mortal pain," says 141,16—unintelligibly in the context. But how long had the quest gone on? The answer depends on the age of Parzival, who had not yet been born at the end of the First Fragment, and who is now here talking with the grief-distracted Sigune as a youth newly set out from home on adventures. Once again we guess his age as sixteen, by which token Schionatulander must be thirty at least, and the quest must have gone on for fourteen or fifteen years. And were the dog and leash never recovered? *Parzival* contains no hint of an answer. Yet, as the present study will reveal, we are not wholly without clues as to what happened after stanza 170.

Critics have lavished praise on this unfinished work. Jacob Grimm found it superior to *Willehalm* and even to *Parzival*. Editor Karl Müllenhoff (1879) termed it the supreme piece of Middle High German poetry. Twentieth-century commentators have been more reserved, suggesting that it was an "experiment" or that the difficulty of its stanza pattern led to its abandonment. Margaret Richey (1961) has reverent praise for it and yet defines it as

> . . . a lyrical recreation of epic (i.e., narrative) material derived from *Parzival*, constructed therefore not as a straightforward tale but as a series of situations with threads of connecting narrative, . . .

As to the time of composition, there is an *apparently* idle span of years between *Parzival* and *Willehalm*—1212 to 1216, at a guess—when the poet might have undertaken—and abandoned—*Titurel*, and without some knowledge of *Parzival* the First Fragment is unintelligible. To those unattested years Richey would date the poem's beginning; then she would have Wolfram work alternately on both *Titurel* and *Willehalm* and leave both poems unfinished at his death (around 1220). We distrust this on-again-off-again schedule, which, we feel, was designed to accommodate Richey's impressions of the *Titurel* Fragments as the creation of an aging, nostalgic, and probably ailing poet. To our notion, both Fragments are sure-handed, with no sign of deliquescent poetic powers. A hint of illness, and perhaps of aging, *is* to be found in *Willehalm* (4,15), and we are persuaded that *that* unfinished work was composed last in Wolfram's career. Nor can we believe that metrical difficulties caused the abandonment of *Titurel*. Abandonment was forced by the large-scale *Willehalm*, we feel, and death cut *that* work short around 1226, rather than around 1220.

We here submit our own suggested chronology for *Parzival* and *Titurel*:

1 In the 1190s, probably before 1194—a first and shorter version of *Parzival*, based on Chrétien's "Perceval," and representing the later Books III through VI, possibly also VII through IX. (Might this version be the one reflected in *Wigalois*?)

—Th. C. van Stockum: *Wolframs* Parzival *und das Problem der Quelle*, in *Neophilologus*, XXVI (1940), pp. 13–24; p. 23: So will es mir also vorkommen, dass die—heute—wahrscheinlichste Lösung für das Quellenproblem des Parzival diese ist: Wolfram habe zunächst nur den Perceval des Crestien gekannt, im Verlauf seiner Arbeit jedoch—und zwar spätestens bei der Abfassung des 9. Buches—das Gralwerk des "Kyot" kennen gelernt, das ihn zu einer Umarbeitung der Bücher 3 bis 6 (bzw 8) teilweise auch der Bücher 1 und 2 (Anjou!), veranlasst habe und auch für die Fortführung der Erzählung nicht ohne Einfluss geblieben sei.

—Fourquet (1949), p. 249: "Si l'on admet avec nous que le *Parzival* a été composé en deux fois, et qu'il y a eu un *Urparzival*, . . ."

2 Also around 1194–95—a Schionatulander romance, in quatrains, *begun* on the basis of a source work to be identified in pp. 70 ff. below and now represented by the *second* Fragment of *Titurel*.

3 From about 1200 to about 1212—the final version of *Parzival*, incorporating material furnished since 1194 about

the Gahmuret story, about the Angevins, about the Grail dynasty, and so on.

Though the *name* "Schionatulander" is used, the personage is introduced only as a man already dead. The story of the quest for the dog's leash is reserved for the unfinished Schionatulander romance, i.e. *Titurel*.

4 From about 1212 to about 1216—composition of the *First* Fragment of *Titurel* as a prologue to the Schionatulander romance and closely coordinated with Books I and II of *Parzival*; and excision of the original prefatory matter of the Schionatulander romance, (now unusable on account of the *new* First Fragment), leaving the *second* Fragment of *Titurel* to begin, in harsh abruptness, with: "They had not long been thus encamped."

5 In the 1212–1216 period—Landgrave Herman of Thuringia (died April 25, 1217) procured for Wolfram a manuscript of the French poem of *Aliscans*, (*Willehalm* 3,8–9), perhaps with the request that it be turned into a German poem.

—From preparatory study of *Aliscans* the name "Ahkarin" was carried over into *Titurel* 40,2 and into *Willehalm* 45,16 for the Baruch left nameless in *Parzival*. The name of "Acarin" seems to be unique in *Aliscans* 1428. With less certainty about the source, parallel claims might be made for the name "Berbester" and for the "heathen" title of *admirât*: both occur in *Titurel* and in *Willehalm* but not in *Parzival*.

6 Before 1217—work on *Willehalm*, possibly at Landgrave Herman's urging, obliged the poet to discontinue work on his Schionatulander romance,—with the result that no more of it was ever composed.

Herewith we proceed to our prose translation of Wolfram's two *Titurel* Fragments, the first complete rendering into English.*

* Our translation follows, primarily, the *Titurel* text in pp. 206–248 of Volume III of Marta Marti's re-edition, 1927–1932, with supplementary notes, of Karl Bartsch's three-volume edition of *Parzival* and *Titurel*, 1870–71. We also consulted Albert Leitzmann's text of *Titurel* in *Altdeutsche Textbibliothek*, No. 16, Tübingen, 1958 reprint of the 1928 printing, pp. 163–184; original edition 1905.

Discrepancies between these two texts are mentioned in footnotes in the few cases where the differences seemed significant.

The First Fragment: Stanzas 1–131*

As long as strong Titurel could still bestir himself, he   1
made bold to take himself and his men into battle. Later on,
in old age, he said: "I learn that I must renounce the spear-
shaft, which once I wielded gladly and well. If I could bear
arms," said the doughty man, "the air would be honored   2
with the snapping of spears from my hand and splinters would
give shade from the sun. Many crests upon helmets have caught
fire from my sword's blade.

"If ever I received noble love's solace, if love's sweet-   3
ness bestowed its blessed power upoon me, and if ever greeting
was given me by a lovely woman, all that has now become
wholly alien to me in my sad yearning. My good fortune, my
self-restraint, my steadfastness and good sense, and   4
whatever high praise my hand achieved by gift-giving and in
combat, these young successors of mine cannot undo. Indeed,
my entire race cannot help but inherit love ever true, together
with loyalty. I well know that self-restraint and stead-   5
fastness are close to the heart of a man who meets with women's
smiles. Never will those two things be far apart, except at death
alone: otherwise they cannot be sundered.

"When I received the Grail, after the annunciation   6
which the noble angel host brought me in its lofty power, I found
my entire Rule inscribed thereon. Before *me*, that gift had never
been vouchsafed to human hands. The lord of the Grail must
be chaste and pure. Alas, sweet Frimutel, of my children   7
I retained none for the Grail save you alone, so receive now the
Grail's crown and the Grail, my fair son!

"My son, you have in your time tilled shield-work   8
with spear-charges, and whenever your wheel stuck fast I res-
cued you unfailingly out of the knightly press. Now, my son,
you must fight alone: *my* strength is about to desert both of us.

"God has granted you, my son, five noble children,   9
and they are a much-blessed and noble company here for the
Grail. Anfortas, and Trevrezent the swift: may I live to hear their

* The numbers in the right-hand margin indicate the stanza numbers of the
original.

fame grow loud before all other fame! Your daughter, Schoy-
siane, has so many excellences in her heart that the   10
world thrives in blessings from them; Herzeloyde is of the same
mind; praise of others cannot silence the praise of Urrepanse de
Schoye."

Knights and ladies heard this speech. Sorrow could   11
be seen in the heart of many a templar[1] whom he had delivered
many a time out of hard straits when he was defending the Grail
with his own hand and with their help. Thus Titurel the strong
had become Titurel the weak, from both advanced age   12
and the strain of illness, and upon Muntsalvaesche Frimutel
worthily possessed the Grail: *that* was the thing of uttermost
desire[2] across the realm of earth.

Two of his daughters were of the age ripe for noble   13
love in a beloved's arms. Many kings from many lands wooed
Schoysiane's love in seemly fashion, but she bestowed it upon
a ruling prince: Kiot of Katelangen won Schoysiane.   14
Never was lovelier maiden seen beneath sun or moon, and in
her he found reward for his many virtues. Toward high renown
his heart was ever undismayed by cost or action. Amid splendor
she was brought home and received there with rich   15
display. King Tampunteire, his brother, came to Katelangen,
and wealthy princes were there: such lavish marriage festivities
had not been seen for many a year. Kiot, the country's lord,
had won fame by his generosity and bravery, and his   16
prowess was far from impaired whenever combat was required
with onrush of horses and wherever men rode in resplendent
array to the joust for the sake of women's reward. Did ever
prince win dearer wife! And what heart's bliss he felt,   17
as was Love's will for both of them! Alas for that. Now his grief
draws near. Thus ends the world: sweetness for all of us must
ever turn bitter in the end.

---

[1] The knights defending the Grail castle and its territory are "templars," but
not "Templars," as explained on pp. 203–205 below.

[2] "The thing of uttermost desire" = *der wunsch*, "the wish." This term occurs
13 times in *Parzival*; in P 235,21–24 Wolfram says: ". . . the perfection (*wunsch*)
of Paradise. . . . That was a thing called the Grail, which surpasses all earthly
perfection" (*erden wunsches überwal*).

At the proper time his wife presented him with a   18
child.—God spare me such a dweller in my household, for
whom I should have to pay so dearly! As long as I have my senses,
such a wish will hardly come from me!—In death Schoysiane,
the sweet and steadfast, bore a daughter, who was to   19
have much goodness about her. All womanly honor was in her,
and she practiced such great loyalty that it is still talked about
in many lands. In this way the prince's sorrow was   20
interlaced with loving joy: his young daughter lived and her
mother lay dead. That is what he had from those two. Schoy-
siane's death helped him borrow the loss of true joy and the
gain of grief for ever more.[3] Then the lady was with sorrow
committed to earth, though first she had to be   21
embalmed with aromatics and balsam, because it was necessary
to delay burial for a long time: from all parts many kings and
princes came to the interment.

The prince had his land in fief from his brother Tam-   22
punteire, who was known as the King of Pelrapeire, and he now
begged him to confer it upon his little daughter, since he was
himself renouncing sword, helmet, and shield. Duke Manfilot
beheld much grief in his noble brother,[4] and that was   23
a bitter sight to his eyes. From grief, he too renounced his sword,
so that neither of the two sought noble love or jousting any
more.

"Sigune" was the name the child received in bap-   24
tism. Her father, Kiot, had paid a dear price for her, because
through her he was bereft of her mother. She by whom the Grail
first permitted itself to be carried, that was Schoysiane. Then
King Tampunteire took the little Sigune with him to   25
his daughter Kondwiramurs. Kiot kissed her, weeping greatly.
Kondwiramurs was also an infant at the breast. The two of them
grew up as playmates, and in such a way that no word was ever
spoken about their loss of renown.

At that same time Kastis died, who had also wooed   26

[3] The metaphor of "borrowing" is oddly muddled.
[4] There are *three* brothers: 1 King Tampunteire, 2 Prince (*vürst*) Kiot, and 3
Duke Manfilot. The latter two now renounce knighthood in order to live as pious
hermits.

the fair Herzeloyde at Muntsalvatsch. Upon that lovely lady he had bestowed Kanvoleiz, and Kingrivals too, and in both those cities his head had worn the crown before princes. Kastis never won Herzeloyde as a wife, and it was in Gahmuret's   27 arms that she yielded her virginal self. All the same, she, sweet Frimutel's child who had been sent there from Muntsalvatsch,[5] became the mistress over two lands.[6]

Then Tampunteire died, and fair Kardeiz also, who   28 in Brubarz wore the crown,[7] and this was in the fifth year of Sigune's being cared for there. Whereupon they had to part, those two girl playmates young and not old at all. Queen Herzeloyde thought of Sigune and most earnestly begged   29 to have the child brought to her from Brubarz. Kondwiramurs began to weep at the thought of losing her company and her steadfast affection.

(The child said, "Dear father, let me have   30* a box full of dolls,[8] now that I am going to my aunt's, and I

---

[5] In P 494,13–14 it is stated that: "The men God sends forth secretly (from the Grail); the maidens leave openly."

[6] P 494 also explains that King Kastis married Herzeloyde at Munsalvaesche but died on the journey home, so that the marriage was not consummated. Nevertheless he willed her his two lands: Waleis (capital city Kanvoleiz) and Norgals (capital city Kingrivals), by virtue of which his "virgin widow" became *Queen* Herzeloyde.

[7] Tampunteire and his son Kardeiz(-1) were successive kings of Brubarz, capital city Pelrapeire.

[8] In dubious stanzas 30, 31, 33, 34, and 36 Wolfram either echoes his own works or is being echoed by a subsequent, unidentified poet. *Willehalm* 33,24–25 speaks of Wolfram's own daughter's doll, which, splendidly arrayed as it is, cannot equal the attire of certain pagan knights.

Similar to 31,3 "My care sleeps . . . ," P 550,10 has "Our good fortune wakes," i.e., is not asleep.

Like 31,4, both P 379 and *Willehalm* 390 speak of using up the Black Forest (in SW Germany, ca. 240 km/150 m SW of Eschenbach) for making spears.

33,4 sounds very much like the description of Alice, "the young, pure, sweet, fair girl" in *Willehalm* 154,9.

Dubious stanza 34 has the inner rhymes characteristic of "The Later Titurel;" see p. 37 below.

Dubious stanza 36,3–4 declares that "hybris" of Sigune which we find in stanzas 165 ff. of the Second Fragment and on which the tragic outcome of the story depends.

will be all ready for the journey. There lives many a knight
who will yet engage himself in my service."
    "Bless me! Such a noble child, with such   31*
sensible ideas! May God grant you Katelangen for a long time,
to be its noble mistress. My care sleeps as long as your welfare
wakes. If the Black Forest were in this country, it would all
be made into spearshafts for your sake.")

Thus Kiot's child Sigune grew up with her mother's   32
sister, and whoever saw her preferred her to the radiance of
Maytime amid the dewy flowers. Up from her heart grew grace
and honor together. Let her grow up to the years when praise
is due, and I will report still more praise of her.

    (Of all that may be reckoned as being in a   33*
pure woman's favor, not so much as a hair's breadth of it
was omitted in her sweet self. She was the stainless scion,
undefiled and without fault, noble Schoysiane's very child
and of quality identical, this chaste, young, pure girl.
    Now we must also take thought of Herze-   34*
loyde the pure: she could not detract from *her* renown, and I
credit that lady with true goodness. As the very fountainhead
of all womanly honor, she well deserved having her praise
increased in all lands.)

The virgin widow, Frimutel's daughter: wherever   35
praise of women was spoken in her early years, no other's praise
resounded so loud and clear. Her fame traveled afar to many
kingdoms, and before Kanvoleiz her love was won with on-
slaughts of spears.

    (Now hear strange wonders about the   36*
maiden Sigune. When her little breasts became rounded and
her wavy hair began to turn brown, then pride rose in her
heart and she began to be haughty and frivolous, yet she did
so with womanly kindness.)

How Gahmuret left Belacane, and how he splendidly   37
won Schoysiane's sister, and how he broke away from the

French queen:[9] all that I will pass over in silence here, and I shall tell you about a maiden's love.

To the French Queen Anphlise there was a lad en-   38
trusted; he was born of princely stock and of high lineage, and he could not do other than shun all things that destroy renown. When all princes shall have been born, none shall ever strive better for fame. When Gahmuret received a shield from   39
Anphlise,[10] the noble Queen presented him with this lad. We must ever praise him, for he had the true sweetness of a boy. He will be the lord of this adventure. Through him I rightly salute all youths. This same lad traveled with the An-   40
gevin across into heathendom to the Baruch Ahkarin, and Gahmuret brought him back again to Waleis.[11] When lads witness valor, it helps them if they are ever to become men.

I shall tell you something of the lad's lineage. His   41
grandfather was Gurnemanz of Graharz, who could split iron, and he did so in the joust with many an onslaught. His father's name was Gurzgri and he died "for Schoydelacurte."[12] Mahaute was his mother's name, a sister of Ehkunat, the rich   42
Count Palatine who was known as "from strong Berbester." His own name was Schionatulander. In his time such high renown was won not by just one man or another. The fact that I did not mention noble Gurzgri's son before the maiden Sigune   43

---

[9] The three lines 37,1–3 allude to most of the subject matter in Books I and II of *Parzival*. Gahmuret abandoned his first "wife" Belacane in P 54–58, at the end of Book I; P 61–100 describe the tournament at Kanvoleiz, in which he won Herzeloyde as his bride; his original "lady" was Queen Amflise of France, and P 87–96 tell how that queen contested the awarding of Herzeloyde as tournament prize and how a "court of law," i.e., a "court of love," found in Herzeloyde's favor.

[10] I.e., at his knighting.

[11] The word "presented" = *lech*, "lent." Marti's note suggests that Schionatulander was already 15–16 years old at the time. He must, rather, have been 11–12 years old: he accompanied Gahmuret to the East, parallel to P 13–14, and Gahmuret brought him back to Christendom and then on to Waleis; some 2–3 years must elapse before the two of them go to the aid of the Baruch a *second* time, parallel to P 101 ff.

"He *will be* the lord of this adventure" means the future hero of the present story. Compare P 338,7, where Parzival is "the lord of this tale," i.e., of *Parzival*.

[12] "Schoydelacurte" ("Joy of the Court") is the name of an *adventure* in *Erec*. See the List of Proper Names.

was because her mother had been sent forth from the rich Grail and her high birth and fair kinfolk gave her precedence. All the Grail company are elect, ever blessed here   44 and destined for unfailing fame hereafter. Now, Sigune was also of that same seed which was strewn abroad in the world from Muntsalvatsch and received by those capable of salvation. Wherever any of that seed was brought from that land,   45 there it unfailingly bore fruit, and it also fell as a hailstorm upon wrongdoing.[13] Hence Kanvoleiz is renowned afar, and in many languages it was termed the capital city of loyalty. O well for thee, Kanvoleiz, that they tell thy steadfastness and   46 the heartfelt love that dwelt—and not too late—in thee! Early, rather, love rose there between two young people, and proceeded so clear and pure that the whole world could not discover any of its own impurity in them.

Proud Gahmuret reared these young people, with   47 each other, in his household. When Schionatulander was still short of maturity[14] he was, in spite of that, bound in his heart's distress by Sigune's love. Alas for that! They are still   48 too inexperienced for such suffering. But where love is caught in youth it lasts longest. Age may renounce love, but youth still dwells in love's bond, and love is undeprived of power. Alas for Love! What did your power avail between children?   49 Yet one who has no eyes could see you even if he were blind. Love, you are of all too many kinds, and not all the scribes together could ever exhaust the description of your nature and your ways. Even an actual monk, even a true hermit,   50 is entreated "for love's sake," so far as their wills are obedient, however little they may be inclined to do many things; and love compels the knight in arms. Yet love takes up so little room.

Love has seized upon   the narrow and the broad,   51
Love here upon this earth   and in heaven also walks before God;
Love is in all places save in hell.

[13] The "seed" are the men of the Grail family, whom God sends forth secretly, and the daughters, who leave openly, for the doing of good in the world; P 494,13–14 and note 5 above.
[14] We guess Schionatulander's age as 13–14 at this point.

Strong Love will weaken in her strength   if   wavering   doubt   and
                                                  inconstancy with her dwell.

Unwavering and undoubting both was the maiden   52
Sigune, and Schionatulander too, and in their sorrow great love
was mingled.[15] I would tell you a great deal about their child-
hood, except that it would take too long.

> (Their modest manners and the quality of   53*
> their lineage—for they were born of purest love—constrained
> them to proper conduct, so that outwardly they hid their love
> in secrecy while inwardly they suffered torment in their
> hearts.)

Schionatulander also had occasion to learn shrewd-   54
ness from many a sweet embassy which the French Queen An-
phlise secretly dispatched to the Angevin. These he performed,
and many a time he averted their sorrow from them. Avert now
his own as well! Schionatulander often   noticed   how   55
his cousin[16] Gahmuret could speak with manly sense and how
he could ease himself from love's pain. Many baptized[17] folk
said that about him, and so did the noble heathen.

All you who practice and undertake love, harken   56
now to maidenly sorrow and to manhood in its travail, for of
these things I mean to relate adventures to those who have ever
found the pangs of yearning because of heartfelt love.

Sweet Schionatulander took courage as his associ-   57
ation brought him into sorrows manifold, and he said: "Sigune,
rich in help, help me, noble maiden, out of my sorrows and you
will be most helpful. *Duchesse* from Katelangen, let   58
me be cured! I hear that you were born of a family that could

---

[15] Editors radically disagree on the meaning of this unclear sentence. We un-
derstand it as anticipatory of the story not yet recounted.

[16] "Cousin" renders Marti's "his maternal aunt's son" (*sîner muomen sun*),
which is confirmed by 126,4 below. Leitzmann prints *sîn oeheim*, "his uncle."
But MHG kinship-terms waver in meaning. 75,3 and 88,3 use *mâc/mâge*, "kins-
man." See also stanza 95.

[17] "Baptized" = Marti's *toufbaern*. Leitzmann prints *tiuschen*, "German."

never abstain from being helpful with their rewards if someone
found love's sorrow for their sakes. Preserve your salvation by
your treatment of me!"[18]

"*Bel ami*, tell me, fair friend, what you mean. Let   59
me hear if your will agrees with mine, if your plaintive entreaty
is to be of any avail. If you are not fully clear about it, you should
not be overhasty."

"One must seek mercy where mercy dwells. Lady,   60
I desire mercy, and you must grant me that through your mercy.
Noble companionship befits young people. Who can find true
mercy if it never finds expression?"

She said: "You must declare your suffering and your   61
need for comfort where they can help you better than I can, else
you may commit a sin by asking *me* to avert your misery; for I
am a mere orphan among maidens and far from my people and
my country."

"I am well aware that you are a great lady over a   62
country and a people. I am not asking for anything like that,
but only that your heart should peer forth through your eyes
to behold my suffering. Now help me at once, before love of
you destroys my heart and my joy."

"If anyone loves in such a way that his love is dan-   63
gerous to so dear a friend as you are to me, the word 'impro-
priety' will never be used by me to designate 'love.' God knows
I have never known love's loss or love's gain."

> (*Here manuscripts seem to have lost Schionatulander's stanza of
> reply, which apparently contained a masculine noun such as
> "Cupid" or "Lord Amor."*
> "The Later Titurel" *supplies a new reply for Schionatulander in
> H-694, then a new Sigune-stanza in H-695, and then a new Schi-
> onatulander-stanza in H-696, before resuming its paraphrase of Wol-
> fram's lines in H-697.*)

"Is 'Love' a 'he'? Can you parse 'love' for me? Is it   64
a she'? If Love comes to me, by what pet name shall I call it?

---

[18] I.e., Do not commit a mortal sin by refusing to help me.

Shall I keep it among my dolls? Or will Love in its wildness be unwilling to fly to my hand? Can I coax Love to come to me?"

"Lady, I have heard—about women and about men—   65
that Love can so draw the bow for old and young that it shoots thoughts painfully[19] and unerringly hits whatever runs or creeps or flies or swims."[20]

"Schionatulander, as soon as you are out of my sight   66
the thought overwhelms me that I am bereft of joy until I secretly catch sight of you again. I grieve for this more than once in a week's course: it happens all too often."

"Then, sweet maiden, you have no need   67
to inquire of me about love. Without your asking, you will come to know love's loss and gain. See how love now turns joy to sorrow. Do justice to love before love destroys both our hearts! I had already recognized love from hearing about it, sweet   68
maiden. Love is of the thoughts, as I can attest for myself. Steadfast affection compels its being so. Love steals joy out of my heart as not even a thief would do."[21]

She said: "Can Love steal its way into hearts so that   69
neither man nor woman nor maiden can escape its swiftness? Does anyone know what it is that Love is avenging on people who never did it any harm, that it should shatter their joy?"

"Indeed it is mighty, for greenhorns and graybeards   70
alike. No scholar lives who could praise to the full its worth and its wonder. Now let us both strive for its help. With affection unimpaired, love cannot deceive anyone with faithlessness."[22]

"Oh, if only Love could provide help otherwise than   71
by surrender of my free person for you to command as your possession! Your youth has not yet rightly earned me: you must first serve me by fighting under the protection of your shield. Be so advised beforehand!"

---

[19] The figure is that of Cupid (or Lord Amor) with bow and arrow, reinforcing the impression of a stanza lost after 63.

[20] I.e., all living things in the four departments of the animal kingdom. Leitzmann less appropriately reads: ". . . flies or runs or walks or swims."

[21] The double stanza, 67–68, for Schionatulander breaks the symmetry of this dialogue, but Marti's transposing of 68 to the position of 66 solves nothing.

[22] Editor Marti labors to make sense of this abstruse line.

"Lady, as soon as I have strength to use weapons,　　72
here meanwhile and then hereafter I shall undertake those bit-
tersweet labors so my service may try to win your help. But help
me now so I may succeed in winning you later!"

This was the beginning of their love-bond in words,　　73
at the time when Pompeius summoned his armed host with
might up before Baldac, and the noble Ipomidon likewise. Out
from their army many a fresh spear was shattered. Gahmuret
rode to the encounter by himself, with only his own　　74
shield,[23] though undeniably he had great forces of men, for he
possessed the crowns of three countries.[24] Thus Love drove
him to death,—which he received at the hands of Ipomidon.
Schionatulander had been unhappy about the　　75
expedition because Sigune's love wholly undid his high courage
and his joy. Nevertheless he had set off with his kinsman.[25]
That was heart's sorrow to Sigune, and to him as well. Love
rode with the two men, stalking them both.

The young prince took leave of the maiden in private.　　76
"Alas," he said, "how shall I live so love will make me rich in
joy and yet keep me from death? Wish me well, sweet maiden:
I must leave you and go among the heathen."

"I am fond of you, loyal friend, but tell me: is this love?　　77
As things are, I shall forever be wishing for the rewards that
high joy will obtain for us both. All waters will burn before love
dies in me."

Much beloved remained behind: beloved also went　　M 78
away. You have never heard tell of maids or matrons or　　L 81
manly men who could more fondly love. Of that, Parzival later
was witness in Sigune at the linden tree.[26]

---

[23] Having neither a supporting army nor a "cause," Gahmuret fought as a
love-knight (*Frauenritter*) for his own fame and to win the admiration of his lady.
P 101 says he fought eighteen such lone jousts after his marriage to Herzeloyde.
Though P 106 does not specify *Frauenritter* status, P 586 includes him in a list
of knights who died for love.

[24] I.e., his native Anjou since the death of Galoes and the two kingdoms,
Waleis and Norgals, which he acquired by marriage to Herzeloyde.

[25] Here "kinsman" (*mâge*); compare note 16 above.

[26] (*zer linden*): At the second of four encounters with Sigune Parzival found
her *in* a linden tree (P 249,14; *ûf einer linden*) clasping in her arms the embalmed
corpse of Schionatulander.

From Kingrivals[27] King Gahmuret secretly de-   M 79
parted from kinsmen and vassals, so that his going   L 78
was entirely concealed. For the expedition he selected twenty
lads of high lineage and eighty squires in armor, but
without shields. Five spendid horses, quantities of   M 80
gold, and jewels from Azagouc followed him on   L 79
his travels, but of shields there departed but one alone.—A shield
ought to choose a fellow-shield so the second shield could say
"Bless you!" if the first shield sneezed. Neither   M 81
his heartfelt fondness nor the Queen's love had   L 80
yet become estranged in any way, and, as her habit was, the
Queen gave him her undershirt of white silk that had lain against
her own white skin; it had also lain against something brown
by her hip. He wore it into the massed jousting before Baldac.

From Norgals to Spain and on to Seville he traveled,[28]   82
this son of bold Gandin, who was to bring tears to many eyes
when they learned how his journey ended. His high praise was
never a stranger to baptized folk or to the heathen. This I speak
in very truth and no wise to mislead.   83

Now we must turn our thoughts to the young price from Gras-
waldan,[29] whom Sigune, his chaste *amie*, held in thrall,—she
who drew joy up out of his heart the way a bee draws sweet-
ness out of flowers. His languorous sickness resulting   84
from love and the loss of his high spirits to the increase of
cares wrung many a pang from the Graharzois: he wished an
easier death than (his father) Gurzgri had found at the hands of
Mabonagrin. If ever a future joust is dealt by his hand   85
with shock of shattering spears through shields, he is still too frail
now for such rigors, because strong love makes him weak, and
the fact that his thought dwells unforgettingly on gracious
love. While other young nobles on meadows and high-   86

---

[27] Kingrivals, capital of Norgals,—as more private than Kanvoleiz, capital of
Waleis?

[28] I.e., to his cousin Kaylet's capital, Toledo, southernmost point in Christian
Spain, whence permission might be arranged through Moslem Spain to the port
city of Seville.

[29] Pp. 101–105 below explain "Graswaldan" at length. For the term "Grahar-
zois" in 84,3 see also p. 101 below.

ways were jousting and fighting, he, from his pain of yearning, had to avoid those things. Love made him weak when it came to hearty joys. When little children learn to stand upright, they first have to steady themselves on chairs. Now grant him to love nobly! Then he cannot help but think of how   87 to steady himself up, and of how his lifelong fame, in youth as in age, can overcome all falsity. I know that if a grown prince tried to learn this, a bear can sooner learn the Psalter.

Schionatulander endured many pains in secret be-   88 fore the noble Gahmuret, watchful as he was, noticed those hidden sorrows and how his dearest kinsman was wrestling with love's torment,—and he suffered every moon as the seasons came, winter and summer alike. Perfect he was,   89 from innate nobility, in his figure, his complexion, his lustrous eyes, and in such glimpses as could be gotten in his flashing glance scarcely to be distinguished from sheer sunlight:[30] what made him so was not tattered fickleness but the full-width cloth of strong love.

Gahmuret's heart was also disquieted by love,   90 whose heat and burning had at times scorched his fair skin, so that he knew something about despondency. Of love's help he had received some share, though he also knew its oppressive hours. Crafty as love may be, it cannot help but show,   91 and to someone with Love's all-seeing, practiced eye its power cannot be hidden. It is also a T-square, I've heard tell, and it sketches and weaves designs better than bobbins and shuttles can do.[31] Gahmuret perceived the hidden oppression   92 and how the young Dauphin[32] from Graswaldan was devoid of joy. He took him aside to a field off the highway:[33]

"How is it that Anphlise's page is in this condition? Your

---

[30] We take this to mean glimpses of his flashing glance in so far as his glance was not obscured by his helmet.

[31] The T-square signifies that Love is a Master Builder; Love is also a maker of tapestries of intricate design.

[32] The distinctive title of "Dauphin" applied only to the ruling Counts of Albon in what—after Wolfram's time—became the independent state of Dauphiné in SE France. It is discussed in pp. 105–108 below.

[33] Wolfram envisages a *land* journey, perhaps the land journey from Toledo to Seville.

sadness does not sit well with me. I am involved to   93
an equal degree in your pain. The Roman Emperor and the Ad-
miral of all the Saracens[34] could not, with all their wealth, al-
leviate it. Whatever it is that has brought you to sighful anguish
must also put *my* joy in pawn."

Now, you must believe that the noble Angevin   94
would gladly have helped the yearning young Dauphin if he
could.

"Alas," he said, "why has your face lost its shining glances?
In you Love robs itself. I divine that you are in love: 95
its marks are all too plain to behold. You must not keep your
secrets from me, seeing we are so close of kin, both of us drawing
life from one family tree and closer related than through the
mother who grew from a borrowed rib.[35]—Oh, you fountain-
head of love, you blossoming bough of love, I am now   96
forced to pity Anphlise who, in her womanly goodness, lent[36]
you to me! She reared you as if she had herself given you birth,
she looked upon you as if you were her own child, so dear are
you still to her as you ever were. If you keep your secret from
me I shall be wounded in my heart, which was *your*   97
heart ever, and if your loyalty dishonors itself by withholding
such great distress from my knowledge. I cannot trust your de-
votion after having so unreliably done wrong."

Sorrowfully the lad said: "I will tell you, provided   98
I may keep your good will and favor and provided I am not even
more afflicted by your anger. For reasons of propriety I con-
cealed my sorrow from you. Now I must speak the name of
Sigune: she has been victorious[37] over my heart. You can, if you

---

[34] The mightiest monarchs in the world: the Roman—i.e., German—Emperor
and the "pagan" Caliph, here termed *der admirât*, as in *Willehalm* 434. The word
= OF *amirail*, itself a corruption of Arabic *amîr*, "prince." Modern French *amiral*
and English "admiral" both developed sea-going connotations alien to the older
forms.

[35] I.e., they are not merely fellow-humans descended from Eve. See Genesis
2:21–22.

[36] "lent" = lech, as in 39,2, where we translated it as "presented . . . with."

[37] "has been victorious" (*hât gesiget*) clearly puns on the name "Sigune" and
MHG *sic/sige* (modern *Sieg*), "victory," thus casting some doubt on the inter-
pretation of "Sigune" as an anagram of OF *cousine*; see under "Sigune" in the
List of Proper Names.

choose to do so, lessen my painful burden. Now let   99
me remind you of the French Queen: if ever I bore a share of
your sorrow, then, in return for that, take . . . (*a word or two
missing*) me out of my weakness. My slumbering thoughts were
never as dangerous as a waking lion's.[38] Let me remind
you also of what seas and lands I have traveled   100
for your sake and not because I was poor and in need of pay. I
have left kinsmen and vassals behind, and Anphlise as well,
my noble lady. I must make up for all that in you, so let your
help be given! You can well deliver me from   101
imprisoning bonds. If ever I become the master of a shield, if
ever I am under helmet and bearing my own expenses across
the lands, then my helpful hand will achieve praise. Meanwhile,
be my protector, so your defense may save me from Sigune's
painful constraint!"

"Ah, frail lad, what forests you must first use up   102
in jousting if you are to know the love of the *Duchesse*! Noble
love is granted according to rule, and a brave man with talents
will win her sooner than a wealthy coward. All the same, I am
delighted to hear that your heart rises so high aloft.   103
Where was there ever a tree's stem so admirably leaved along
its boughs? She is a gleaming flower on heath, in forest, and on
meadow. If my little niece[39] had you in her power, oh, happy
are you for that lovely report! Of Schoysiane, her
mother, it was exclaimed that God Himself and   104
His art made a special point of creating her beauty, and Sigune,
Kiot's daughter, inherited Schoysiane's sunny radiance: so
say the well-known opinions of her. Kiot, the pursuer of
fame in the sharp press of combat, the ruler of   105
Katelangen before Schoysiane's death robbed him of joy! In all
truth, this is how I hail the child of those two: Sigune the vic-
torious[40] on the battlefield where maidens chaste and sweet

---

[38] Marti understands: My thoughts when asleep were like the thoughts of a
lion asleep with one eye open; my waking thoughts are those of a lion alert.

[39] "my little niece" = *mîn müemel,* literally "my little maternal aunt;" Lexer's
dictionary defines it as "friend."

[40] *Sigûne diu sigehafte;* see note 37 above.

are chosen![41] For her who has triumphed over you   106
you must triumphantly strive in faithful service. Therefore I will
delay no longer, but for your help I shall enlist her noble aunt.[42]
Sigune's radiance shall make your own color bloom like the
glowing flowers.[43]

Then Schionatulander spoke thus: "Now your com-   107
fort and your loyalty will burst the bonds of all my sorrows
asunder, since with your favor I love Sigune, who has long been
robbing me of joy and cheerful spirits."

Well might Schionatulander have reckoned on help   108
if he desired it.

But we must not forget the great distress endured by the child
of Kiot and Schoysiane. Before receiving the seeds of comfort
she had to live without joy. When the princess from   109
Katelangen had been long tormented by cruel love—her
thoughts had struggled hard and all too long for her to try to
conceal it from her aunt—the Queen perceived with agitated
heart what Sigune was suffering. Very like a dewy
rose all wet from redness had her eyes become, and   110
her lips and face were awry from distress. Then her modesty
could not conceal the lovely love in her heart, which was
grieving for a boy-knight far away.[44]

Then from love and loyalty the Queen said: "Alas,   111
child of Schoysiane! Until now I have been bearing all too heavily
a different grief which I feel for the Angevin, but a new thorn
is growing into my sorrow now that I am aware of your grief.
Tell me, are you worried about your country and your   112
people? Or is comfort from me and your other kinfolk so far
away that their help cannot reach you? What has become of your
sunny glance? Alas, who has stolen it away out of your cheek?

---

[41] Apparently a coy reversal of the notion of Valkyries as "choosers of slain
heroes" from the battlefield, even to the use of the old word *wal*, "battlefield."

[42] I.e., Herzeloyde.

[43] Our translation only half-reflects the complex word play of: *Sigûnen glanz
sol dîne varwe erblüen nâch den bliclîchen bluomen.*

[44] "For a boy-knight" = *nâch kintlîchem recken*; the technical term *recke* meant
a knight in distant foreign lands.

Homeless maiden, now your homelessness makes me   113
pity you. For all that I wear the crown of three lands, I must be
accounted poor unless I live to see your sorrow disappear and
unless I discover the real reason for all your grief."

"Then with sorrow I must tell you all my anguish.   114
If you think any the less of me, your grace may sin against me,
because I cannot give it up. Admit me to your favor, sweet love.
That beseems us both. May God reward you! All   115
loving tenderness that ever mother bestowed on her child,
that same devotion I find here steadfast in you,—I who am so
poor in joy. You have preserved me from the sense of homeless-
ness, and I thank your womanly kindness for that. Your
counsel, your comfort, your favor, I need these one and   116
all because I suffer yearningly for a friend's sorrow. With
anguished torment that cannot be averted, he harries my wild
thoughts: my whole mind is held in bonds by his bonds.

I have these many evenings   kept my gazes   117
From windows over heathland   fixed on highroad and the shining
brookfields
All in vain: I never see him coming.
Thus my eyes must dearly   pay with tears for love of my beloved.

Sometimes I leave the window   for the ramparts,   118
There to peer out eastwards   and to westwards for a glimpse of him
Who has this long, long time constrained my heart.
I may be justly charged with grown-up love and not with childish
yearnings.

Or I may journey   down a river,   119
Peering out for   more than thirty miles of distance
In hopes that I may hear some tidings of him
That might relieve the weight of   grief I bear for my fair friend.

Where is my gladness gone? and   how can my high spirits   120
Have left my heart deserted?   A sigh of sorrow now must follow
both of us,

Which I had wanted only I should suffer.
I know that yearning grief will drive him   back to me, but now he
lives without me.

Alas!, his coming home is   all too precious,   121
Chills assail me as I crave it,   craving too, I lie in crackling flames,
I am ablaze with Schionatulander,
I feel his love as fire like   Agremuntin's that breeds the salamander.[45]

"Alas," said the Queen, "you speak as with the   122
wisdom of the wise. Who has given you evil counsel? Now I
fear the French Queen Anphlise may have taken revenge on me
in her anger: all your wise words have been prompted by her
lips.[46] Schionatulander is a rich prince of high rank.   123
His nobility and modesty, however, would never have ventured
to the point where his youth would have made a claim to your
love unless proud Anphlise's hatred were taking vengeance on
me in her spite.
    "She reared that boy from the time he was weaned.   124
If she has not, from treachery, given the advice that has so griev-
ously troubled you, you may offer him many joys,—and he you.
If you are fond of him, do not let your desirable self waste away:
offer it to him with honor. Let your eyes shine again,   125
and your cheeks, your chin! How would it become such youthful
years if your bright complexion faded over this? You have min-
gled all too much grief with your brief joy. If the young Dauphin
has destroyed your joy, he may well make you rich   126
again in joy. Many excellences and much love he inherited from
his father, and from the Dauphine Mahaute who was his

[45] We imitate the irregular metrics of this lyric passage and end it with the
final rhyme of the original; stanza 121 has the irregular rhyme-scheme: a b a b
in the German. (Eight lyric poems of Wolfram's are preserved.)
    For salamanders in the fiery mountain of Agremuntin see under "Agremun-
tin" in the List of Proper Names.
[46] Herzeloyde "stole" Gahmuret away from French Queen Anphlise; she fears
Anphlise may now be luring Schionatulander and Sigune away from her, "in
revenge."

mother, and from his aunt, Queen Schoette.[47] I am sorry
you are his *amie* so early. You will inherit the love-   127
pangs that Mahaute felt for the Dauphin Gurzgri. Many a time
her eyes saw how he won the prize in many lands as he fought
under helmet.

Schionatulander will surely rise in renown. He was   128
born of people who do not allow their fame to decline,—and
their fame has grown broad and long. Grant him comforting joy
and do not let him bring sorrow upon you. No matter how much
your heart within you smiles upon him, I am not   129
surprised. How well he must look under the shelter of a shield!
Upon him will fall many teardrops of fire as they spark from his
helmet under sword-strokes when fiery rain is heavy.[48] As
though painted, he sits mounted for the joust: who   130
could portray him then.[49] Never, I think, in any woman's son
was so little overlooked in forming a manly countenance that
was made for women's kindness. His glance will make your eyes
sweet again, and I bid you reward him for that with your love."[50]

Thus, then, was authorized love with love em-   131
braced. Steadfastly toward love their two hearts were undis-
mayed by love.

"Oh, how happy I am, my aunt," said the Duchess,[51] "that
I may now, with your permission, so love the Graharzois before
the eyes of the whole world!"[52]

---

[47] The Dauphine Mahaute and Queen Schoette of Anjou were sisters—a re-
lationship declared only here, hence their respective sons, Schionatulander and
Gahmuret, must be first cousins. See note 16 above.

[48] In a daring metaphor the sparks struck by metal against metal (swordblows
on helmets) are equated with the tears being shed by ladies anguished over the
contestants' fates.

[49] Schionatulander "is a picture."

[50] We take this "command" as the formal authorization of a guardian for Si-
gune's *betrothal* to Schionatulander. If the betrothal conveyed marital rights, as
we think it did, then in stanzas 166 and 168 below Sigune's unreasonable demand
is exclusively her fault.

[51] Here "Duchess" = *herzoginne*; *Ducisse* in 58,1 and *duzisse* in 102,2 were
"Wolfram's Old French."

[52] Sigune's delighted outcry parallels Schionatulander's in 107.

The Second Fragment: Stanzas 132—170

They[1] had not long been thus encamped when   132
they heard a hunting dog[2] loudly racing toward them in full,
sweet cry on the red-stained track of a wounded animal. The
dog was stopped for a time, and for that I am still lamenting—
for friends' sakes.

When they heard the forest ringing so loud with   133
uproar, Schionatulander—from boyhood he was noted for
overtaking the swiftfooted, except Trevrezent the pure, who out-
ran and outjumped all who practiced such knightly sports—he,
Schionatulander, thought to himself: "If someone is   134
to overtake that dog, let knightly legs do it."—He will sell his
joy so doing, and buy himself everlasting grief.—Up he jumped
in the direction of the barking, intending to catch the dog. Since
the fleeing quarry could not enter the wide woods   135
except by passing in front of the Dauphin, his trouble is all the
greater: future grief it brought him. Now he hid in a dense
thicket.

Then, dragging its leash, along came Duke Ehkunat's[3] dog,
which had slipped from that prince's hands, tracking   136
the arrow-cut bloodstains.—May she[4] who in high spirits had
sent this dog forth never send forth another, because it hunted
down the proud Graharzois and later robbed him of many
joys.—As it broke out of the underbrush onto the   137
trail, an Arabian collar could be seen tightly wound around its

---

[1] "They" = Schionatulander and Sigune, who are also the "friends" of 132,4;
Wolfram "sides with" favorite characters. Attendant maidens are mentioned in
156,1 below, and it may be assumed that Schionatulander is not without male
servants out here. See note 17 below.

[2] "Hunting dog" = (*der*) *bracke*, archaic English "brach/brachet," from Old
High German *bracco*, via Old French, a dog that hunts by scent, a sleuthhound.
Hotspur, rather than hear his lady sing in Welsh, would have his brach howl
in Irish; *1 Henry IV*.

[3] To avoid ambiguity, the name of Duke Ehkunat is brought up from stanza
151.

[4] "She" = the lady Clauditte, who sent the dog to Ehkunat (146 and 149
below).

neck and studded with precious and bright jewels: they flashed in the forest like the sun.

The dog was not all he caught. What else did he catch besides the dog? Let me tell you. Grief lined with trouble[5] he   138 had to confront undauntedly, and great strife and struggle ever after. For him the dog's leash was indeed the beginning of times lost to joy.[6] He carried the hound in his arms to   139 Sigune the fair.

The leash was a good twelve fathoms[7] long and made of ribbon-silk of four colors: yellow, green, red, and brown was the fourth; wherever the strips ended they were clasped together by an ornament. At those points there were rings white   140 with pearls, and the hand's-breadth sections in between the rings were not stinted for precious stones. Each section had four strips of the four colors and each strip was a finger in width.— If *I* ever catch a dog on a leash like that, *it* will stay with me even if I let *him* go.—When these strips were spread   141 out smooth between the rings, there was writing to be found inside and outside, and of costly materials. Now harken to adventure,[8] if you will be so kind! With golden nails the gems were firmly   attached   to   the   strand.   Emeralds   formed the letters, intermingled with rubies, and there were   142 diamonds too, and chrysolites and garnets. Never was a leash better dogged, and the dog was very well leashed. You can guess which one *I* would take if the dog were the alternate choice. Of samite green as the Maytime forest a ribbon was sewn   143 to form the collar, studded with jewels of many kinds, and a woman had composed the wording: Gardeviaz was the dog's name, which in German signifies "Watchways."[9]

---

[5] The metaphor is that of cloth garments with linings.

[6] Here, between 138 and 139, may have come a stanza about the colors of the dog, the stanza H-1151 of "the Later Titurel;" see pp. 71 ff. below.

[7] "Fathom" (*klâfter*) = about 6 feet, from middle-fingertip to middle-fingertip of the outstretched arms. Thus the leash must be almost 72 feet long.

[8] "Adventure" meant a story, particularly one of a strikingly unusual kind.

[9] The German is *Hüete der verte,* literally "Heed the path(s)."

The Duchess Sigune read the beginning of the   144
story:

> Though this be the name of the dog, the word befits noble
> human beings. Let man and woman watch well their ways
> that they may travel here in this world's favor, if salvation is
> to be their reward yonder.

She read further on the collar, but not yet down the   145
leash:

> Whoever watches well his way will never find his repu-
> tation up for sale in the changeful and unsteadfast market-
> place, for praise dwells so strong in pure hearts that eyes will
> never overlook it.

Dog and leash together had been sent as a love gift   146
to a prince, and she who sent it was a young reigning queen.
In the text down the leash Sigune read who that queen was, and
who that prince was, too, for both were perfectly clear.
She had been born in Kanedic, and her sister was   147
Florie, who had given her heart, mind, and self as *amie* to Ilinot
the Briton,[10] and everything she had, save her body in passion's
embrace. She had brought him up from childhood until his set-
ting out as a knight, and she cherished him above all things
won. Under helmet he found his death in the quest   148
for her love. If I were not breaking my knightly code, I would
curse the hand whose joust brought him death. Florie died in
that same joust, though spearpoint never came near her body.[11]
She left a sister who inherited her crown. Clauditte   149
was this maiden's name. Her modesty and goodness brought
her the reward of strangers' praise and the praise of those who
knew her as well. Her renown was so proclaimed through many
lands that never did anyone contest it.
The Duchess read further along the leash about this   150
maiden.

[10] Ilinot is King Arthur's son, hence, as it were, Crown Prince of "Britain."
[11] I.e., she died of grief.

The princes of her realm asked her for a master over them, to be chosen by tribunal. For them she summoned a court at Beuframunt[12] to which came rich and poor in untold numbers, and they left the choosing to her. *Le duc* Ehkunat de   151 Salvasch Florie was the one she preferred in her heart, and he had also chosen her for his *amie*. There his heart counted for more than her crown.[13] Ehkunat aspired to the ideal of all princes, for he watched well his way.[14] His youth, together with the right of disposition of her kingdom thus   152 accorded to her, persuaded her, and, with the choosing left up to her, the maiden chose worthily. Would you like to hear her friend's name in German?—He was Duke Ehkunaver of Flowering Wildwood:[15] that is what I heard him called.—Since his name was "of the Wildwood," to the Wildwood she   153 sent him this wild[16] letter—this dog, namely—that roamed the ways of field and forest, as by nature he would. The writing on the leash declared further that she herself intended to watch her womanly way.

While she was reading, Schionatulander was angling   154 wih a feather-bait for perch and trout—and also for the loss of his joy, so that afterwards he was seldom to be glad. The Duchess untied the knot in the leash in order to read further down the length of the writing. The leash was tied fast to the tentpole. I am distressed by that untying. Ah, if only   155 she had refrained from doing that! Gardeviaz was straining with all his might on his rope, begging the Duchess for food, and she was going to give him something to eat. Two attendant maidens hurried out beyond the tentropes to fetch it.   156 I bemoan the Duchess's white, soft hands. If the leash cut them, what can I do about it? It was rough with jewels. At one bound Gardeviaz was off and away in pursuit of canine quarry. He had

[12] An actual town, Bauffremont, in Lorraine.
[13] Clauditte cared more for love than for the fact that Ehkunat was only a duke, whereas she was herself a queen.
[14] *er phlac siner verte.*
[15] The troublesome name is explained in the List of Proper Names, under "Ehkunat."
[16] A pun on *wiltlich*, "odd; wild," and *wilde*, "Wildwood."

escaped from Ehkunat too in just that fashion that   157
same day. She called to the maidens. They had procured some
food for the dog and were hurrying back to the tent with it, but
he had slipped in between the tentsides and could be heard far
out in the forest. He ripped some of the tentcloth off   158
the holding pegs, and now as he came on the fresh red trail he
made no secret of it: he hunted quite openly and not at all se-
cretly. From that, there came much grief for noble Gurzgri's son
to endure.

Schionatulander had been catching the big and the   159
little fish with his rod, down where he was standing with his
white legs bare for the coolness in the clear, swift brook. Now
he caught the sound of Gardeviaz's barking, and it rang to his
undoing. He threw down his fishing rod and swiftly   160
ran over stumps and through brambles, but still he got nowhere
near the dog. Trackless wastes took him so far afield that he
found neither dog nor quarry, and the wind carried even the
sound away. His bare legs were badly scratched by   161
the brambles, and his white feet also came in for their share of
wounds from the briers as he ran, so he was easier to follow
than a wounded animal. He had them bathed[17] before he came
into the tent.

There he found Sigune with the palms of her hands   162
scraped gray as a jouster's hand whose spearshaft has glanced
off his opponent and burned across his bare skin: just that way
the leash had torn across the Duchess's hand. She saw all the
cuts on his legs and feet. She expressed pity for him,   163
he expressed pity for her.

Now I must turn this story bitter, as the Duchess began to
beg him for the writing on the leash. The loss of it will now lead
to the shattering of many spears.

He said: "I have heard of very few dog-leashes   164
with writing on them. *Books* of writing, and in French, I do know,
and I have not neglected to acquire that skill. I would read you

---

[17] "He had them bathed" (*er hiez sie twahen*) implies the presence of male
attendants.

whatever was written in them. Sigune, sweet girl, say the writing on that leash is of no concern to you!"

She said: "There was an adventure on that leash.   165
If I cannot finish reading it, I do not care about my whole country of Katelangen. All the wealth that anybody could offer me, even if I were worthy of accepting it, I would give it all to have that writing. I do not say this, noble friend, to make you   166
angry, or to anger anybody, but if both of us were to remain young to the end of our days and if your service were still to go on seeking my love, you would first have to get me that leash by which Gardeviaz was tied here."

He said: "Then I will gladly strive for the leash on   167
that condition. If it must be won in combat, I will lose life and fame or else bring it back to you. Be merciful, sweet girl, and do not keep my heart so long in bondage to you!"

"Favor, and all that a girl should do for her fair and   168
noble friend, I will grant you, and no one shall prevent me, if you fight for that leash that the dog was trailing along when you brought him to me."

"My service shall faithfully strive for it. You offer   169
a rich reward. But how shall I go on living until such time as my hand can bring it to you, so I may receive your favor? I shall seek it near and far. May Fortune and your love guide me!"

Thus to each other they made do with promises   170
and with good will. Oh, to think how this beginning of much grief was to end! Greenhorn and graybeard alike shall hear true report of this undaunted man[18] whether his fame soars or sinks low.

---

[18] Marti prints *verzageten*, "daunted," but admits it must mean "*un*daunted." Leitzmann prints *unversageten*, "undaunted."

·II·

"THE LATER TITUREL"
🎠 🎠 🎠

IT WAS THE CURIOUS FATE of these Titurel fragments of Wolfram's to be incorporated, in slightly modified form, into a novel-length stanzaic romance which scholars term "The Later Titurel" (*Der Jüngere Titurel*). Since late stanzas of this poem were quoted in the sermons of Berthold of Regensburg, who died in 1272, the compositional date of "around 1270" is inferred. Down to the end of the Middle Ages this poem enjoyed the highest esteem *as a work of Wolfram of Eschenbach*, and, as "Wolfram's *Titurel*," it was revived and praised by German Romanticists at the beginning of the nineteenth century,—until it was pointed out that, at least in some manuscripts, the poet gave his name as Albrecht. This Albrecht was then identified by the Romanticist Sulpice Boisserée as Albrecht of Scharfenberg, the author of lost poems entitled *Merlin* and *Seifrid von Ardemont*, and despite strong denials of this identification by subsequent critics the handbooks of literary history have gone on listing "The Later Titurel" as a work by "Albrecht von Scharfenberg." Either way, the author remains obscure except for what can be deduced from the text itself. More will be said on this troublesome point in the concluding portion of the present chapter.

An astonishing total of 57 manuscripts is known, most of them fragmentary, to be sure. Among medieval works this number is surpassed only by the genuine works of Wolfram: 84 manuscripts of *Parzival*, 76 of *Willehalm*. As a gauge of popularity we may compare: 34 for the *Nibelungenlied*, 25 for Hartman's *Iwein*,

23 for Gotfried's *Tristan*, 13 for the Old French poem of *Aliscans*, "about 8" for *La Chanson de Roland*, to say nothing of *Beowulf* or *Sir Gawain and the Green Knight*, each preserved in a single manuscript. "The Later Titurel" was also imitated by German poets of the late Middle Ages, one after another, in their metrics and otherwise. Around 1491 Count Gerhard von Sayn, in his will, recommended the poem to his sons as the model of all virtue and honor. And in 1477 the new invention of the printing press turned out a printed "Later Titurel" as companion piece to the printed *Parzival* of the same year.

With the Reformation the work lapsed from favor. Linguistic change was, in any case, making it ever more difficult to read, and gradually a stage was reached where only antiquaries knew of it, often only from hearsay. Such, however, was the general fate of medieval German books. The very existence of the *Nibelungenlied*, for instance, was forgotten.

Around 1800, amid the Romantic revival of interest in things medieval, both German and general European, one of the rediscovered books was "The Later Titurel." In 1810 B. J. Docen issued his "First Open Letter on *Titurel*" (*Erstes Sendschreiben über den Titurel*), which praised the splendid scope and all-pervasive mystical sense of the poem, its moral content, its verse form and its exalted language. Its author, Docen confidently assumed, was Wolfram of Eschenbach. To the "Open Letter" were appended the actual Wolframian fragments, which Docen had just discovered, and these were identified as "a pre-Eschenbachian forestudy" by an unknown, lesser, predecessor!

In an article of the following year, 1811, August Wilhelm Schlegel wrote that *Wolfram* was the author of the fragments, in which case "The Later Titurel" must be by someone else, but this correct estimate went unheeded by many. Partisan spirits preferred pre-judgment to judgment. In 1813 the Catholic Romantiker Joseph Görres published the post-Wolframian poem of *Lohengrin*—an exceedingly dull work—and in his Introduction cited *Parzival, Titurel*—i.e., "The Later Titurel"—and *Lohengrin* as three masterpieces, with *Titurel* as "the seal, jewel, and noble gem" of the three and as "the fair, gleaming altar piece" in this trio of poems about the Grail. In 1829 a study by K. Rosenkranz, entitled *Über den Titurel und Dantes Komödie,* found that the work breathed the very spirit of Roman Catholicism, that it was the supreme achievement of the German Middle Ages, equal to *The Divine Comedy* and matched in modern times only by *Faust* (i.e., *Faust. Part I*). The author was still assumed to be Wolfram of Eschenbach.

Within that same year, 1829, the prestigious critic Karl Lachmann reviewed the Rosenkranz study, saying that *Wolfram* could never have composed "so tedious, dead, and affected a work" as this and that Albrecht's *imitation* of Wolfram was "intolerably silly" (*unleidlich albern*). These remarks produced consternation. Moreover, Lachmann repeated them in the Preface to his 1833 edition of Wolfram's works, and since that edition long remained the standard one the judgment was widely advertised.

Manuscripts, chiefly fragmentary ones, were now being discovered in rapid succession, revealing grave disparities, while the 1477 printing had become a rarity. The urgent need for a new printing was finally met in 1842, when K. A. Hahn published a version in 6,207 quatrains (24,828 long lines) on the basis of MS B (Heidelberg), but with faulty stanzas, from 5,908 on, amended on the basis of MS A (Vienna). (Compare the 24,812 *short* lines of *Parzival*.) Sad to relate, this 1842 book remains to this day the only "complete" "Later Titurel" in print! Quotations here will necessarily be made from it, with stanza numbers preceded by the letter H (for Hahn).

With more manuscripts came more problems. Besides verbal discrepancies there were discrepancies in the order of stanzas. Some manuscripts contained whole sets of stanzas not to be found at all in others. In "Group II" of the manuscripts, for instance, H-439 is followed by 42 stanzas of praise to the Blessed Virgin (*Marienlob*) which do not occur elsewhere. The formidable editorial task was at last undertaken by Werner Wolf in 1931, resulting in a 500-page Volume I, dated 1955. This offers, page by page, *a* text with multiple variants of 1,957 quatrains, bringing us as far as H-stanza 1920. The Wolf numbering is given at the left, the Hahn numbering at the right, with 37 new stanzas indicated by a dash. The 137-page Introduction traces the history of the poem and provides an extensive description of the manuscripts. Wolf's Volume II, dated 1964, continues the text to stanza 3236 in his numbering. Death prevented further installments, but, under the date of 1952, Wolf issued an 80-page booklet of selections, the last 15 pages of which contain the conclusion of the total poem. Thus roughly half of "The Later Titurel" still remains accessible only in the Hahn edition of 1842.

The Metrics of *"The Later Titurel"*

At first glance Albrecht's quatrains look very much like Wolfram's quatrains as described on page 2 above, and the end rhymes are still: a—a—b—b. The significant difference lies with a pair of inner rhymes at the ends of the first and third *half*-lines, producing the effect of a *seven*-line stanza. To take an example, Wolfram's stanza 139 (in Marti's edition) reads:

Er truoc den hunt an dem arm   Sigûnen der clâren.
daz seil was wol zwelf klâfter lanc,   die von vier varwe bortsîden wâren,
gel, grüene, rôt, brûn diu vierde,
immer swâ diu spanne erwant   an einander geworht mit gezierde.

In recomposed form this appears as Albrecht's stanza H-1152:

Er truoc den hunt so ENGENGE—sigunen hin der klaren—
Zwelf clafter mit LENGE—daz seil des varwe da vier von siden waren—
Gel broun gruene und ouch rot die vierde—
Immer swa die spanne erwant—so warens wol geworht mit richer zierde.

(Hahn's only "punctuation" was dashes between metrical units and a period at the end of a stanza; he began each line with a capital letter, regardless of sense. Wolf's text provides normal punctuation and capitalizes only sentence beginnings.)

The sense of H-1152 is so little altered from Wolfram's 139 that

our prose translation of the latter on page 29 above is still valid
or very nearly so, but Albrecht's contriving of those inner
rhymes tended to contort still more an already contorted style.
Critics who fancy that Wolfram's difficult stanza pattern led him
to abandon his poem should note that Albrecht's more difficult
stanza pattern did not discourage him from composing in excess
of 6,207 stanzas.

Style

Late-medieval readers apparently relished these "difficult"
stanzas, just as they admired the unrelieved stateliness of the
poem's diction, characters, and action. Albrecht is a wordy, if
earnest, poet. He doles out his story in small bits, reluctant to
broach a narrative point without first reflecting upon the pre-
vious one. He is fond of long descriptions, eulogies and elegies,
and odds and ends of bizarre lore. Extended allegorical inter-
pretation is a favorite device with him. Yet he never loses dig-
nity. Never does he fall into the insipidities of Ulrich von Tür-
heim, whose poem of *Rennewart* (around 1246) completed, after
a fashion, Wolfram's unfinished *Willehalm*. He is a poor story-
teller, his characters are lifeless, and he has no sense of humor
at all, but "The Later Titurel" is *not* "intolerably silly," as Karl
Lachmann angrily said in 1829. On the contrary, it has passages
of striking beauty. At times it even conveys a sense of awe. What
the author lacked was the ability to express fully the grandeur
of his own concepts. Above all, the plan of the total poem is
imposingly grand.

The Over-all Plan of the Poem

The poem opens with a prayer to God, which expands the
first 44 short lines of Wolfram's *Willehalm* (1,1 to 2,14) into 76
quatrains (304 long lines), or, with Wolf, into 85 quatrains (340
long lines). Biblical allusions and religious comment account for

the increased bulk. The author's piety is genuine, but the stark and exalted might of the *Willehalm* prayer has here become a diffuse and over-lengthy religious meditation.

The true beginning of the work is at H-77 (Wolf 86), following which the reader gradually comes to perceive a vast double-poem organized as follows:

399 H-stanzas (H-77 to H-475)—the story of Titurel's ancestry and youth, his establishment of a *gral*-temple on the hill of Muntsalvatsch, and his life as first king of the *gral*. H-475 hints ominously at unseemly rivalry among Christians for possession of the *gral*.

5,488 H-stanzas (H-476 to H-5963; = 21,952 long lines)—the romance about Schionatulander and Sigune.

244 H-stanzas (H-5964 to H-6207)—the story of how the *gral* was removed to "India" and of how Titurel proclaimed the nature of the *gral* just before his death, apparently at the age of five hundred.

The two *gral* portions of the poem, to a total of 643 H-stanzas, can be read as a continuous and self-contained work, wholly without reference to the central romance. Indeed, H-475 leads directly into H-5964, a fact which suggests to the present writer that those two portions were composed uninterruptedly and that the intrusion of the central romance between them may have been a second idea. As for the central romance, it has only minimal connection with the Titurel-*gral* portions and can also, therefore, be read as an independent poem. Both parts of the work are coordinated with the scenario of Wolfram's *Parzival*— the romance much more so than the other sections—but with surprising discrepancies and contradictions. Above all, the central romance incorporates, in modified form, all 170 stanzas of Wolfram's *Titurel* Fragments, bridges the gap between them, and goes on to recount a complete story about Schionatulander, Sigune, and the dog's leash. Whether this complete story represents the intended scenario of Wolfram's *in*complete story is a point long debated. Our answer to that question will be given below.

In scholarly investigations of "The Later Titurel" the lion's share of attention has gone to the two Titurel-*gral* sections, with only small concern for the central romance. Here that procedure, is reversed: our primary concern is with the story of the young lovers and the fateful dog. We proceed first, however, to an account of the Titurel-*gral* sections, and readers already familiar with these may pass directly to page 70 below.

The Story of Titurel and the Gral: First Part (H-77 to H-475)

1. (H-77 to H-256)—The topic of these 180 stanzas is the ancestry of Titurel, a subject about which Wolfram says not a word anywhere. H-77 acknowledges that silence:

> *Der von Provenzale   und Flegetanis parluere*
> *heidenisch von dem grale   und franzoys tuents kunt vil aventuere.*
> *daz wil ich diutsch,   gan iz mir got, hie kunden.*
> *swaz Parzival da birget,   daz wirt zu liehte braht an vakel zunden.*

Even in Wolf's edition, as cited, these lines are difficult; we understand:

> He of Provence   and speaker Flegetanis
> set forth many a tale   in heathen (? Arabic) and in French
>   about the *gral*.
> These I intend to relate here,   if God so permits me, in German.
> What *Parzival* conceals   will be brought to light without
>   kindling of torches.

Flegetanis was the heathen stargazer and *fisiôn* (natural scientist) who, in P 453-4-5, read the name of the Grail in the constellations and whose book on that subject was found, discarded, in Toledo, and read by Kyot. "Kyot the well known Provençal" was Wolfram's nine-times-invoked informant: P 416, 431, 453, 455, 776, 827; in P 416,25-30 Kyot "saw this tale of

Parzival written in heathen (*heidensch*) language. Whatever he told (*gesprach*) of it in French, I (Wolfram) . . . am telling further in German." (The word *parluere* = Old French *parleor*, modern *parleur*, "speaker.")

The sense would seem to be that *two* sources—the verb *tuent* is plural—furnished the matter of *Parzival*, one source heathen-written and the other French-oral, and that everything suppressed from those sources in the telling of *Parzival* will be revealed in the present poem about Titurel. Here and in other cases through much of the poem the poet implies that he *is* Wolfram of Eschenbach; the self-identification as "Albrecht" comes late and, we think, grudgingly.

The Wolfram-imposture also marks H-78, which begins: "*I have so often been asked by noble people for information about who that noble, chaste, pure man was*" who sired the Grail dynasty, "*that obligation compels me*" to relate the ancestry of Titurel.

Titurel was of the race of Troy, which, through *Eneas*, became the race of Rome. His great-grandfather was Senabor—an anagram of "Porsena"?—who ruled the land of Cappadocia. (Cappadocia, now east-central Turkey, is mentioned only incidentally in the Bible, in Acts 2:9 and 1 Peter 1:1.) His grandfather was Barillus, named for the beryl (H-90), the sea-green gem called *beryllos/-us* by the Greeks and Romans. The sources did not say whether Senabor was present at the Lord's baptism, but Barillus, together with his brothers Sabilor and Assibor, was an early Christian. The Emperor Vespasian, after besieging thirty-times-thirty-thousand Jews in Jerusalem, brought these three brothers to *Römischen landen* (H-105), gave them princesses in marriage, and assigned them, respectively, to France (*frankriche*), Anjou (*antschowe*), and Cornwall (*kornuwale*). The historical Vespasian completed the conquest of Jerusalem in 70 A.D. and ruled over the Roman Empire until his death in 79, hence Barillus and his brothers must have come west in the 70s,—unless Albrecht confused Vespasian (as medievals sometimes did) with the Emperor Tiberius, who died in 37 A.D., four years after the traditional date for the Crucifixion.

Upon Vespasian's own daughter Argusille Barillus begot a son, Titurisone, whose name suggests Vespasian's own son Titus, Emperor from 79 to 81. Titurisone married a princess of Aragon named Elyzabel, and their son in turn was named, two-thirds for his father, one-third for his mother, "Titur–el." An angel preannounced his birth.

A model child, Titurel learned books, knighthood, the love of God, and a bit about courtly love, but he understood that the poet Ovid might be "a goblin, a spirit out of hell" (*ein schrat, ein geist von helle*, H-180). Another warning against Ovid is sounded in H-250. Father and son warred jointly against heathens, and when Titurisone died Titurel continued the struggle alone. By age fifty, when he still looked thirty, he rejoiced to see very few heathens left in western lands (H-245). At that same point in his life the *gral* was entrusted to his care.

As H-stanzas 416, 431, and 607 all stress, Titurel then reigned as first king of the *gral* for 400 years, i.e., until age 450. That was his age when he abdicated kingship in H-476, which is a recomposed form of Wolfram's stanza 1, and at the end of the poem he dies at age 500. Thus the action of "The Later Titurel" belongs to those final fifty years of Titurel's life. If this literary arithmetic is meant to put the story "in King Arthur's time," Albrecht overshoots the mark by a century. Compare the inscription in golden letters which, according to Malory's Book XIII, appeared on the Siege Perilous: FOUR HONDRED WYNTIR AND FOUR AND FYFFTY ACOMPLYVYSSHED AFTIR THE PASSION OF OURE LORDE JESU CRYST OUGHTE THYS SYEGE TO BE FULFYLLED. Malory's date works out to 487 A.D. The death of Arthur is given as 537 in *The Annals of Wales*, as 542 by Geoffrey of Monmouth (XI,2). Albrecht's date cannot be accurately reckoned but it would seem to place Titurel's death around 600.

2. (H-257 to H-415)—Upon Titurel at age fifty and still in youthful bloom an angel conferred the *gral* (*im . . . gebnde was*; H-257). Directly he summoned his cousins of Anjou and of Cornwall to give lands in fief for appropriate establishment of the precious object. The site selected is a hill, presently called Muntsalvatsch, at the center of the impenetrable *Fareis zu salvatsch*

(H-282; Wolf prints *Foreist Salvasch*). The angel guided Titurel to the place, which is craggy and densely wooded for thirty miles in all directions. H-stanzas 284–5 list the known and the unknown trees of this forest, including the incombustible *aspindê* of which Noah built his ark.[1] Despite the inland location one wonders if that central height was not a poet's imaginary analogue to Mont Saint Michel. (See page 219 below.) In any case, the location is *not* in Spain.

Around Muntsalvatsch hill a wall was built (H-292,4), and then the summit of the hill was made level for the construction of the *tempel* Muntsalvatsch. The description of this *tempel* in H-stanzas 311–415 is one of the most memorable passages in the total poem. About the great hall (*palas*), says H-310, "you" have heard in *Parzival,* hence it is not described. There were dormitories (*dormter*) connected with the main complex by a cloistered passageway (*kriuzgang*), and both the great hall and the dormitories faced south. The pathless land on all sides was called *Salvaterre*; Wolfram's term was *Terre de Salvaesche*.

The *tempel* was emplaced upon the hill's summit, which was formed by a natural crag of pure onyx. Gold, jewels, and *lignum aloe* were almost exclusively used in the structure, though columns of bronze supported the dome; only the chairs were made of wood. The jewels were such as to provide warmth in winter and coolness in summer. Everywhere there were crucifixes, madonnas, statues, and chandeliers. The organ was over the west portal. Incense filled the air. Costly vessels were on the high altar and on the numerous side altars, the most precious item for each being a rich ciborium (the chalice with domed lid in which consecrated Mass wafers are stored). In a leafy tree made all of gold, mechanical birds sang as breezes stirred the branches; four angels with trumpets were poised on the outer boughs. Around the base of the dome were seventy-two—Wolf insists: twenty-two—galleries. In the dome, of pure sapphire, a clockwork (*orolei,* from Latin *horologium*) moved a golden sun, a silver

---

[1] The *aspindê* wood, which neither burns nor rots, is three times named in *Parzival* (490, 741, and 812), but with no mention of Noah's ark.

moon, and the various planets against a sky studded with stars made of carbuncles (garnets). Cymbals of gold sounded the times of the seven days. Beneath the crystal pavement swam mechanical fish and fabled sea-creatures. In short, this *tempel* was a smaller replica of God's cosmos.

To some of the Romanticists of the early 1800s all this seemed like a dazzlingly beautiful confirmation of their vision of the Catholic Middle Ages. In 1835 there appeared a book by Sulpice Boisserée entitled *On the Description of the Holy Grail in the Heroic Poem "Titurel,"* in which three plates offered architectural designs of the *tempel*. The Gothic structure, 100 fathoms (*klafter*) in diameter (ca. 180 meters/550 feet), was envisaged as having 72 side chapels, a dome supported (necessarily) on a forest of pillars, and with light introduced through a tier of windows high up in the arc of the dome. Albrecht's concept derived, in Boisserée's opinion, from Hagia Sophia in Constantinople and from two sacred buildings in Jerusalem, the Church of the Holy Sepulcher and the renowned Islamic Dome of the Rock.

In 1841 the Wolfram scholar San-Marte suggested incidentally in his two-volume *Life and Works of Wolfram of Eschenbach* that Albrecht's inspiration was the Church of Our Lady (*Liebfrauenkirche*) erected 1242–53 in Trier, as one of the earliest Gothic structures in Germany. (It was destroyed in World War II.) The same idea was advanced in 1872 by Ernst Droysen in *The Temple of the Holy Grail according to Albrecht von Scharfenberg*, but a review of this book, by H. Otte, declared that Albrecht's description was merely a dilettante's analysis of the Trier *Liebfrauenkirche* architecture.

Passing over further books and articles, a 1917 dissertation by Blanca Röthlisberger, *The Architecture of the Grail Temple in "The Later Titurel,"* sought to reconcile previous studies but claimed that the architecture was not Gothic, but Romanesque. Julius Schwietering's 1923 article, *Medieval Literature and Plastic Arts*, found Albrecht's description a poet's fancy rather than the plan of a real architect. Meanwhile the noteworthy studies of Friedrich Zarncke had pointed up the need for a reliable "Later Titurel" text on which to base conclusions about this temple. The eclectic text presented by him was found unsatisfactory by Werner Wolf, whose own editorial work began with criticisms of Zarncke. Then, while Wolf's own work was under way there appeared in 1942 a thick volume by Lars-Ivar Ringbom, proposing a radically new idea.

According to this Swedish writer, the "original" of the Grail Temple was the Zoroastrian holy city of Shiz—the holy city of the Magi—constructed amid the wild nature of Azerbijan Province of northern Iran by Sasanian ruler Khusro II (better known in the West as Chosroes II), who, from 580 to 628, controlled a vast empire that included Jerusalem. In 624 this Zoroastrian holy city of Shiz was destroyed by Byzantine Emperor Heraclius. Reproduced in Ringbom's book were three aerial photographs taken by the American expedition on behalf of the Institute for Iranian Art and Archeology. These show a crater lake centered on an upward-thrusting block of stone, the outer slopes of which resemble onyx. Here was "the Throne of Solomon" and also the omphalos of the Zoroastrian world. As for the city of Shiz itself, it was ancient and figured in legends long before the time of Khusro II; that monarch's reconstruction was only one reconstruction in a series. But since the destruction of 624 the site has lain neglected. To the Moslem conquerors of 635–642 that place was an abomination.

Wolf was fascinated by the reports of Shiz but he stopped short of claiming that it was Albrecht's model. To be sure, the Emperor Heraclius was the subject of a French romance, *Eracle*, by Gautier d'Arras, ca. 1164, and one Master Otte made a German adaptation of it (to which Wolfram unclearly alludes in P 773,22). Both Master Otte's poem and the medieval *Kaiserchronik* (Chronicle of Emperors) allude to Shiz as "the Earthly Paradise," but neither work begins to supply the multiple details of the Grail Temple, and other channels of information are unknown.

In short, there is no consensus as to the origins of Albrecht's description of the Grail Temple. If H-stanzas 311–415 represent *only* a poet's flight of fancy, then we must concede that Albrecht soared on mighty pinions.

3. (H-416 to H-475)—The *gral*, we were told in H-309,1, "hov-

ered" and allowed no one to touch it, but now, as of H-417, an angel placed it in the tabernacle constructed for it. Then writing appeared upon it, designating a wife for Titurel in the chaste orphan princess Richaude, daughter of a deceased King Frimutel *in Spangen lant*. From Spain the Princess Richaude was fetched to Muntsalvatsch, the marriage took place, and for twenty years the couple knew great love (H-434). Then, after bearing Titurel twelve children, Richaude died "in her youth."

Of these twelve children only two are named for us, daughter Richaude-2 and son Frimutel. The former is extrapolated from P 84,10, where *Rischoyde* is mentioned as Kaylet's wife and a cousin to Herzeloyde. Albrecht terms Kaylet, quite properly, *fillirois de* Kastel, i.e., heir apparent to the kingdom of Castile, with capital at Toledo, and we are told that he wooed and won Richaude-2 as his bride. For son Frimutel a consort is found in Klarisse, daughter of the converted heathen Granat de Grosie. Klarisse's death is announced in H-469, but of the five children she bore to Frimutel only the two males are mentioned: Anfortas, who undertook love service prohibited by his vows, and Trevrizent, swift of foot and expert at horsemanship. Titurel is more than four hundred years old when he sees these grandchildren of his.

H-475 abruptly and ominously states that Christians now began unseemly rivalry for possession of the *gral*, and H-476 (which rephrases Wolfram's stanza 1) begins the account of Titurel's abdication from kingship of the *gral* in favor of Frimutel and the account of Sigune's ancestry. Therewith the poem passes to the 5,488 stanzas of the central romance.

The Story of Titurel and the Gral: *Second Part (H-5964 to H-6207)*

As if no interruption had occurred, H-5964 continues directly from H-475 by saying that evil neighbors were all about Salvaterre: *Iz wart diu Salvaterre   alumb gemalvisînet,* and the next stanza adds that there were also lapses of faith within. The most urgent prayers avail nothing, the *gral* must be removed to a far and permanent home.

Humbly the self-exiles set out, fed by the *gral* as they traversed many realms to arrive at the port of Marseille. A scent of lilies wafting from Paradise urged them on, the mariners rejoiced at their rich pay, and they sailed. Titurel was with them and the *gral* was their guide. At the island city of Pitimont, five hundred miles from the nearest land, they tarried for four days. The inhabitants gladly took the food and wine supplied by the *gral*, and they begged King Parzival to stay and rule over them, but on the fifth morning the voyagers resumed their journey. The island folk renamed their city *Grals* and built a temple with seventy-two—Wolf says twenty-two—galleries.

Surviving losses incurred by sailing too close to the Lodestone (*magnes . . . dem steine*), they reached "India," where, as Feirefiz explains, the ruler is called Prester (Priest) John because (H-6034,4) "on earth the name of priest is higher in worth than kings." His realm encompasses all of Asia, and he dwells close to Paradise, i.e., the Earthly Paradise, but with a brilliantly shining mountain intervening. A stream with jewel-silt flows from the mountain, the curative herb *assidôse* flourishes on the streambanks, crops of pepper grow nearby, and we are told of methods for harvesting pepper. We hear also of a second mountain called Olimpius, and of a sandy sea on the shores of which live the Jews, and of the fiery mountain of Agremonte where salamanders weave *pfelle* in the fire; five stanzas detail the process of gathering the *pfelle*.

In his land of *Tartarie* Prester John is a mighty hunter, also a mighty warrior who slays 200,000 heathens in a single battle. His palace and its service are rich beyond compare. In the vast courtyard a hundred and twenty-five steps, apparently in concentric circles, ascend to a pillar which supports an enormous ciborium, and over the ciborium, apparently like a hovering Eucharistic wafer, is a mirror that reflects the movements of any enemies that may be astir in the monarch's provinces.

This entire description anticipates what the travelers see upon arrival. Out to meet them comes Prester John in his splendor.

To his inquiry of what the *gral* may be, Titurel replies at length (H-6167–85) and then begs to be deprived of the sight of the *gral* so that he may at last die; (compare P 480,25–29 and P 788,21–30). His wish is granted, he dies, and sumptuous burial is accorded him.

No German tongue, declares the closing stanza (H-6207), ever composed so worthy a poem as this: the souls of all who read it or copy it cannot miss being "paradised."

The Gral *in "The Later Titurel"*

Titurel's definition of the *gral* for Prester John marks the grand climax of our poem and we quote the essential stanzas (H-6172–7) translated from the last pages of Wolf's 1952 booklet of excerpts:

6172 In olden times a host brought the *grâl* to earth,
   a stone in high splendor. People decided to fashion a dish from it.
   Jasper and flint it is called;
   from it the phoenix lives anew whenever he burns himself to ashes.

6173 That same fair dish was befitting for Jesus Christ;
   were anything on earth a thousand times more precious, or even nobler,
   that too would beseem Him as a dish
   for His sublime Eucharist, of which His disciples partook along with Him.

6174 With these qualities the *grâl* transmits its holiness.
   It has preserved them unimpaired ever since the angel deigned to bring it to me on the mountain of *bhaltenunge*;
   in this realm it is now for the first time preserved from all change.

6175 A second costly dish, very noble and very precious,
   was fashioned to duplicate this one. In holiness it has no flaw.
   Men of Constantinople assayed it in their land,
   (finding) it richer in adornment, they accounted it the true *grâl*.

6176 Joseph of Arimathea recognized the true one,
(he) who early and late loves Jesus Christ in pure truth.
Rightly he preserved the dish secretly
until the angel brought it to me, (the one) called *grâl* in angel tones.

6177 Thus have I known it for half-a-thousand years.
Any who do not now shut it away from my sight, he incurs great sin.
To this land it has now come home:
the soul shall fare home to Paradise, the body here turns to loam.

Space here will permit comments on only a few points in this grandiose final scene, and we begin with the first of the quoted stanzas above, (H-6172, but in Wolf's form).

6172 *Ein schar den grâl ûf erde   bî alten zîten brâhte,*
einn stein in hôhem werde.   mán ein schüzzel dar ûz würken dâhte.
jáspis et silix ist er genennet,
von dem der fênix lebnde   wírt, swenn er sich selb zu aschen brennet.

The first line echoes P 454,24 (which purports to be a quotation from the heathen writing of stargazer Flegetanis): *ein schar in ûf der erden liez* (A host left it on earth). That the "host" was "of angels" is clear from Wolfram's added remark that "it" flew high aloft beyond the stars. P 471 identifies these angels as those who stood neutral in the war between Lucifer and God, but P 798 retracts this heterodox notion, saying *those* angels are "eternally lost." (Dante likewise pronounces the neutral angels damned: *Inferno* III, 37–42.) Wolfram specifies no alternate bringers or keepers of the *grâl*, nor does he name time or place for the *grâl*'s descent to earth. Our impression, however, is that the time was soon after the creation of the world. With Albrecht, on the other hand, our impression is that the descent was at the beginning of the Christian era and that the place was probably Palestine. For a long time after being entrusted to Titurel the *grâl* "hovered" (H-309), until an angel placed it in the tabernacle of the *grâl* temple. Possibly Albrecht associated it with the star of the

Magi in Matthew 2:9, which traveled and hovered: "*Et ecce stella, quam viderant in oriente, antecedebat eos, usque dum veniens staret supra ubi erat puer.*" This idea would fit with the return of the *grâl* "home," to "India." We may also recall in passing that Shiz was the holy city of the Magi.

Line 2 terms the *grâl* "a stone," as does P 469,2. In P 235 Parzival sees that stone effortlessly carried by Repanse de Schoye in solemn procession, as if its size and weight were slight, and in P 469–470 Trevrizent repeatedly calls it a stone. No color is mentioned, though it is carried on a green *achmardi* (a silken fabric).

P 469,7 gives the "name" of the stone as *lapsit exillis,* a meaningless expression for which Marti lists (Introduction, p. XXXVII) nine Latin variants proposed by scholars. Wolf says that in all manuscripts of "The Later Titurel" seen by him the "name" is *jaspis et silix* (with the Latin conjunction *et*). Conceivably this was the "name" intended by Wolfram and garbled by copyists.

Jasper is "an opaque variety of colored quartz, usually reddish, yellow, or brown," says Webster's New World Dictionary, but Latin *iaspis* in the Vulgate Bible is understood to be green,— in Exodus 28:20 and 39:13, where it is one of the twelve gems on the breastplate of the High Priest, in Ezechiel 28:13, and in Revelations 4:3, 21:11, 18, and 19, all reporting celestial visions. "The Later Titurel" rather stresses the color green in association with good objects and good characters,—Schionatulander's banner, for instance. In Catholic symbolism green normally signifies "hope." Note also the jasper in the mosaic floor on which the Wonder Bed stands (P 566,21) and, among other prophylactic jewels, in the adornment of Anfortas's sickbed (P 791,13).

Albrecht's *silix* is Latin *silex*, "flint," apparently for kindling the phoenix's death-fire. Flintstone is also a variety of quartz, usually brown, black, or gray in color. How the single *grâl*-stone can be *two* stones is not apparent. See P 469,8–10 for Wolfram's immediate juxtaposition of phoenix and *grâl*-stone.

In line 2 ein *schüzzel* (Acc. fem. sing.) = modern *eine Schüssel*, "dish, charger (i.e., platter); bowl; tureen," from Latin *scutella* (with a short *u*), "a small, flat dish; a tray." (*Scutella* with a long

u yielded OF *escuëlle,* modern *écuelle,* "dish, soup-dish, bowl."
Unfortunately the etymology leaves unclear the size and shape
of the object. The rest of the clause is evasive: *man,* "people,"
"they," "someone," "decided to fashion," "got the idea of fash-
ioning," a "dish" out of it; no hint of who, how, or why, but
prior to the Last Supper and most plausibly in Jerusalem. About
the duplicate *grâl* in Constantinople the present writer knows
nothing.

With the notion of the *grâl* as Eucharistic "dish" and with the
introduction of Joseph of Arimathea into the story Albrecht con-
tradicts Wolfram outright. Where both Chrétien and Wolfram
spoke of "the Grail," Albrecht speaks of "the *Holy* Grail."

The earliest known work containing this idea is the 3,514-line
French poem *Le Roman de l'Estoire dou Graal* (often termed the
Joseph d'Arimathie), composed by Robert of Boron certainly before
1212 and probably before 1201. Subsequently this poem was
retold in prose, and two copies of the prose version are extant,
along with Robert's original poem. From the one version or the
other Albrecht is most likely to have derived his idea of the *grâl*
as a Christian relic connected with Joseph of Arimathea. We
summarize the French poem briefly:

> Robert of Boron's *Roman de l'Estoire dou Graal**
> Through most of this poem the object in question is termed
> a "vessel" (*veissel*). It is first mentioned as a household object
> in the home of "Simon" where the Last Supper was held.
> The Gospels leave the house-owner unnamed, but a reading
> of Matthew 26:6 down into 26:18 will reveal where the name
> came from, and Robert is oddly careless about Biblical details.
> Using this *veissel,* "Christ made His sacrament," (line 396).
> (In Matthew 26:6–13 and Mark 14:3–9 Jesus eats in the home
> of Simon the leper, in Bethany.)
> Then: "A Jew found the *veissel* in Simon's house, took it
> for himself and kept it, for Jesus was led out from there and
> brought before Pilate" (397–400). For reasons unstated the
> Jew gave the *veissel* to Pilate, and "Pilate put it safely away

* Quotations are from an unpublished translation by the present writer.

until such time as it was reported to him that they had de-
stroyed Jesus" (436–8). Again for unstated reasons Pilate
gave the *veissel* to Joseph of Arimathea, who, after taking the
dead Jesus down from the cross, used it to catch the blood
flowing from the wounds of Christ, (563–572). Thus the *veis-
sel*, or "dish," is both a Last Supper relic *and* a Crucifixion
relix, associated with both the bread *and* the wine.

When, four days later, Joseph denies concealing the body
in order to encourage rumors of a Resurrection, the malicious
Jews throw him deep down into a round tower in the house
of an unnamed rich man and abandon him to die. There the
risen Christ appears to him amid dazzling light (717 ff.), en-
trusts him with "the large and precious *veissel*," and, using
symbolism of the Mass, identifies the *veissel* with the altar
chalice—*not* the ciborium.

Joseph long remains so immured, living in the light of the
veissel and presumably furnished by it with food and drink.
Lines 961–1748 relate how Emperor Vespasian's son Titus,
who was suffering from leprosy, was cured at sight of the
lady Veronica's veil (*suaire*), which bore the impress of Jesus'
countenance. (This miracle was originally told of the Emperor
Tiberius, the ruler at the time of the Crucifixion, in a work
called *Cura sanitatis Tiberii*, but by the late twelfth century
Titus had been substituted as beneficiary of the miracle in a
chanson de geste called *La Destruction de Jerusalem*.)

Vespasian is so impressed by his son's cure that he orders
Pilate to reopen the case of Jesus,—forty years after the fact,
where Tiberius could have done so within days or weeks after
the Crucifixion,—and the investigation ultimately brings Ves-
pasian to Palestine and to Joseph's prison, (1749–2012). Let-
ting himself down by a rope into the round tower, the em-
peror finds Joseph alive, cheerful, and ready with Christian
instruction beginning with Lucifer's war against God and the
fates of the fallen angels, (2013–2306).[2]

The third, last, and most interesting portion of Robert's

---

[2] In July of 67 A.D. the actual Vespasian, not yet emperor, had the Jewish
General and future historian Flavius Josephus brought up out of "a deep pit
communicating on one side with a wide cave" where he was hiding and even-
tually made that same Flavius Josephus his trusted advisor. (See Flavius Jose-
phus: *The Jewish War*, pp. 207–212 of the Penguin Classics translation, 1959;
revised 1970.)

poem (2307–3514) relates how Joseph of Arimathea, with Vespasian's permission, led a party of Christians westwards and ultimately "to the vales of Avaron" (i.e., of Avalon), guided not so much by the *veissel* itself as by the Holy Ghost speaking in its presence.

Lines 2657–74 finally disclose the "name" of the *veissel* as *Graal*, "for none shall see the Graal . . . without its pleasing him" (*qu'il ne li agree*). Successive wordplays emphasize the connection of the name with the Old French verb *agreer*, "to please," with a supposed derivation of the word "*Graal*" from Latin *gratia* and *gratus*. In lines 929–936, however, Robert mentions "the large book" (*le grant livre*)—which he does not have—and in which "are written the great secrets that are named and called the Graal" (. . . *Qu'en numme le Graal et dit*).

"The Later Titurel" concurs with Robert's poem on the major point of equating the *gral* with the Eucharistic "dish" of the Last Supper, but with no hint of a Crucifixion relic containing Christ's blood. Both works connect the *gral* dynasty with the Emperor Vespasian and his assignment of Christians to "western" lands. Both connect the sacred relic with Joseph of Arimathea, the French poem making him a character of primary importance, the German poem mentioning him only in its final pages, where H-6176,3 says he "preserved the 'dish' secretly." Both works, however, dwell at length on a journey of faithful attendants who remove the precious object afar, the one to Avalon in the extreme West, the other to "India" in the extreme East.

Yet it must be noticed that, between 1200 and 1230, other French poems presented the *Holy* Grail as a Last Supper relic, sometimes connecting it with the wine chalice of the Mass, and it may have been a widespread tradition to that effect which led Albrecht—or even obliged him—to "correct" Wolfram on this crucial point.

The Name "Muntsalvatsch"

In H-6174 Albrecht "translates" his own term *Muntsalvatsch* as "the mountain of *bhaltenunge*," an interpretation not readily perceptible for Wolfram's *Munsalvaesche*. English meanings of this troublesome word include "maintenance," "preservation," "protective guard," "keeping (of a secret)," "custody," and so on. Forms of the corresponding verb occur in 6174,2 (*behalten*) and 6176,3 (*behielt*), both translated above as "preserved." In H-289 the mountain is *behalten* from Christians, Jews, and heathens,—meaning that *nobody* can find it without divine guidance. Kolb (p. 135) lists further occurrences. In Kolb's opinion *Muntsalvatsch* signifies either "rescued mountain" (*der errettete/ bewahrte Berg*) or "mountain of the rescued" (*der Erretteten/Bewahrten Berg*), i.e., a waiting place for nearly perfected souls just short of Paradise: in other terms, a *purgatorium*, a last way station between the world and God's eternity. Perhaps *berc der bhaltenunge* might be rendered into English as "Mountain of Safeguard." See also further details under "Muntsalvatsch" in the List of Proper Names, pp. 187–88 below.

Be it noted also that in *Parzival* there is no removal of the *gral* to "India" or anywhere else: on this important point Albrecht is again "correcting" Wolfram.

Review: "The Later Titurel" versus Parzival

The Titurel-*gral* portions of Albrecht's poem deal with seven topics which we now succinctly review for their relationships with Wolfram's *Parzival*.

1. TITUREL'S ANCESTRY.—Titurel is a descendant of "Eneas," and hence "a Roman," by way of his grandfather's marriage to a daughter of the Emperor Vespasian. The paternal line goes one generation further back, to Senabor, an early Christian in Cappadocia. His mother was a princess of Aragon. To his father and to two uncles Vespasian assigned "western lands," so that Titurel is hereditary King of "France," with cousins ruling "Anjou" and "Cornwall." In the last fifty years of his five-hundred-year lifetime he is a contemporary of King Arthur. As King of the Gral and living in the Gral territory he is nowhere fitted into the history of Gaul or France; indeed, nothing at all is said about his secular kingdom.

We take this historically impossible and poetically shabby account to be Albrecht's invention. In *Parzival* Titurel is enfeebled and bedridden, and in the *Titurel* Fragments we see him only at the moment of his abdication from the *gral* kingship, but Wolfram nowhere mentions a specific age for him. In his advanced years he is a contemporary of King Arthur, but his family origins are left in total mystery.

2. THE GRAL TERRITORY.—A single angel brought the *gral* to Titurel and guided him to the place where it was to be established, on the hill of Muntsalvatsch at the center of an impenetrable wilderness called *Salvaterre*.

In *Parzival* a host of angels brought the *gral* to earth, where and when is not said; its passing into Titurel's guardianship is left mysterious. The description of the *Terre de Salvaesche* is conveyed in scattered remarks. Albrecht borrowed and expanded these details in a single continuous description of *Salvaterre*, and though he accepted Wolfram's data his description gives the impression of being rearranged.

3. THE GRAL TEMPLE.—The justly famous account of the *tempel* which Titurel built to house the *gral* is entirely without basis in *Parzival*. Albrecht seems to retain Wolfram's Grail *castle* by casually referring to its great hall (*palas*), but his interest is almost exclusively centered on the stupendous *church*, which he seems to place contiguous to the north side of the castle. The source or sources of inspiration for this church remain a matter of debate.

4. TITUREL'S LIFE.—From age fifty until age four hundred Titurel ruled as King of the Gral. At age four hundred, obeying written instructions that appeared mysteriously on the *gral*, he married Richaude-1, the chaste orphan princess of "Spain," begetting upon her in the twenty happy years of their union twelve children, only two of whom are named: his son and successor Frimutel and a daughter, Richaude-2, who married Kaylet of Castile. At age four hundred and fifty he abdicated his kingship of the *gral* in favor of Frimutel, who at that point has the two sons, Anfortas and Trevrizent. Daughters Schoysiane, Herzeloyde, and Repanse de Schoye are mentioned only subse-

quently. Upon Frimutel's premature death Titurel saw grandson Anfortas become King of the Gral.

Frimutel and Kaylet appear in *Parzival*, and Richaude-2 is there mentioned once as Rischoyde, but there is no mention of Richaude-1 or the twelve children. Supplementary details seem to be of Albrecht's invention.

5. REMOVAL OF THE GRAL TO "INDIA."—Christian dissensions outside and inside of Muntsalvatsch required the translation of the *gral* to a safe and permanent home in "India," whence it may originally have come. Titurel, now approaching the age of five hundred, Parzival, as the new King of the Gral, Feirefiz, and all the other members of the *gral* dynasty are members of the voyage to the East.

Wolfram knows nothing of all this. In *Parzival* the *gral* remains in the "west," and the only voyagers to "India" are Feirefiz and his bride, Repanse de Schoye; these two will be the future parents of Prester John, (P 822,21–823,10).

6. PRESTER JOHN'S "INDIA."—This entire section contradicts Wolfram outright. Albrecht's source was some version of that notable forgery, the "Letter," in Latin and dated to some year between 1165 and 1177, which the Oriental Priest-King "John" sent—according to the variant preserved manuscripts—either to Emperor Manuel I, or to German Emperor Frederick Barbarossa, or to Pope Alexander III. That document and relevant materials are presented in Friedrich Zarncke's two studies, of 1876 and 1879, entitled *Der Priester Johannes*; H-stanzas 6034–6458 (in Zarncke's eclectic text) are there included and cross-referenced to the "Letter." Albrecht selected details at will, omitting as he chose, and expatiated at length on what he borrowed.

7. THE NATURE OF THE GRAL.—Just before his death Titurel publicly proclaims the nature of the *gral*. His definition salvages Wolfram's repeated identification of the *gral* as a (small) stone but insists upon the reshaping of the stone into the "dish" which served in Christ's institution of the Eucharist at the Last Supper. This "dish" passes successively into the possession of "Simon," of a thieving Jew, of Pontius Pilate, and of Joseph of Arimathea, who ultimately brings it to "the vales of Avalon." In this ac-

count Albrecht again contradicts Wolfram outright, following a Grail tradition known to us in a French poem by Robert de Boron before 1212. Wolfram's mysterious "Grail" has here become the Christian relic termed "the *Holy* Grail."

The Story of Schionatulander and Sigune (H-476 to H-5963)

At H-476 Albrecht turns abruptly from his account of affairs at Muntsalvatsch to his long central romance, beginning the latter precisely where Wolfram began in stanza 1 of the First Fragment. The Wolframian quatrains, each reworded to introduce that pair of inner rhymes,—including the dubious stanzas: 30, 31, 33, 34, 36, and 53—recur in sequence but with 164 additional stanzas interspersed among them as H-476 through H-780. As before we are told of Titurel's abdication of the *gral* kingship in favor of his son Frimutel, the ancestries of Sigune and Schionatulander, the departure of Schionatulander with Gahmuret for the East, and the stylized colloquies about love. The bulk has been more than doubled—295 stanzas in place of Wolfram's 131—but no new narrative elements are broached.

H-781 proposes to resume the story of "the young *talfin*" but what follows is an account of Gahmuret's (second) expedition to the Baruch and his death before Baldac. (We use the familiar spellings, rather than Albrecht's "Tschinotulander," etc.) The matter is extrapolated from *Parzival* 13–14, 101–2, and 106–7–8 (where Schionatulander was not so much as mentioned), and though the story is well retold, it contains no new actions.

At H-985 the small role of the messenger Tampanis (P 105,1) is initiated—to no purpose, since Tampanis and Schionatulander share (H-1048–50) in the delivery of the doleful tidings of Gahmuret's death and the delivery of the bloodstained tokens, at sight of which Herzeloyde faints. The return from Baldac is by way of Morocco (*Marroch*), Seville, and King Kaylet's land of *Dolet in Yspanie*.

At a convocation of all her nobles the Queen entrusts her three kingdoms of Waleis, Norgals, and Anjou (H-1075–7) to Schio-natulander. Eight days later—P 112 says fourteen days later—she gives birth to a son, and H-1080 says, as *Parzival* did not, that the infant was *baptized* "Parzival." At H-1087 Herzeloyde withdraws to *wuesten Solitane* (Wolfram's *Soltane*).

Deputy ruler Schionatulander now proclaims a great tournament at Kanvoleiz. Guests include King Arthur, Kaylet of Spain, Ehkunat of Berbester (Schionatulander's uncle), and Gurnemanz of Graharz (Schionatulander's grandfather). Later, Schionatulander and Sigune visit Herzeloyde in Soltane, and on this occasion the deputy ruler carries the little boy Parzival about in his arms. The story-time is between Books II and III of *Parzival.* Riding away from Soltane and into a forest, the chaste lovers spend the night beneath the tent that once belonged to black Razalic, Prince of Azagouc, (and before that to Isenhart, P 27 and 61), the very tent, of vast proportions, that Gahmuret pitched (in P 59,21 ff.) outside of Kanvoleiz at his first arrival there. These events occupy 359 stanzas, H-781 to H-1139, (or 1,436 long lines).

"They had not long been thus encamped," begins H-1140, and now follow the 39 stanzas of Wolfram's Second Fragment recomposed as the 49 stanzas, H-1140 to H-1188. As before, the dog with its jeweled leash is caught and lost again and Sigune promises her love on condition that Schionatulander recover that leash at any cost.

The chaste lovers return to Kanvoleiz, but Sigune is inconsolable until Schionatulander mounts his horse Trakune (Dragon) and sets out (H-1256) on his quest. Meanwhile the dog has been caught by King Teanglis of Talimon and Teseac. Admiring the leash, this king lacks the knowledge of letters for reading its jeweled legend, so he winds the leash back around the dog's neck and rides as the animal may guide him. A mile away Orilus von Lalander is encamped, and in a joust (H-1266 ff.) he wins the prize away from King Teanglis.

After various adventures Schionatulander arrives near King Arthur's encampment and successfully engages several knights who come out to meet him,—Keie, Segremors, etc., (H-1329–

80), much as Parzival does in P 284–299, but with no Gawan to bring the hero amicably into the court circle. Instead, Ehkunat of Berbester arrives, starts to challenge the newcomer, and then recognizes him by his coat of arms as his own nephew. The two proceed to Arthur's court, where Schionatulander is knighted.

Ehkunat hears the story of the dog and its leash and is embarrassed that both his wife's and Clauditte's names are mentioned in the jeweled inscription. Orilus, with Jeschute, is also at court, and Jeschute has possession of both dog and leash. When inquiry is pressed as to the rightful ownership of the precious quarry, Orilus maintains that he caught the dog as it was running away from King Teanglis and hence it belongs to him. Schionatulander is to challenge his truculence in a future duel "before Nantes." Meanwhile the knights and ladies favor Orilus's claim. From a reading of the leash before a small company King Arthur learns of the death of his son Ilinot in love service to the lady Florie, and the king mourns his loss. Nevertheless he now proclaims high festival and tournament on the plain of Floritschanze, (= ? Wolfram's *Jôflanze*).

Almost a thousand stanzas are devoted to this festival. The roster of guests culls names from both *Parzival* and *Willehalm* and from other sources, as well as princes from such realistic places as Saxony, Thuringia, Hesse, etc. Wolfram usually avoided naming Germans as participants in his narratives. On the third morning, when "princes under three-times-six-years-old" were to perform (H-1631), there is an interruption as weary travelers arrive bearing gifts from the Baruch Akerin. On the fourth day another digression grants Sigune the joy of hearing the complete message on the jeweled leash as King Arthur bids a scribe (*schriber*) read the message aloud to the whole assemblage.

The inscription occupies 54 stanzas, the first ten of which (H-1836–46) freely vary both Wolfram's 144–153 *and* Albrecht's own paraphrase of them in H-1158–67. There are elaborate conceits and wordplays about Ehkunat's title of "Flower of the Wild," but the remaining 44 stanzas (H-1847–90) constitute a show-piece. As a refrain, the fourth line of each stanza consists of the words: *nu huete wol der verte* (Watch well your ways), as a translation of the dog's name *Gardivias* (i.e., Gardeviaz). The recipient of the message is adjured to observe patience, humility, modesty, faith in *Ecclesje*, mercy toward the poor and toward widows and orphans, and above all to abide by the knightly code. He should have eyes like the ostrich to avoid shame, ears like the lynx against bad company, a throat like the crane to hold back over-hasty speech, etc., etc. If he dances, let him put twelve flowers in his chaplet,—such "flowers" as loyalty, moderation, steadfastness, humility, and so on; also "sweetness" (*süeze*), "for that is called 'love' (*minne*)." "Do not disdain the dog's name," the jeweled inscription concludes, but "Watch well your ways!" This sermon in symbols was admired, we infer, by medieval readers as the epitome of the Christian-knightly code.

Near the close of the festival the brothers Orilus and Lehelin swear fealty to Schionatulander (H-1897), as do twenty other princes. It should be mentioned that Anfortas, still young and unwounded, is one of the guests on this occasion, (H-1756). The chaste lovers return to Norgals, whence Schionatulander must soon set forth to answer yet another appeal for help from the Baruch of Baldac.

Accompanied by Ehkunat he sets out, after sorrowful leave-taking from Sigune. They go first to visit Kaylet in Toledo, but they *sail* from "the harbor of Marseille (*marsilie*)" (H-2524), not from Seville. The nautical cries of the sailors are in Old French.

A storm drives the ship off course and into the harbor of Patelamunt in the land of Zazamanc (*zazamantz*). At that city a blacks-versus-whites tournament is held, as in Book I of *Parzival*, and various personages from that Book are encountered anew. We also hear of apes and she-apes in these regions, and of parrots that speak German, (H-2554). But, unlike Gahmuret, Schionatulander has no love adventure with a black lady. Eventually the party reembarks and sails *eastwards* (H-2628,2). A second storm drives them ashore in the land of *Maledic alterre*, where hostile natives attack them.

News of their plight reaches the Baruch, who comes in person to escort them to Baldac. With great pomp they are greeted by "the Admiraless" (*atmerinne*) Klarissilie, who is attended by a thousand ladies—a hundred of them crowned queens, while acrobats and equestrian performers entertain the assemblage before a great statue of the god Apolle.

An immense war is now detailed through more than 1,400 stanzas, with battle "troops" successively announced as in *Willehalm* 341 ff. at the second battle of Alischanz. The commanders bear names borrowed from both *Parzival* and *Willehalm*, and Albrecht traces the *future* lineage of the Baruch Akerin down to Terramer, the heathen invader—of some 300 years later—in the poem of *Willehalm*! A heathen messenger from "India" also reports (H-2959) about Feirefiz, who already wears jeweled raiment and has the ecidemon device soldered onto his helmet. (We would not have guessed that Feirefiz was old enough yet for such military display.)

By stanza H-4359 Schionatulander has recrossed the sea and is again riding to visit Kaylet. By H-4382 he has rejoined Sigune at home. In nearly 2,000 stanzas the *story* has not advanced an inch.

Presently Sigune goes to pay a visit to Herzeloyde in Soltane; Schionatulander is not allowed there lest he bring impressions of knighthood and martial things into that retreat. *Bonfis, kyrfis, beafis* is growing up,—in P 140,6 *bon fîz, scher fîz, bêâ fîz* were the only names the boy knew for himself,—and H-4391 reports that he spends all his time shooting at birds *uf der vogelweide* ("on the bird meadow"). The story-time is parallel to P 118, just past the beginning of Book III.

On the plain of Floritschanze King Arthur, *der brituneise*, holds festival in honor of the heroes returned from the East and his guests admire their Oriental trophies, including elephants and camels. News comes (H-4437) that Orilus has slain Galoes, the son of Gandin, i.e., Parzival's uncle and the ruler of Anjou; P 80, 91–92, and 134 placed that event before Parzival's very conception, and besides, we thought Schionatulander was the deputy ruler of Anjou. Ehkunat and Kaylet, as staunch allies of Schionatulander, express (H-4441–2) their strong opposition to Orilus. Then comes further word: the brothers Orilus and Le-

helin have laid siege to Kanvoleiz, Schionatulander's capital city;
loyal vassal Turkentals has been slain in that siege (H-4452; =
P 128,8), along with other faithful defenders.—Albrecht is now
inching his story forwards.

Yet Schionatulander, instead of rushing to recapture Kanvo-
leiz, departs with King Arthur "in the direction of Arles" (*gein
arle*), where the Emperor Lucius is invading. Geoffrey of Mon-
mouth (ix, 15 ff.), Wace, and Layamon all place this war against
the Emperor Lucius late in King Arthur's career, just before
treachery at home brought him back to Britain and his final bat-
tles. And now too, H-4652 reports that Orilus has made himself
sole ruler of Waleis and that he shares with his brother Lehelin
the rulership of Norgals, a statement that does not quite square
with P 128 and 141.

Returning from Arthur's war, Schionatulander faces Orilus in
a duel (H-4861–83), the subject of contention being primarily the
dog's leash, which is still in the lady Jeschute's possession,
rather than territorial claims. Though Orilus is unhorsed, the
encounter is inconclusive, and not until H-5009–58 do these op-
ponents fight again: then Schionatulander meets his death at
the hands of Orilus.

In H-5068 ff., the youth Parzival, still in fool's garb, comes
upon the distraught Sigune holding the newly slain Schio-
natulander across her lap; Albrecht has now come up parallel
to P 138–141 (Book III).

After the youth goes on his way, Sigune remains five days
without sustenance, until King Arthur arrives. He brings spices
for the embalming of Schionatulander's corpse, but Sigune de-
clines his offer to convey the dead man to Graswaldan for burial.
At H-5178 Parzival comes upon Sigune a second time, as in
P 249–255 (Book V), sitting *in* a linden tree with Schionatulan-
der's embalmed corpse in her embrace. Directly after he leaves
her Cundrie *la sorcière* (*Kundrie larsusiere*) comes to her and re-
ports that *yesterday* a youth visited the *gral* castle but, beholding
Anfortas's agony, did not inquire its cause. How long (beyond
five days) Sigune has been sitting in the linden tree is not said,

but P 142–249 puts months between Parzival's two meetings with Sigune.

For a time (H-5234 ff.) we hear about Indian Queen Secundille and about Parzival's half-brother Feirefiz (*Ferafis*), whose conquests as listed in the thirty *lines* of P 770 are now expanded into thirty *stanzas.*

At H-5366 Sigune is still sitting in the linden tree as before. Various persons now come to mourn with her,—her father, Duke Kyot of Katelangen, (in contradiction to P 805); Repanse de Schoye, the Grail Bearer, with Anfortas himself, despite his grievous wound, (H-5372); Gurnemanz of Graharz with his daughter Liaze; and so on. At last, at Sigune's request, a hermitage is built for her "at Muntsalvatsch, by a cliff's edge and over a clear brook" (H-5463). Thither, we are told, she retired, and Bishop Bonfacie blessed this *fontsalvacie* (Wolfram's *Fontâne la salvâtsche*) against evil spirits, but we are surprised to learn that the hermitage is adorned with jewels and gold: that was not our impression from P 437 (Book IX).

A lapse of years is now indicated by brief mention of Parzival's conquests, in *romanie,* through wild Greece, in Cappadocia, Asia, and Provence, always in the service of the *gral* and of noble ladies. To this period also belongs the death of Grail King Frimutel in love service to Floramie, daughter of King Flordibintze and Queen Albaflore, rulers of Flordibale, a kingdom rich in rivers and in harbors toward the west. These names do not occur in P 251, where Sigune told Parzival that Frimutel had perished in love service, presumably some considerable time ago.

From the beginning of the Schionatulander-Sigune story "The Later Titurel" adjusted its story-time to coordinate with the story-time of *Parzival,* primarily with Book II and the early Book III of the latter work. With Albrecht's bringing of Parzival to Sigune in the linden tree there is a sudden leap from Wolfram's Book III to Wolfram's Book V; now comes a greater leap, from Book V to Book IX, as Albrecht brings Parzival to Sigune's hermitage. About five years have elapsed, according to P 460 (and according to Chrétien's "Perceval," 6220–1, Roach ed.), but Albrecht is now hurrying toward the end of his narrative. The account of the visit to the hermitage is told in a mere two stanzas (H-5773–4), apparently because the reader is expected to recall the extended scene in P 435–442 of Book IX. This, says H-5774, "is told in full in another book." Five lines later we are told that Sigune "died alone in the forest," and presently there is mention of her burial in the same coffin with Schionatulander, parallel to P 804–5 in Book XVI, but nothing is said about the fact that it was Parzival who gave the lovers joint burial. Independent of anything in Wolfram, Albrecht adds that from the uncorrupted mouths of the lovers two vines, luxuriantly green, grew forth to entwine the common tomb.

Just as we are assuming that the story of Schionatulander and Sigune has been brought to this sad conclusion we are startled to find H-stanzas 5792–5828 devoted to a stirring account of the vengeance taken in their names. The avenger is Ehkunat, who now meets Orilus in a final and violent duel. The place is before the city of Prurin, where Jeschute's brother Erec once unhorsed Orilus (P 134). The savage contest is waged, first on horseback with spears, then on foot with swords, and finally as a desperate wrestling match, and it ends with Orilus's being slain. The ferocity of Albrecht's description surprises us.

Through most of the battle Jeschute lies in a swoon. The body of Orilus is buried in a convent within the city of Prurin, and there Jeschute mourns him with hideous cries that no one can abide hearing, until she herself dies less than a year later. In these statements the shadowy figure of Jeschute belatedly takes on form as a villainess-accomplice frantic with grief and perhaps with remorse.

During the struggle the fateful dog is also present, off to one side, its gorgeous leash glittering in the sun. Suddenly the leash catches fire, and then, with a vigor and vividness unmatched elsewhere in the long poem, H-5811 says:

The dog too caught fire—it was ermine(-white) of pelt—
Inwardly it was made of fungus—the fire caught so swiftly because—
It was the demon's (*or* dragon's) nature to produce fire—

Der bracke must ouch brinnen—der was von harm velle—
Von swammen was er innen—da von daz feur vienc er hie so snelle—
Der tracke was von rehte feur gebende—

By the end of the duel the infernal element has consumed dog and leash totally.

Unwilling even now to relinquish his narrative, Albrecht goes on to tell how Ehkunat is recovering from the serious wounds dealt by Orilus when news is brought to him that Anfortas has been cured and that Parzival has become King of the Grail; (= P 795–6, Book XVI). Seventy-three further stanzas (to H-5917) make final disposition of surviving characters, and the 46 stanzas of H-5918–63 relate a story about Parzival's son Lohengrin, which is rather at variance with Wolfram's account of Loherangrin in P 824–6. At H-5964 the story of Titurel and the *gral* is resumed from where it broke off in H-476.

Meanwhile, at H-5883, amid those addenda to the Schionatulander-Sigune story, the author of "The Later Titurel" gives his name as "Albrecht."

Who Was Albrecht? and Who Did People Think He Was?

Abruptly and awkwardly H-5883 states:

> *Die auentuere habende—bin ich albreht vil gantze*
> *Von dem wal al drabende—* . . .

"Having the adventures, I am Albrecht, trotting back all in one piece from the battlefield" and from an encounter with a certain prince (*fursten*) who could, but shall not, be named. The knightly metaphor masks the admission of not having found financial support from an unnamed "prince." Naturally one inquires: Albrecht *who*?

In 1835 Sulpice Boisserée asserted that the poet was Albrecht *von Scharfenberg.* His assertion was based on Ulrich Füetrer's *Buch der Abenteuer,* composed in 1490, using the stanza pattern of "The Later Titurel," for Duke Albrecht IV of Bavaria. In that work a poet named Albrecht von Scharfenberg is praised as the equal of Wolfram and Gotfried and as the author of poems called *Merlin* and *Seifrid von Ardemont*, both of which had been lost before 1800. "The Later Titurel" is not mentioned. The *Merlin* catches our attention, since Robert de Boron composed a *Merlin* as a continuation of his "Joseph d'Arimathie;" its 502 opening lines are preserved in the "Joseph" manuscript, and if the rest is lost, two later prose reactions of the complete poem survive. If Albrecht used ideas from the "Joseph" in the final portion of "The Later Titurel," he might plausibly have composed a Merlin poem on the basis of Robert de Boron's continuation of the "Joseph." But with the *Merlin* of Albrecht von Scharfenberg lost without a trace, there is no way of judging the matter.

Boisserée's identification was widely accepted. It passed into the histories of literature and into library catalogues, where it still remains. In 1883 a study by Reinhold Spiller denied the identification outright, and others have agreed,[3]—but not all. Werner Wolf (1955), for one, takes "Albrecht" to be "Albrecht von Scharfenberg." We, as readers, have our choice between two equally obscure authors.

The "prince" whose patronage failed to materialize has, however, been identified. In a scrap of manuscript discovered in 1817 by Boisserée and mislaid until 1902 some twenty-three quatrains may be read, in which the poet again gives his name as Albrecht—but not "of Scharfenberg"—and praises a Bavarian *prinz* called *duc Loys et palatinus*. After erroneous identification by Boisserée, this *prinz* has now been identified with fair certainty as Ludwig der Strenge, the very powerful Duke of Bavaria who, in 1272–3, expected to be, but was not, elected Emperor. In the electoral disappointment of October 1, 1273, may be found, in Werner Wolf's plausible opinion, the reason why patronage money was not forthcoming. Further in Wolf's opinion, it was

[3] K. Nyholm: *Albrechts von Scharfenberg "Merlin,"* in *Acta Academiae Aboensis,* Series A: *Humaniora,* 33/2, Åbo, 1967, and H.-G. Maak: *Zu Füetrers "fraw Eren hof" und der Frage nach dem Verfasser des Jüngeren Titurel,* in ZfdPh 87 (1968), pp. 42–46.

the application to Duke Ludwig that forced Albrecht to drop his impersonation of Wolfram of Eschenbach and acknowledge himself as "Albrecht." This point in turn forces *us* to reconsider the whole poem of "The Later Titurel."

The poem, we recall, opened with an over-long prayer in first-person singular and in the manner of the opening prayer of *Willehalm,* but without declaring the speaker's name as Wolfram declared *his.* At the outset of the story proper, H-stanza 77 (quoted on page 40 above) claims the same source works that Wolfram claimed for *Parzival,* heathen Flegetanis and Kyot the Provençal, implying that *Wolfram* is now about to disclose information which he suppressed from those sources in *Parzival.* In H-227–231 and again in H-252 Lady Adventure is addressed (as in P 433,7), and both times Lady Adventure's reply is addressed *to Wolfram.* H-2352, imitating P 143, addresses the long-deceased poet Hartman of Aue as if he were still alive, and H-2381 alludes to Wolfram's patron, "Herman the Count by misdeeds unstained," who had been in his grave since 1217. Hundreds of proper names are reused from both *Parzival* and *Willehalm,* Wolfram's stylistic mannerisms are mimicked again and again, and we have mentioned how closely the scenario and story-time of the Schionatulander-Sigune story are coordinated with *Parzival.* It is little wonder that medieval readers were persuaded that "The Latter Titurel" was a work of Wolfram of Eschenbach.

But what about the "I am Albrecht" of H-5883? Did medieval readers ignore that declaration? Wolf admits to some bafflement on this score, but he has a persuasive explanation. A special manuscript, he thinks, must have been prepared for the imperial candidate, to accompany the application for patronage. To that special manuscript were added six new stanzas—A through F in Wolf's 1955 edition—between H-475 and H-476, and one new stanza—marked A by Wolf—just before H-1140, i.e., preceding the recomposed versions of Wolfram's First and Second Fragments, respectively. In the set of six, "Sir Wolfram" is absolved of any blame for poetic imperfections in the new poem, and in the single stanza before H-1140 it is acknowledged that "The Later Titurel" is reworked from an author "of some fifty years ago" (*di lenge wol von funfzic jaren*). In preserved manuscripts these extra stanzas are differently combined and intruded into the text at points where they make no sense; six of them appear, for instance, in Hahn's text as 885–890. One infers that Albrecht did not mind deceiving the public at large about his identity but that he did not venture to deceive the powerful Duke of Bavaria.

What financial support Albrecht did or did not receive after 1273 is unknown, but H-5883 must have been added soon afterwards, possibly after another refusal of patronage. Wolf thinks that Albrecht then finished up everything from H-5883 to H-6207 and suggests completion of the work by ca. 1275, whereas the present writer feels that the Titurel-*gral* portions of the poem,—as witness the smooth "join" of H-475 with H-5963,—were completed in advance. This would explain how H-stanzas 6179–84 were quoted in the sermons of Berthold of Regensburg, who died in 1272. It is the section between the slaying of Orilus and the resumption of the Titurel-*gral* narrative that shows the frayed ends of workmanship and the author's reluctance to admit to himself that he had said all there was to say. It was naturally amid those miscellaneous "extra remarks" that he included the declaration of "I am Albrecht." We feel that the admission was made grudgingly but almost of necessity: the Wolfram-impersonation had been undone by the application to Duke Ludwig.

As for the bewildering discrepancies in the text, they are probably to be explained by Albrecht's issuing his poem in installments and by rewrites between installments. The discrepancies were certainly "early." In a poem of 1462 Jakob Püterich von Reichertshausen remarks: . . . *wol dreissig Titurelen/ hab ich gesehen, der Kainer was rechte* (I have seen maybe thirty *Titurels*, and not one of them was right).

About the author of "The Later Titurel" the only reliable information must be deduced from his poem. His name was Albrecht. He shows clear evidence of being widely read in Latin, French, and German books. His exclusively aristocratic characters and his strictly aristocratic point of view mark him as a member of the knightly class. Several clues indicate that he was a Bavarian, including his language, which retains Bavarian characteristics even in manuscripts made by non-Bavarians. He intensely admired the works of Wolfram of Eschenbach, even to the point of pretending to *be* Wolfram, yet he did not hesitate to contradict and "correct" him at will. His Roman Catholicism was sincerely devout but marked by an excessive concern with cult objects and religious symbolism. Wolf thinks he may have become a churchman late in life. Two centuries of praise for his poem do not include a single allusion to the man.

"The Later Titurel" is his only known work, unless, of course, he was "of Scharfenberg" and also composed the lost poems of *Merlin* and *Seifrid von Ardemont.* How he learned his poetic craft we do not know, but it is unlikely that his first and only project was the daring and unique one of encapsulating a long Schionatulander romance within a two-part romance about Titurel and the *gral.* Even his sustained impersonation of Wolfram was a brilliant conception.

The plan of his poem is grand, as we have said; its execution is faulty. The acting personages rarely act. He could excellently describe *things* but failed to portray human beings. He was utterly without a sense of humor. He totally ignores the comic adventures of Gawan in *Parzival;* he banishes the very name of Gawan from his own poem, and where Wolfram alternated serious and comic heroes, Albrecht alternates two serious themes. There are no jokes at all, whereas Wolfram could often be whimsical and occasionally brutally off-color. Albrecht shuffles the facts of history like a pack of cards; ideals and other-world concerns occupy him exclusively. His poem gives the effect of a very long saint's legend, where stasis and color are primary principles and where a dreamy, if wholly sincere, religiosity is the prevailing quality. A mournful sense of the transitoriness of all earthly things dominates the total work.

·III·

SOURCES OF THE
SCHIONATULANDER STORY
🎠 🎠 🎠

NINETEENTH-CENTURY SCHOLARS, A. W. Schlegel, Karl Lachmann, and in particular Karl Bartsch, were inclined to think that Albrecht's central romance about Schionatulander was guided by more Wolframian text than the 170 quatrains of the *Titurel* Fragments. No scrap of preserved writing confirms this assumption, nor is there any record of an oral transmission of Wolfram's plan to Albrecht some forty years later. The discontinuity of the two Fragments lent color to this impression.

In H-stanzas 923–955 Gahmuret's death "before Baldac" is narrated with such dignity that Bartsch felt Wolfram's work must underlie these stanzas and that Wolfram's "original" could be recovered, primarily by eliminating the inner rhymes but also by imitating Wolfram's style. Bartsch's reconstruction of the "original" of these stanzas is printed in Marti's edition (III, 251–260), followed by similar reconstruction of Schionatulander's leave-taking from Sigune and the beginning of the search for the lost dog. Divested of the cloying inner rhymes, these verses almost persuade us that *Wolfram* so composed them. They remain, however, as testimonials to Bartsch's linguistic expertise, but since Bartsch's time scholars have agreed that it is a hopeless task to recover lost writing in this way.

Between Wolfram's first and second Fragments *any* sensible person can infer that Gahmuret was killed "before Baldac" and that Schionatulander returned safely home; the death at Baldac is, moreover, told in *Parzival* 106–108. Albrecht did no more than extrapolate his material from *Parzival* 106–108. That he *re*told the episode well is not remarkable: on occasion Albrecht *could* compose good verse. But significantly, no new *actions* are reported. And why should Wolfram have repeated himself this way from one poem to another?

We feel sure that Bartsch's reconstructions were no reconstructions at all and that the passages in question are Albrecht's, and only Albrecht's, first creations. Yet the lurking suspicion persists that Albrecht was, somehow or other, extending Wolfram's original scenario. Our present purpose is to explore that notion further.

The Dog

Other, miscellaneous stanzas reconstructed by Bartsch appear on Marti's page 250, and one of these is particularly significant. It reworks H-stanza 1151, which, if it had a genuine Wolframian original, would fit between stanzas 138 and 139 of the Second Fragment. It begins:

> *Der bracke was harmblanc gevar—ein klein vor an der stirne—*
> *Die oren lanc rot was sin har—* . . .

Wolf's 1955 text adds nothing but a more rational punctuation, and Bartsch's reconstruction differs only in eliminating the inner rhyme to make the first half-line read: *Harmblanc was der bracke*. The sense, either way, is the same:

The hound was ermine-white of color—a little way down its forehead—
Its ears were long, red was its hair— . . .

From the awkward word-grouping we visualize a *red* dog with a white spot over the eyes. But H-5811,1 (quoted on pp. 64–65 above) clearly describes the dog as "ermine(-white) of pelt" (*von harm*[1] *velle*), so that we visualize a *white* dog with red ears. The latter impression is surely the correct one, and just as surely it betokens a supernatural dog from a source in Keltic story.

In Keltic tradition animals from the Otherworld, the land beyond death, may be of various colors[2] but most commonly they are white with red ears. At the opening of the first narrative of *The Mabinogion*, for instance, the hero encounters the Lord of the Otherworld with a pack of dogs that are "brilliant shining white, and their ears red." In pages 90–91 of *Arthurian Tradition* . . . ,[3] R. S. Loomis cites Welsh and Irish tales, as well as French Arthurian and German Arthurian derivatives from them, in which supernatural animals have this coloration, most often horses or dogs, occasionally other species. In the German poem of *Wigalois*, contemporary with *Parzival*, lines 2543–9 (Kapteyn edition) describe a horse as "white as a swan . . . but its left ear and its mane were cinnabar-red." In *Parzival* 339,29 Gawan's horse is "Gringuljete with the red ears," but the name (= Chrétien's *Guingalet/Gringalet*) represents Welsh *guin-calet*, "white-hardy."

That Gardeviaz—Albrecht spells "Gardivias"—comes from the Otherworld is clear from H-5811, where he is said to be "inwardly of fungus" and where he burns away to nothingness, mysteriously, in hellish fire. Amid the slow stateliness and *bienséance* of "The Later Titurel" such a vivid and uncharacteristically imaginative *action* is startling, and we find ourselves exclaiming: "Albrecht never invented that motif! This is something out of Keltic story!" And certainly the motif is independent of Wolfram. Immediately we are reminded of the Otherworld dogs in the opening scene of the *mabinogi* of *Pwyll Prince of Dyfed*,

---

[1] MHG *harm*, French *hermine*, and English "ermine" all derive from *Armenius mus*, "Armenian mouse." Modern German says *Hermelín*.

[2] See Katharine Briggs: *An Encyclopedia of Fairies*, New York, 1976; pp. 83, 140, 247, etc.

[3] Roger Sherman Loomis: *Arthurian Tradition & Chrétien de Troyes*, Columbia University Press, New York, 1949.

Further references to this book will be indicated simply by "Loomis."

the first, and one of the oldest, of the eleven tales of *The Mab-inogion*.

Because of this and other parallels to be discussed presently we formed the hypothesis that the story about Schionatulander and the dog derives ultimately, not in direct line of descent from the *mabinogi* of *Pwyll*, but from that area of Keltic story of which the *mabinogi* of *Pwyll* is the only preserved example in Keltic literature. Not that either Wolfram or Albrecht knew Welsh or this *mabinogi*! The immediate source of the Schionatulander story would need to be a French derivative of the *mabinogi*, which is dated soon after 1050. But before any discussion is possible it is incumbent upon us to state the essentials of Albrecht's Schio-natulander romance.

Albrecht's Basic Scenario

Setting aside all the wars and tournaments and voyages and multitudinous embellishments, the Schionatulander story, as Albrecht tells it, is a very simple one.

> The dog sent by the lady Clauditte to her ami Ehkunat escapes from Ehkunat, comes into the possession of the chaste lovers Schionatulander and Sigune, and escapes again. Sigune stipulates recovery of the dog and its story-bearing leash as her condition for granting her love, and the youth accepts her terms.

Thus far Wolfram's Second Fragment and H-stanzas 1140–1188.

> Dog and leash are next captured by King Teanglis, only to be lost anew almost at once to Duke Orilus, who bestows them upon his devoted *amie* Jeschute. At Arthur's court Ori-lus becomes Schionatulander's vassal, but during the latter's absence in the East he turns disloyal and seizes Schionatu-lander's lands. Returning lord and faithless vassal fight a duel in which, not territorial claims, but possession of the dog is

the primary issue. This fight ends inconclusively, but in a later encounter Orilus kills Schionatulander. Still later, Ehkunat, the hero's constant friend, meets Orilus in desperate combat and slays him. In the course of this duel the watching dog and its jeweled leash burst into supernatural fire and burn away to nothingness.

We marvel that Albrecht should stretch so tenuous a story to nearly 22,000 lines.

The essential characters, we observe, are the two males, the hero and his foe, with Ehkunat as avenger emerging belatedly into the foreground as a third primary personage. At the same point the dog also becomes "a character" after having been so long a mere object. The three ladies count for very little. Wolfram had indeed *begun* to make Sigune a memorable personage, but Albrecht, once he had repeated what Wolfram had to say about her, found little else to say about her. His Jeschute and Clauditte are mute shadows, mere pretexts alleged to motivate their lovers.

Two male roles, at first inspection quite different from Schionatulander and Orilus, are the focus of attention in the Welsh *mabinogi*; a third male, offstage, may not be related to our purpose; and two (not three) offstage ladies complete the cast of characters.

Pwyll Prince of Dyfed[4]

Pwyll Prince of Dyfed (southwest Wales, approximately modern Pembrokeshire) went hunting once in Glyn Cuch (the valley of the River Cuch which separates Pembrokeshire from Carmarthenshire). When his dog-pack, in pursuit of a stag, leads him far from his companions he sees the stag brought down in a forest clearing by another pack of dogs such as he had never seen before.

> The colour that was on them was a brilliant shining white, and their ears red; and as the exceeding whiteness of the dogs glittered, so glittered the exceeding redness of their ears.

---

[4] We follow the translation of *The Mabinogion* by Gwyn Jones and Thomas Jones in Everyman's Library 97, 1948, New York, E. P. Dutton & Co.; pp. 3–9.

He drives the strange dogs off and baits his own pack on the stag. Just then the owner of the rival pack arrives. He is Arawn, king of Annwn (the Afterworld; pronounce: ah-NOON), clad in a brownish-gray garment, with a hunting horn slung from his neck, and riding a dapple-gray steed. The ensuing altercation is quickly appeased when Pwyll agrees to kill a rival king from Annwn, Hafgan ("Summer-white"), a year from tonight "at the ford."

For the intervening year Pwyll and Arawn exchange shapes and live in each other's kingdoms, each sleeping with the wife of the other without either wife's perceiving the deception. Both kings pass the year pleasantly but chastely. A year and a day hence the kings shall meet again at this very spot and reexchange shapes.

On the anniversary night Pwyll meets Hafgan in the middle of the ford and deals him a mortal blow. As Arawn had instructed, Pwyll refuses to deal Hafgan a second blow, much as the latter begs to be put out of his misery. Hafgan dies. Pwyll adds Hafgan's kingdom to his own, and on the morrow—a year *and a day*—keeps his appointment with Arawn in Glyn Cuch. Each resumes his true shape, and in the times that followed there was strong friendship between them.

Folklore underlies this detached episode, (which is followed by wholly new story matter). Arawn, in his brownish-gray garment, is Winter, Hafgan is Summer, and the duel "at the ford" is a seasonal encounter,—probably on the night of October 31st. The supernatural alliance glorifies Pwyll and the rulers of Dyfed, whose progenitor he is, but why Arawn needs a mortal to slay Hafgan for him is unclear. More about this episode may be found in Loomis, pp. 131–3; 264; and 449 ff., and there it will be seen that Arawn, here quite benign, is more particularly the personification of the Winter Storm.

A Lost French Lai *about Schionatulander*

From the area of Keltic story represented by the *mabinogi* we assume the derivation of one or more versions in the Old French language, most likely as *lais* in verse. We have in mind courtly narrative poems in octosyllabic couplets, running to a total of 400 lines perhaps,—the average length of the twelve *lais* generally attributed to Marie de France,—and dealing with love. Such poems were derived from Keltic sources, usually Welsh or Breton, normally had (it is believed) a Breton prose stage followed perhaps by a French prose stage, and ended in French versions of rhymed verse.

We now present a freely improvised scenario for such a continental *lai* derived from "the area of story represented by the *mabinogi*."

Where the (nameless) wife and queen of Arawn was deceived into believing that Pwyll-in-Arawn's-shape was actually her husband, it is easy to imagine a story-variant where, without discovering the deception, the wife became resentful of her "husband's" neglect.

> As a wife aggrieved she sought rescue by a mortal. She stole one of Arawn's hunting dogs—inevitably a white one with red ears, furnished it with a message attached to its collar, and dispatched it to the mortal man. Out of its master's control the dog went wild, escaped from the mortal man, and came into the possession of a third party, who did not perceive that the creature was taboo. Arawn came upon the "thief," slew him forthwith, and blasted the disloyal dog with a thunderbolt out of his winter-storm clouds.

No such poem need have existed; this is mere invention on our part. We do, however, believe that a particular French *lai*, now lost, existed under some such title as the *lai* of *Li Joenet de la Lande*, "The Youth from the Moor," a phrase which Wolfram took as the name "Schionatulander," and that this particular *lai* served both Wolfram and Albrecht as the basis for their Schionatulander romances, the unfinished one and the finished one alike. Our purpose now is to reconstruct this lost *lai* as far as possible by examining the several acting personages, including the dog Gardeviaz. Necessarily we must take one personage at a time, and we begin with Orilus.

Orilus

Wolfram.—In *Parzival* 129–137 the youthful hero, on his second day out from home, comes upon a lovely lady asleep in a rich tent. She is Jeschute, Duchess of Lalander. From her the lad steals a kiss, a ring, a brooch, and some of her lord's food and then rides merrily on his way. The fire-eating husband returns from hunting, believes the worst about his wife, and punishes her by dressing her in rags and making her ride a starveling horse. (Note how this "punishment ride," as a motif out of Keltic story, had already served both Chrétien and Hartman as Erec's humiliation of Enide.) Jeschute's punishment continues "more than one whole year," until Parzival (in P 256 ff.) chances upon the pair, defeats Orilus in a joust, and compels him to three pledges: acceptance of the innocent explanation, reconciliation with Jeschute, and surrender at Arthur's court to Orilus's own sister, Cunneware de *Lalant,*—oddly, not *Lalander.* In his defeat Orilus fulfills these three pledges and becomes, as far as we can see, a kindly husband and a loyal knight of Arthur's. Ten further allusions to Orilus as far as P 545 (Book X) do not alter this impression. His identification in 545,29 as a Burgundian (*Burgunjoys*) seems to be a gratuitous detail. We also recall Wolfram's reluctance to portray villains. In short, Wolfram's Duke Orilus de Lalander is a distasteful, though not malignant, character who turns wholly to the good and thereafter recedes gradually from the reader's view.

Albrecht.—In "The Later Titurel" Duke Orilus de Lalander, beloved of the lady Jeschute, is a major character, not a secondary one, unrelievedly arrogant, brutal, disloyal to his oath, and in ever increasing degree malignant. To the tent episode no allusion is made, nor to Orilus's gracious surrender at Arthur's court. Nowhere does he turn to the good, even temporarily. He is evil from the start, and in his final duel with Ehkunat displays a startling ferocity. As for Jeschute, who never speaks a word in "The Later Titurel," we infer that she is the faithful mirror of her lord's ego, and in her name *he* stubbornly keeps the dog and leash, consistently maintaining that they are rightly his.

Even his duel with Schionatulander is fought for the dog and leash, not for the territories he has usurped from Schionatulander.

Where, we ask, did Albrecht get his notion of Orilus as evil and ferocious? Certainly not from the *Titurel* Fragments, where he is not so much as mentioned. True, Sigune did tell young Parzival (in P 141) that Orilus murdered both Schionatulander and Galoes, Parzival's uncle, and Albrecht repeats these charges. Wolfram seems to forget and forgive them, and Albrecht does not dwell on them. Sigune also said that Lehelin, Orilus's brother, had seized two kingdoms of Parzival's; at a much later point in story-time Orilus and Lehelin together usurp Schionatulander's two kingdoms,—the very same ones that he is said to be defending in the name of young Parzival. Yet even in transferring the usurpation, Albrecht allows the political-territorial motif to lapse: when Orilus and Schionatulander face each other in combat it is for possession of the dog and leash, not for territorial claims. In our opinion, Albrecht only very tenuously connected his Orilus with the Orilus of *Parzival* because he was following the outlines of the lost French *lai* of *Li Joenet de la Lande,* where the Orilus-character *was* both evil and ferocious and where he *did* slay "the youth from the moor" in dispute over the possession of the dog and leash.

Chrétien.—Nor did Albrecht go back to Chrétien for his new concept of Orilus. The tent episode, in "Perceval" 636–833 (Roach edition), agrees with Wolfram's account, and, as noted, "The Later Titurel" makes no allusion to it. With only minor discrepancies, "Perceval" 3691–4140 presents Orilus's change of heart in Wolfram's terms; again, "The Later Titurel" ignores Orilus's change of heart. About kingdom-stealing the French poem says nothing at all.

In one detail Chrétien's Orilus-character *is* ferocious: the corpse of the Schionatulander character is *beheaded* (*avoit trenchie la teste*). Otherwise the French lines 3428–3690, parallel to *Parzival* 138–141, present "a maiden" (*une pucele*) distracted with grief for the death of her *ami* (3441), who is simply "a knight" (*un chevalier*, 3454) and who has just been slain by "a knight" (*uns chevaliers*, 3464).

Not until the following episode, at 3817, is the slayer-knight's name given as *li Orgueilleus de la Lande*. Note Wolfram's *der stolze Orilus* in *Parzival* 133,5. By this name we understand "the haughty[5] knight of the moor." Gaulish *landa* passed into French as *la lande*, "moor, heath, wasteland;" borrowed into Middle English as *laund(e)*, it took on the meaning of "open treeless space," (Ernest Weekley) and developed into modern "lawn." Loomis regularly speaks of "the Proud Knight of the Glade." Wolfram first gave him the title of *duc*, and Albrecht echoes that title.

[5] In Chrétien's *Erec* 2121 (Roques edition) *li Orguelleus de la Lande* appears as a jouster at the tournament "in the plain below Tenebroc," where he accepts Erec's challenge. Erec unhorses him by a blow "on the shield, before his breast" and leaves him lying on the ground as he rides to meet his next challenger.

As Hartman's *Erec* retells the episode, the tournament is held between "Tarebrôn and Prûrîn" and the defeated jouster is "a doughty (*vrum*) man, the arrogant Lando" (*der hôchvertige Landô*), line 2576.

In *Parzival* 134 Orilus boasts that Jeschute's brother Erec well knows his prowess, "although he unhorsed me in the lists at Prurin."

In *Diu Crône* (see p. 157 below) a list of Arthur's guests at the castle of *Tintagûel* in *Cornôalle* includes *Von der Lande Orgoillos*, line 595.

At the same tournament, knight Riwalin, speaking of the undependable nature of Fortune, remarks that Fortune can sometimes lead a man to disgrace,

". . . as befell *Orgolois de la Lande* at Parzival's hands when he avenged the *halsslac* ("blow on the neck," or "box on the ear," or "slap in the face") that he struck him with his spearshaft in retaliation for an insult (*unvuoc*) committed in speaking just when he was amicably receiving him; . . ." (lines 5980–6).

This "recollection" does not tally with *Parzival* 260 ff., which reports the only encounter between Parzival and Orilus. Might it be that *Diu Crône* is recalling the scene from what we believe was the earlier version of *Parzival*, composed in the 1190s?

In any case, we observe that the Orilus-figure is regularly "haughty" and regularly humiliated for his haughtiness.

Like "Gurnemanz of Graharz," the Orilus-figure appears in several continental romances, suggesting that his narrow role is a mere residue from a much broader role that he once enjoyed in Keltic story. "The Later Titurel" is alone in granting him larger scope, and we feel that, in granting him that larger scope, "The Later Titurel" retains more of the ferocity and malignancy of the original Keltic character.

This Duke of Lalander is properly "haughty." His prototype was Arawn, Lord of the Otherworld, and for all his benignity in the *mabinogi* of *Pwyll*, he was much more than a personification of Winter; he was King Death in person.

If it seems implausible that a mortal—Ehkunat—should slay "King Death in person," such an idea is not unique in Arthurian story. Erec does just that (in Chrétien's *Erec* 4815–30, Roques edition) when he kills the Count of Limors. There "Limors" is a castle, but *li mors* in Old French meant "the dead man," probably translating Breton *ar Maro*, as a circumlocution for Death personified; see Loomis, pp. 164–5. Moreover, though this Count's name is Oringle, Loomis (p. 489), citing from the Foerster edition of *Erec,* notes that in three cases the scribe wrote "*Orguilleus* de Limors," not "Oringle de Limors."

In other words, Arawn as "Lord Death" was the prototype and the "haughty knights" in all three authors are his literary descendants. By chance, the Orilus of "The Later Titurel" is nearest to the prototype in arrogance and ferocity; if we had the lost *lai* of *Li Joenet de la Lande* these features would not seem to be emphasized "by chance."

Ehkunat

In Wolfram's *Titurel* Fragments Ehkunat is, so far as we can determine, a benign personage, maternal uncle of the hero, the *ami* of the lady Clauditte, and the intended destinee of the jeweled message on the dog's leash. In "The Later Titurel" his role is vastly expanded, as the role of Orilus is vastly expanded, but in the opposite direction: Albrecht makes him the noblest of knights and most loyal of friends, the dauntless avenger of his slain nephew Schionatulander, the slayer of Orilus, and the undoer of evil.

In making him so, Albrecht disregards three allusions to an offstage Ehkunat in *Parzival*, which, minor as they are, have an odd ring to them. In 178 Gurzgri (Schionatulander's father) is said to have ridden with "Mahaute in her beauty, whom her *haughty* (*stolzer*) brother Ehkunat had given him for a wife." It is true that *stolz* occurs also as a laudatory term, or even as a "mere epithet," but we incline to take it as "haughty" in 178,19. In P 321 Gawan is accused of having murdered King Kingrisin of Ascalun in the very act of greeting him, yet P 413 and P 503 agree that it was "the proud (*stolze*) Ehkunat," and not Gawan, who perpetrated that foul deed.

An arrogant Ehkunat capable of murder by treachery seems incompatible with the Ehkunat of "The Later Titurel" *and* of Wolfram's *Titurel* Fragments: can Clauditte's "Flower of the Wild" be a villain? In fact, there seem to be discrepancies between the two Ehkunats of Wolfram himself, the one in *Parzival* and the one in the *Titurel* Fragments. Since both Wolframian Ehkunats are offstage characters the matter cannot be immediately resolved, but there is no doubt that the Ehkunat of "The Later Titurel" is a perfect flower of chivalry and a major personage in the story. (Even more dismaying is the possibility that there are two different Ehkunats, one a Count and one a Duke, in Wolfram's *Titurel* Fragments; we believe there is only one, primarily because Albrecht thought there was only one, but the complex matter is discussed under item "Ehkunat" in the List of Proper Names, p. 168 below.)

Flutre lists no name corresponding to "Ehkunat" in any of its spellings; nor any corresponding name in "Es-" closer than one obscure "Escorant;" but Bartsch (p. 142) thought it was probably the equivalent of the Arthurian knight "Equinot" (son of Count Haterel) in Hartman's *Erec* 1669. Jean Fourquet (p. 257) confidently asserts the same, and we agree. The *h* is otiose, like many an *h* in MHG names, and we should not pronounce "E*h*kunat," as commonly, but "Ekunat;" the French "Equinot" should be pronounced "Ekinot."

Chrétien's *Erec* has no name corresponding to "Equinot" in Hartman's line 1669, and Flutre, besides having no "Equinot," has no "Haterel" either. We propose that (French) "Equinot" is a shortened form of *Herlequinot/Hellequinot*, with *-ot* suffix (as in "Lancel*ot*;" see Loomis, p. 190), the basic name being *Herlequin/ Hellequin*. In the French poems of the "William cycle" this

yielded *Hernaut/Ernaut/Arnaud* as the name of one of William's
brothers, also the *Arnalt* of *Willehalm*. Its component parts are:
Herla (= Wotan!) and *quin*, (Germanic) "king," and it is the name
of "the Wild Huntsman" who leads his troop (*mesnie*) across the
sky as the personification of winter storm.[6] Alternate names
listed by Loomis, p. 264, fn 8, are: Wodejäger, the Grand Veneur
of Fontainebleau, and Herne the Hunter of Windsor Forest (as
in Act V of *The Merry Wives of Windsor*). In further development
the name became "Harlequin."

The Wild Hunt figures in the folklore of various European
peoples, and details about it vary, as does the name of its leader,
the Wild Huntsman himself. In Welsh lore the leader's name
was most commonly Gwyn ap Nudd ("son of Nudd"), Nudd
being probably identical with the Keltic god Nodens and also
with Wolfram's *Noyt* (in *Parzival* 178 and 401). His particular
locale was "Avalon." That name might designate the Keltic is-
land of the dead far out in the western sea, or again it might
designate the legend-haunted, if normal-seeming, town of Glas-
tonbury in western England; in the Welsh language that town
has always been known, and still is known, as *Inis Avalon*, "the
Isle of Avalon." Landlocked it may be, where it lies at the foot
of the high hill of Glastonbury Tor, but almost until the begin-
nings of recorded history the mighty and isolated hill was re-
flected in a shallow lake (since dried up) and human inhabitants
clung to its lake-shore base. As Geoffrey Ashe relates in *King
Arthur's Avalon*, (New York, 1958; p. 26), Gwyn, "King of the
Fairies," brought the spirits of the dead upon the winds to the
top of, or into the interior of, Glastonbury Tor and, after assem-
bling them there, guided them on to Annwn, the Welsh Hades.

Likewise a leader of the Wild Hunt, and likewise associated
with Avalon, was the unclear Welsh figure of Avallach, hardly
to be distinguished from Gwyn, says Ashe. King Arthur himself

---

[6] See Spitzer: *Arnaud*, in *Mélanges de Philologie romane . . .* , Paris, 1949, pp.
107–112, and Frappier: *Les Chansons de geste du cycle de Guillaume d'Orange*, (Vol.)
I, Paris, 1955, pp. 104–6. Also Ernest Weekley's *Etymological Dictionary*, under
"Harlequin."

In Katharine Briggs's *An Encyclopedia of Fairies*, op. cit., some of the relevant
items, alphabetically listed, are: *The Fairy Rade, Gwyn ap Nudd, King Herla, Wild
Edric*, and *The Wild Hunt*.

was sometimes termed the Wild Huntsman (Ashe, pp. 98–99), as was Arawn (Loomis, p. 132). Wotan, as King Herla, was another alternate, though not localized at Avalon, and in French-language areas Herlequin/Hellequin.

At some French stage in the evolution of our story, we think, "Equinot," as the name of the Wild Huntsman and as a shortened form of *Hellequinot*, was substituted for the Wild Huntsman of older Keltic versions,—Arawn, or Avallach, or Gwyn ap Nudd. But somehow the Wild Huntsman figure—"King Death in person"—had acquired the appellative of *li Orgueilleus de la Lande*, thus permitting the inappropriate shift of the name "Equinot" to the hero's friend, the benign character in the story. Possibly the shape-shifting in the *mabinogi* of *Pwyll* contributed to the confusion of names, the genuine Arawn being indistinguishable from Arawn-in-Pwyll's-shape. From the confusion there may have developed conflicting notions of "Equinot," to account for the treacherous villain Ehkunat in *Parzival* 413 and 503 and for the apparently benign Ehkunat of the *Titurel* Fragments—and for the seemingly good Arthurian knight listed by Hartman as *Equinot fil cont Haterel*. We infer that the Ehkunat of "The Later Titurel," as a paragon of chivalry, reflects the *good* character mislabeled "Equinot" in the *lai* of *Li Joenet de la Lande*.

A Related Episode in Wigalois

In any case we think our lai of *Li Joenet de la Lande* was not the only continental derivative "from the area of Keltic story represented for us solely by the *mabinogi* of *Pwyll*." We pause to consider an isolated episode in lines 2207–2318 of the German poem of *Wigalois*.[7]

[7] We translate from *Her Gwigalois, der Ritter mit dem Rade* (Sir Gwigalois, the Knight with the Wheel), edited by J. M. N. Kapteyn, Bonn, 1926. This poem of 11,708 lines in tetrameter couplets was composed by Sir Wirnt von Gravenberg in 1208–1210, as the 1847 editor Franz Pfeiffer claims, but not all scholars are agreed. The text alludes to Hartman's *Erec* and *Iwein* and to the character of Jeschute in *Parzival*; Wolfram himself is praised in 6343. Besides 3 complete manuscripts and fragments of 30 more, the work is known in a prose Volksbuch form after 1400.

Sir Wigalois (or Gwigalois) is riding in the company of a young lady when

> . . . a little brachet-hound (*bräkelîn*) ran past them,—no prettier could there be, white all over, except that one ear was yellow and the other red as blood. . . . (Wigalois) caught the little dog (*hundelîn*) and to her delight put it in her lap. . . . This was past mid-morning.
>
> Without a care they were riding along toward a dark pine forest when out rode a mighty man with coal-black hair, each lock entwined with silk and gold just the way he liked it, and his horse was black and fine. He wore a hat of flowers and garments of green twill (*tymît*). . . . In his hand he carried a club stoutly girded with thongs. I fancy he had ridden with his dogs into the forest. His anger was roused at sighting his little dog (*hundelîn*) and to the girl he said, 'I'll have you know, young lady, that little dog (*kleine hunt*) is mine. Tell me, who gave it to you? This may well cost him his life.'
>
> "This knight here," said she.
>
> "How dare you, Sir, catch my pretty dog? Have him put down on the road this minute or you will never get off with your honor and you will go home with an unsound body."
>
> "This talk is for a woman," said Wigalois the warrior, "and if God keeps us we shall not yield honor and life for so trifling a matter. I doubt the dog is yours. Anything else you ask of us honorably and kindly you may well obtain, but, come what may, harsh language and threats will never make us give you this dog."

Angrily the knight rides off "across the broad fields and toward the great wilderness" to reappear further down the road armed and ready for combat. His emblem is a swan with body represented by ermine fur, beak and feet of gold, but his name is not given. In the joust that ensues Wigalois runs a spear right through him, suffering no harm himself.

> The little dog was liberated by the joust, and, churches being scarce in the region, the lord was left lying there. As for his horse, our knight tethered it to the bough of a thorn bush.

We take this episode to be the *residue* from a lost French *lai* collaterally descended from the *mabinogi* of *Pwyll* and collaterally related to that other French *lai* which we term *Li Joenet de la Lande* and which we think served both Wolfram and Albrecht as the basis for their respective romances about Schionatulander. The nameless knight in summery accouterment is likely to be a derivative from Hafgan. The little dog is one of *his*, not Arawn's, dogs, hence *not* a "prototype" of Gardeviaz. The pretty ingénue who receives the dog as a gift is probably a French addition to the story, analogous to Sigune but by no means similar to Sigune. The role of Wigalois is parallel to the role of Pwyll and involves no vengeance for the slaying of a friend.

The casually mentioned thorn bush, however, is a significant residual detail. As Loomis, pp. 129–131 and 449 ff., shows, a hawthorn bush marked the place "at the ford" where knights derivative from Hafgan are slain in various romances. (The ford is often "the Ford Perilous," OF *li guez perilleux*, and in *Parzival* 583, 600, and 602 it is Gawan who slays the opponent at *Li gweiz prelljus*.) The un-Christian abandonment of the opponent's corpse is likely also to be a survival from a more primitive version of the story, but, despite its rough-and-ready slaying, this brief episode in *Wigalois* is much attenuated from its ultimate Keltic source. Our hypothetical *lai* of *Li Joenet de la Lande* must have been more stark and tragic.

Schionatulander

For the name "Schionatulander" Karl Bartsch suggested two equally plausible explanations: either *li joenet ù l'alant*, "the youth with the (hunting) dog," or *li joenet de la Lande*, "the youth from the moor." (We prefer "moor" to "glade" because we have yet to find a clear case where OF *lande* had the Middle English sense of "glade," though it may well have been significant that the Pwyll-Arawn encounter took place in a forest glade.) The terminal *-er* of "Schionatulander" is the common Germanic ending, as in "New Yorker," "Berliner," etc. The second alternative would have the advantage of associating "the youth" with his murderer, Orilus de *Lalander*, with the same terminal *-er*. We have already noted that the sister of Orilus is Cunneware de *Lalant*, not "de Lalander."

As Orilus's victim Schionatulander may have been a Hafgan-derivative. On the other hand, by taking and keeping the runaway dog he resembles Sir Wigalois, who seems to have been a Hafgan-slayer. Quite possibly he was neither, but a wholly new character introduced into the story situation. Since medieval poems regularly took their "titles" from the names of their heroes, the tale would have been known as "the *lai* about *li joenet de la lande*." Thus Wolfram, we believe, must have thought of his unfinished romance in quatrains as his *Schionatulander*, or as his *Schionatulander and Sigune*; we consider "*Titurel*" a misnomer born of literary confusions of the Romantic era.

In the *lai* the Schionatulander-character must have been "a youth" (*joenet*), not a knighted adult, but of noble birth. Introductory matter must have explained who he and his young *amie* were, but the narrative is likely to have come quickly to the woodland episode in which the runaway dog was captured and lost again. Following upon Wolfram's stanza 170 and Albrecht's H-1188, "the youth" must have taken his *amie* "home,"—he could hardly leave her in the forest,—and from "home" (which Albrecht identifies with Kanvoleiz) he set out on his quest for the lost dog. Perhaps his horse had the name *Trakûne* ("Dragon"), as H-1255 says. H-stanzas 1263–1303 of "The Later Titurel" then relate that King Teanglis of Teseac captured the runaway dog and lost him again, that Schionatulander met Orilus and from him learned part of the truth about King Teanglis, and that Schionatulander rode a successful joust against Teanglis. Later, in H-1329, Schionatulander espies a dog that he thinks may be Gardeviaz, but he cannot get close enough to make sure. In some form or other these adventures may well have been included in the lost *lai*. Very probably the *lai* then brought the characters to Arthur's court, as in "The Later Titurel," where Schionatulander challenges Orilus's possession of the dog and where a joust is appointed "before Nantes" for settling the matter by contest of arms. From that point until H-

5017 Albrecht's digressions lead us far away from the *lai*. Schionatulander's brutal death at the hands of Orilus and before the eyes of Sigune must surely, however, have had its counterpart in the source work.

We imagine that the Schionatulander-character was still "a youth" at his death and that the story-time of the *lai* encompassed nothing like the many years alleged by Albrecht. Upon this *naif* Albrecht superimposed heroics derived from multiple sources and a political role extrapolated almost entirely from Sigune's remark in *Parzival* 141,2–3: "This prince was slain for your (Parzival's) sake because he defended your lands steadfastly." Orilus, as mentioned, usurps Schionatulander's lands—which are allegedly Parzival's lands temporarily defended by Schionatulander,—yet the Orilus-Schionatulander duel is fought, not over usurpations, but over claims to the dog and its jeweled leash. In that significant detail Albrecht reveals how closely he is hewing to the story line of the source work, even to forgetting about his own contrived politics.

The Three Female Characters

SIGUNE.—The *lai* is likely to have provided an *amie* for each of the three male personages, and a prime motivation in the story is likely to have been the male rivalries in love feats for these ladies. What names they bore, if any, we do not know. We imagine the Sigune-figure to have been a docile ingénue, probably nameless. What Wolfram intended by calling her "Sigune" is discussed in pp. 197–9 below in the List of Proper Names. The memorable portrayal of Sigune, as *begun* in the Fragments, dwindles to mere conventionalities in "The Later Titurel," probably because her role in the *lai* contained few *actions*. She was necessarily with her beloved when the dog was captured and lost again near the beginning of the story; she was apparently with him when Orilus killed him; presumably, however, he pursued his quest of the lost dog without having her at his side.

It is our guess that the *lai* contained a concluding statement about her to the effect that after his death "the youth's" *amie* "withdrew from the world" and lived in single-minded devotion to his memory. Where else could Wolfram have found that notion? Chrétien's poem contains no hint of it.[8]

In "Perceval" the Sigune-character is paralleled *only* by that nameless "maiden" (*pucele*) who in her distraction of grief holds the corpse of her slain (and nameless) *ami* across her lap. It is our guess also that the *lai* of *Li Joenet de la Lande* contained a scene much resembling this, with the Ehkunat-character (rather than young Parzival) coming upon the woeful tableau and hearing the "maiden's" lament.

JESCHUTE.—Contrary to anything in *Parzival*, the Jeschute of "The Later Titurel" is a villainess-accomplice to Orilus. Utterly at the command of her lord, she never speaks in the poem and never appears except at Orilus's side. She swoons to behold the duel between her lord and Ehkunat, and after burying Orilus she howls in insane grief until she herself dies. In "The Later Titurel" this mad sorrow of wicked for wicked is doubtless meant to be a contrast to Sigune's devotion in prayer beside Schionatulander's coffin, the decorous mourning of good for good. We fancy that Albrecht's Jeschute followed the pattern of her counterpart in the *lai*.

CLAUDITTE.—In the second episode of the *mabinogi* to which we have repeatedly alluded, Rhiannon, the Queen of the Otherworld, deliberately seeks out Pwyll as love-mate, ultimately marries him, and bears him the semi-divine hero Pryderi. The unknown Welsh author, writing after 1050 or so, gave Rhiannon supernatural attributes but human origins, himself not quite aware, it would seem, that his story once founded the line of semi-divine rulers of Dyfed. Nothing whatsoever is said about Arawn; the narrative seems to take Rhiannon as a husbandless Queen, acting solely on her own initiative, with goddess's powers at first and then becoming a mere mortal. Clauditte may be her literary descendant.

---

[8] Note the wholly different motivation for the hermitess life of Sir Percival's "awnte," a remote Sigune parallel, in Malory's Book XIV.

Quite possibly, however, the Clauditte-character in the *lai* was originally one of the multiple avatars of Morgain le Fay,—as is Erec's wife Enide; Loomis, pp. 100–103,—in which case her nature would have been that of a capricious temptress. Neither Wolfram nor Albrecht provides enough information about Clauditte to make any assessment sure. As a Morgain derivative, she might have been the wife of the Orilus-character in the *lai*, or his mistress, or even a mortal lady held captive by him. We incline to think that guile and deceit were characteristic of the original Clauditte-figure. We note in passing that maiden Queens are often rulers in Wolfram's works,—Belacane, Herzeloyde, and Condwiramurs are conspicuous examples,—and Queens rule in sole authority in other Arthurian romances as well. In actual medieval life such independently ruling Queens are conspicuously absent,—but Keltic story abounds in fairy ladies, once goddesses in some cases, who ruled in sole power over "realms."

Gardeviaz

At all stages of the story's evolution the dog must have been the "character" upon which the plot absolutely depended. He is a *casus belli*, but also considerably more.

In the Second Fragment Wolfram portrays him as a wild and obstreperous animal, rather in excess of what normal canine behavior would warrant. His first approach is in loud and swift pursuit of, apparently, some woodland quarry, but Schionatulander the fleet of foot overtakes and captures him. When he escapes, Schionatulander, for all his fleetness, can *not* overtake him. Twice in a single day he escapes from persons to whom he does *not* belong, first from Ehkunat and then from Sigune. Albrecht reports that he was caught by King Teanglis and escaped again. Yet once captured by Orilus, he remains, literally for years, contentedly in the possession of Orilus and Jeschute without attempting further escapes. We infer that his wild behavior continued only until he found his rightful master, and also that his frantic chasing was in search of his rightful master and not of some woodland quarry. He is still with the evil couple at the conclusion of the story: he sits watching the showdown duel between Orilus and Ehkunat, and he "dies" when Orilus dies.

In short, Gardeviaz is a demonic animal, loyal to his malignant master (and mistress) but treacherous to all others. As a white dog with red ears (H-stanzas 1151 and 5811) it is clear that he was originally a creature out of the Keltic Hades, and we believe that Albrecht could have found this coloration only in the *lai* of *li Joenet de la Lande*. And, as said, we believe that Wolfram worked from the same source, shrewdly adumbrating the dog's demonic nature by the description of his behavior.

H-stanza 5811 says the dog was "inwardly made of fungus" (*Von swammen was er innen*). We take this to mean that a demon of hell fashioned a fungus into the shape of a dog and somehow animated it, perhaps himself inhabiting within the canine shape, so that it appeared to be an actual dog. The demon's purpose would be to wreak the destruction of good human beings. Almost automatically the demon would be a subordinate of Orilus's, from which it follows that Orilus was—for Albrecht—The Devil, the Lord of the Afterworld. Before the higher Force of Good incarnate in Ehkunat the demon flees, leaving his fungus contrivance to burn away in hellish fire. For a parallel, but without the specifically Christian symbolism, we need look no further than to Hoffmann's *Der goldene Topf,* where the witch, who has the illusory human form of old Liese Rauerin, burns to death beneath Archivarius Lindhorst's robe of flame, to be revealed at last as, in essence, nothing but an ugly beet-root (*eine garstige Runkelrübe*). This Märchen motif is common enough, but in Albrecht's handling of it we sense a sternly moral purpose and a quasi-theological turn of mind.

In the *lai* the supernaturalism is likely to have been simpler, more folkloristic, more perceptibly Keltic, and without the quasi-theological devil-lore. On page 76 above we proposed "a freely improvised scenario" to serve as a starting-point for our discussions, suggesting a *faithless* dog blasted by "Arawn" with a thunderbolt borrowed from his winter-storm clouds. Such may have been the case in some transitional phase between the Keltic and French versions of the story, but in the wholly French *lai* of *Li Joenet de la Lande* the Arawn-derivative character would have to be a "realistic" knight divested of all supernatural powers. Our analysis, moreover, has produced the concept of a dog wholly *loyal* to his true master. In "The Later Titurel" the dog "dies" when Orilus dies—and *because* Orilus dies, and such, we think, was the case in the *lai*. There the dog probably withered away, without Albrecht's addition of the fires of hell, to leave a toadstool at the spot of his withering. In Irish tales toadstools sometimes mock the deluded finders of leprechauns' gold.

The Leash

We also suspect that Wolfram (echoed by Albrecht) expanded upon "a smaller detail" by giving Gardeviaz a seventy-foot length of silken leash[9] with an extensive message spelled out upon it in jewels. The gorgeous object surprises and dazzles our imagination so that we suspend our disbelief. In the *lai* we fancy there must have been fewer jewels and a shorter message, perhaps on the dog's collar only. But *any* message at all raises problems.

WOLFRAM.—In Wolfram's Second Fragment two stanzas, 144–145, do report an inscription on the collar. A moral, derived from the dog's name, is stated there: men and women must "watch well their ways" if they hope for the world's favor and heaven's reward. Presumably this moral would have been applied at one or more points of the unfinished story.

Three stanzas, 147–149, begin reporting what is written on the leash proper: King Arthur's son Ilinot perished in love service to Queen Florie, and Florie herself died from the grief of his loss. We take this to be a prefiguration of the fates of the present lovers.

[9] See footnote 7 to Chapter I above.

As Sigune continues reading down the leash, the four stanzas, 150–153, relate how Florie's sister Clauditte, now the reigning Queen, has chosen Ehkunat as her *ami* and how Ehkunat had already selected Clauditte as his *amie*. Just at that point the dog wrenched himself free and Sigune could read no further. These four stanzas constitute an ingenious introduction of characters who have yet to enter the narrative.

Wolfram's three-part composition is astute: an applicable moral followed by two narrative passages, one premonitory, the other anticipatory, and all three parts functional and relevant to the *author's* purpose. But it is passing strange that Clauditte should send her *ami* a message consisting of a moral, an ominous news report, and a review of what her *ami* knew perfectly well.

ALBRECHT.—In "The Later Titurel" the message described above is recapitulated piecemeal and only partially, so that we infer that Albrecht discerned no poetic purpose in the letter. His loose paraphrase in H-stanzas 1836–46—where the Ilinot story is omitted—leads up to his own "message," the forty-four stanzas (H-1847–90) of a sermon on the ideals of Christian knighthood. Forty-four times he repeats the refrain of "Watch well your ways!" and expounds his list of twelve virtues symbolized by (unparticularized) flowers. We note Albrecht's delight in moralizing allegory and his preference for describing "things" rather than human beings. We doubt that even seventy feet of leash-length could accommodate *this* message, and we fancy the world entire would need to be plundered to furnish jewels enough to spell it all out. The long passage is a show-piece, but it is also an excursus from the story. We are more puzzled than before to know why Clauditte should be sending such a "letter" to her *ami*.

But even if, in both poems, there is a story-purpose that we have missed, there remains an awkward question in regard to "The Later Titurel," or, rather, two questions: (1) why should an *infernal* dog carry a sermon-in-jewels about the ideals of Christian knighthood?, and (2) why should the sermon-in-jewels burn away in the same hellish fire that consumes Gardeviaz?

Albrecht gives no forthright answer to the second question in the "miscellany" of (approximately) H-5836 to H-5964, but in H-5964, at the resumption of the Titurel-*gral* narrative, we are told of the unseemly dissensions among Christians which force the removal of the *gral* to "India." Albrecht seems to mean that the era of chivalry is ended and all "Europe" is sinking beneath the weight of evil. With profound pessimism he seems to be reading back into the last stages of King Arthur's reign his own feelings about the sorry political chaos of the Great Interregnum, 1254 to 1273, when the German Empire had, at first, no ruler at all, and then had simultaneous rival emperors, with dismal results for all of central Europe.

Nevertheless it seems incongruous to us that the jeweled leash with its noble "sermon" should, like Gardeviaz himself, burst spontaneously into hellfire and burn away to nothingness. Again we feel that Albrecht repeated—incongruously—what he found in the *lai*. But what did the *lai* report?

Quite probably in the *lai* a jeweled leash, suggestive of a break-away, trailed from the dog's collar, but we doubt that it contained any inscription at all. Whatever message there was is more likely to have been either on the jeweled collar of the dog or attached to the collar. The nature of the message depends on our notion of the Clauditte-Ehkunat relationship, and the information available is too meager to permit a judgment. The message could, with differing estimates of the characters involved, have been a plea for rescue, some injunction, some assignation, some word of love: we do not know. Whatever it was, it doubtless vanished away when the dog vanished away.

Wolfram's Source Work

Significant elements of the *lai* of *Li Joenet de la Lande* have, we believe, been recovered in the sections here preceding, though important elements still remain obscure. Most important of these are: the nature of Clauditte, her motivation for sending a message to Ehkunat, and the original contents of that message, to say nothing of such questions as how she came by the dog and how she was able to direct the dog to Ehkunat. The "story geography" is a puzzle. Location on a realistic map would, of course, be irrelevant, but we would like to have some idea of distances involved and of the relative positions of the acting personages. We assume "home castles" for the characters, as we assume "realistic" human natures for them, with supernatural qualities of literary antecedents reduced to merely residual features. In the case of the dog, not all supernatural attributes could have been eliminated: perhaps he was represented as being a fairy dog from Avalon, like the iridescent Petitcriu that was given to Tristan.

We summarize our findings about

The *Lai* of *Li Joenet de la Lande*

The *lai* must have opened with introductory matter about "the youth" and his young *amie* and then passed soon to the scene of the woodland encampment where the runaway dog was captured and lost again. The tender ages of the lovers were probably emphasized and "the youth's" vow to recover the animal may well have been portrayed as rash.

Some of the story probably followed the dog's own "adventures." A humorous episode may have shown how King Teanglis caught him and lost him again and how Teanglis, because he was illiterate, was unable to find out what was said in the inscription (or message) on the dog's collar (and leash?). Eventually the dog may have voluntarily, even joyously, found "Orilus" (and "Jeschute") and stayed with them.

Plausibly the main characters may have all come together at King Arthur's court, as they do in "The Later Titurel," and there the conflicting claims for ownership of the dog may well have been aired, with the result that the dog was adjudged to "Orilus," the courtiers generally assenting. There too "Ehkunat" might logically appear and encounter "the youth," who was his friend, or his kinsman, or his vassal,—or all of these things. It is difficult to imagine how "Clauditte" could also have appeared at court without causing the plot to unravel then and there.

What adventures and what interval of story-time then ensued cannot be guessed; weeks or months are more readily imagined than Albrecht's lapse of years. Possibly "Orilus" and "the youth" issued their mutual challenges before leaving court, with a rendezvous set for some later time "before Nantes." "The youth's" challenge would have been inevitable in the light of his vow to his *amie*. Alternately, the foes, each accompanied by his *amie*, may have met unexpectedly in open country, with their duel following immediately and with "the youth's" being quickly slain—perhaps also beheaded. Upon the sight of the grief-distraught *amie* with "the youth's" corpse came "Ehkunat," who vowed revenge on the slayer. The corpse was then reverently buried and the *amie* vowed withdrawal from the world and lifelong mourning at her beloved's grave.

Perhaps "Ehkunat" grimly pursued and soon overtook "Orilus," or perhaps the two met only after a search, but the final scene portrayed their savage combat. As "Orilus" was clearly getting the worst of it, "Jeschute" swooned, and as he died, the watching dog vanished into nothingness, leaving a toadstool at the spot of his vanishing. Jeweled collar (and leash?), inalienable from him, vanished likewise. Mournfully "Ehkunat" assumed possession of "the youth's" lands.

As briefly indicated on page 7 of the present work, we believe that Wolfram came to know this *lai*, probably before 1200, between the composition of his first, simpler, and shorter version of *Parzival* on the basis of Chrétien's "Perceval" only and his recasting of the definitive *Parzival* after 1200. He set about turning the *lai* into a romance in quatrains, following the narrative order of his model by first identifying the two principals of his story and then passing to the scene of their woodland encampment where the obstreperous dog was caught and lost again. He stressed the tender ages of the lovers and prepared their tragic destinies in Sigune's excessive demands upon her belovèd and in the too great self-trust that produced Schionatulander's rash vow. Exaltation in immaturity was their common flaw and the poet both admired and deplored that exaltation. Wolfram's early work on his *Schionatulander* romance is now represented by a truncated version of the Second Fragment of *Titurel*.

Meanwhile information was furnished him about Gahmuret, the Angevins, the Grail dynasty, and so on, and he set his *Schionatulander* romance aside in order to recast his *Parzival* in its more complex form. While reserving the story about the quest for the dog's leash for subsequent telling he nevertheless identified the names and fates of Sigune and Schionatulander with the nameless "maiden" and "knight" of Chrétien's lines 3428–3690. From the vow made by the hero's *amie* in the *lai* he elaborated—with no hint whatsoever from Chrétien's French poem—the impressive figure of Sigune as hermitess perpetually at prayer beside her belovèd's coffin. Perhaps that line, P 141,16, so baffling in context, "It was a hound's leash that brought him (Schionatulander) mortal pain," was introduced for the sake of audiences already acquainted with the *lai* or with Wolfram's own plans for his unfinished story.

With Sigune definitively established in *Parzival* as a Grail-dynasty descendant, it remained for the poet to contrive a suitable ancestry for Schionatulander. A paternal line from Gurnemanz of Graharz is described in detail in *Parzival* 177–8,—minus the crucial detail of Schionatulander's descent from that line. (Might "the youth from the moor" in the *lai* have been descended from Gurnemanz?) Schionatulander's mother Mahaute is named in that same passage, but with no mention of the fact that she *is* his mother. Ehkunat is mentioned, but with no hint that he is Schionatulander's maternal uncle. And nowhere in *Parzival* is Schionatulander accorded his title of *talfîn* or his land of Graswaldan. We suspect that all these matters were worked out before *Parzival* 177–8 was composed and that they were all deliberately reserved for the unfinished Schionatulander romance, which we know as the "*Titurel* Fragments."

Suppressed likewise, we think, was the blending of Dauphin Schionatulander's death with the death of Count Guigo IV, *Dalfinus*, of Albon in 1142, as will be explained in the chapter next following here.

Once *Parzival* was completed in final form around 1210 or 1212, we think Wolfram returned to his neglected Schionatulander romance and made a fresh start by composing what we now know as the First Fragment of *Titurel*. Now the genealogies were described, the previously missing titles and lands were supplied, and the narrative was carefully coordinated with Books I and II of *Parzival*. As part of the same project the old introduction to the Schionatulander romance now had to be scrapped, but the splendid woodland scene with Schionatulander, Sigune, and Gardeviaz was largely retained, with the abrupt opening line: "They had not long been thus encamped." Presumably the "bridge" between the newly composed First Fragment and this abrupt opening line of the old, truncated "Second Fragment" would have been the poet's next order of business. But Landgrave Herman of Thuringia had meanwhile obtained a manuscript of the Old French poem of *Aliscans* for Wolfram's use, quite possibly with the request that it be turned into a German poem. About the date of this procurement (and request) we can be sure only of its being prior to April 25, 1217, when Landgrave Herman died. A patron's request is a command, and the poet found himself simultaneously working on the old project and preparing for the new one. The evidence for such simultaneous work lies, we believe, with the unique name of *Acarin* in *Aliscans* 1428, which was introduced both into the (new) First Fragment of *Titurel* (40,2) and into *Willehalm* 45,16 for the Baruch of Baldac left nameless in *Parzival*. With less certainty, the terms "Berbester" and *admirât* seem to be in parallel case. Eventually, however, a second abandonment of the Schionatulander romance was forced by work on *Willehalm*, quite possibly again at the Landgrave's urging, and death claimed the poet before either project was completed.

One troublesome detail requires particular mention: from what source did Wolfram get the dog's name of "Gardeviaz"? There is scholarly consensus that this name represents only Provençal *garda vias*, ("Watch your ways!"); Old French would produce *voies/veies*. Hence the Old French *lai* of *Li Joenet de la Lande* could not have contained the name. A Provençal informant and transmitter (?) of the *lai* is our only suggestion. Informant "Kyot the Provençal" having been declared non-existent, we find ourselves repeatedly obliged to invent him.

Overview

Wolfram's First Fragment is not only coordinated with Books I and II of *Parzival* as to story and characters but, like those Books, it deals with matters antecedent to the main narrative. The 3,454 short lines of those "Gahmuret Books" represent 13.92% of the 24,812 short lines of the total poem. As for the total *"Schiona-tulander"* as envisioned by Wolfram, our guess is: approximately a thousand quatrains (or four thousand lines). Of that number the 524 *long* lines of the First Fragment—counting on the unreliable number of 131 quatrains—would make up 7.63%. Doubtless the proportions would have been smaller for the smaller poem, but the long *"Schionatulander"* lines would have admitted more material, so that these figures may be misleading. But surely Wolfram never intended anything like Albrecht's 21,952 long lines.

Albrecht, we believe, composed, probably in the 1260s, a continuous and complete poem about Titurel and the Grail. To its 643 H-stanzas (77 to 475 and 5964 to 6207) we would add the 76 H-stanzas of opening prayer, imitated from *Willehalm*, to a total of 719 H-stanzas. In our opinion, this is the only poem justifiably entitled *Titurel*.

At some point Albrecht came upon the 170 (not 164) quatrains of Wolfram's *"Schionatulander"* and used them anew in modified form, bridging the gap between them with material extrapolated from *Parzival* 13–14, 101–102, and 106–108 and carrying the story to conclusion by following the outline of the *lai* of *Li Joenet de la Lande*, to a total of 21,952 lines. This second poem he then encapsulated between the unequal halves of his *Titurel*. He interconnected his two stories only tenuously, but he did frequently coordinate the "inner" story with *Parzival*, often inaccurately.

In his "outer" story he repeatedly insinuated (but never de-
clared outright) that Wolfram of Eschenbach was the author. For
more than two centuries his "double poem" was immensely
admired as a work of Wolfram's; then, after three centuries of
neglect, it was revived around 1810, still as "Wolfram's *Titurel*."
Once it was clearly distinguished from the genuine Wolframian
Fragments, the latter were also termed "Wolfram's *Titurel*," with
the lame explanation that the occurrence of the name "Titurel"
in the opening line justified that title. Albrecht's poem then be-
came "The Later Titurel." The confusion is still with us. We
firmly believe that Wolfram left two Fragments of a *Schionatu-
lander* and that Albrecht composed a *Titurel* which *includes* a
Schionatulander romance.

·IV·

SCHIONATULANDER AS DAUPHIN

🐜 🐜 🐜

IN WOLFRAM'S FIRST FRAGMENT, stanzas 41–42 set forth the ancestry of Schionatulander: he is the grandson of Gurnemanz of Graharz, the son of Gurzgri and Mahaute, and the nephew of Ehkunat. The relationships of these persons were stated in *Parzival* 177–8, except for the crucial fact: that Schionatulander had anything to do with the family there described. That point was reserved for the *Titurel* romance which announces that Schionatulander *"will be* the lord of this adventure."

In the *Parzival* passage Gurnemanz names three sons of his slain in knightly combat and their (unnamed) mother dead from grief. Our impression is that this aging, wealthy, proud, and lonely Prince of Graharz is bereaved of all kin save for his cherished daughter Liaze. That daughter-in-law Mahaute also died after Gurzgri's death may perhaps be inferred from the phrase "lost her beauty;" at any rate she does not personally appear in either poem. No mention is made of either Schionatulander or of Gurzgri's presumably younger son, Duke Gandiluz, who, in *Parzival* 429,20 only, is listed as one of Gawan's squires. This extensive family is the more surprising since Gurnemanz's name, in various spellings, occurs in several continental romances with never an allusion to wife or child of his.

About these forebears our List of Proper Names gathers pertinent information under items "Gurnemanz," "Gurzgri," and

"Schionatulander;" also under items "Mahaute" and "Ehku-nat," while information about "Graharz" is presented within item "Gurnemanz," with added remarks in the *Geography* sub-section of item "Waleis." Our immediate concern now is with three points conspicuously made in the *Titurel* Fragments but nowhere mentioned in *Parzival*: Schionatulander's title of *talfîn,* his land of Graswaldan, and his *mother* Mahaute.

As a grandson of Gurnemanz he is "a man of Graharz" (*Grâ-harzoys/Grâhardeiz*), presumably from having been born in that "land" (or city), but he is not "*of* Graharz" because that title belongs to Gurnemanz, who survives him. In his own right he is the ruling Prince of Graswaldan, with the title of *talfîn;* his father Gurzgri before him bore that title likewise, and his mother bore the title of *talfînette.*

Grâswaldân

Schionatulander's "land" of *Grâswaldân* has long been recognized as the (now French) region of Grésivaudan/Graisivaudan to the northeast of the city of Grenoble. From some date prior to 1050 it was claimed by a succession of Counts of Albon as one of their territories among several, but their control over it was probably not secure until the 1130s. It was apparently during Wolfram's lifetime that the ruling Count of Albon began to be known as "the Dauphin," and it was not until many years after Wolfram's death that the greatly expanded territories of the Dauphins came to be known as *le Dauphiné.* For clarity's sake we shall need to begin with a brief account of these Counts of Albon.

Count Guigo I.—In the period 843–888, when Charlemagne's vast Frankish empire was being dismantled, there was formed, in what is now eastern France, an unstable Kingdom of Bur-gundy, which, in 1029, was approaching dissolution. At that point the Burgundian king, Rudolf III, "Do-nothing" (*le Fai-néant*), bestowed the city of Vienne, together with its territo-ries—*le Viennois*—upon his wife, Queen Hermengarde, who

promptly bestowed the total gift upon the Archbishop of
Vienne. Archbishop Bouchard retained the city for the church
but divided *le Viennois,* assigning the northern portion to his
brother-in-law the Count of Maurienne and the southern portion
to Guigo, the Lord (*Sire*) of Vion. These land grants were made
either on September 14, 1029, or on October 22, 1030, and they
were, in embryo, the future "states" of Savoy and Dauphiné,
respectively.

Vion, a small site west of the Rhone, had been ruled all
through the Burgundian period by a father-to-son succession of
Lords (*Sires*), each named Guigo. (Germanic *Wigo,* "warrior,"
Latinized as *Guigo,* became Old French *Guigues* and modern *Gui-
gue.*) With the land grant of 1029/1030 came, it would seem,
elevation to the rank of Count and also a change of "home
castle," from Vion to Albon, another small site further down
the west bank of the Rhone. Thus Guigo VI of Vion became
Count Guigo I of *Albon.* Confusingly, historians opt for either
numbering system for the entire line of these rulers; here, we
shall begin with Guigo I.

Ten years later, in 1039/1040, this ambitious Count Guigo I of
Albon obtained the Alpine town of Briançon, together with two
still more easterly towns, in fief from the German emperor
Henry III. For these places he owed direct allegiance to the Em-
peror, whereas he held the southern *Viennois* in fief from the
Archbishop of Vienne who, in turn, owed allegiance to the Ger-
man Emperor. In between the two sets of holdings lay the region
of Grésivaudan, which belonged to the city of Grenoble. Next,
therefore, Guigo I effected a partition of the city of Grenoble
and its territories between himself and his cousin, Bishop Mal-
lein (*Mallenus*), the prelate retaining the city for the church and
the Count taking Grésivaudan. A document of 1050 styles Guigo
"prince of the region of Grésivaudan."

The Count's lands were discontinous, largely rural, and with-
out a center. In Albon, in Vizille (south of Grenoble), or in Be-
sançon his presence defined his "capital." Between his Rhone-
valley and Alpine holdings Grésivaudan was both the vital link

and his economic mainstay. It was a fertile plain of the sub-Alps, inhabited since prehistoric times (by the Keltic Allobroges and their descendants), spanned by much-frequented roads, and picturesquely situated along the west bank of the Isère River. To the envy of Savoy, it contained prosperous farms, hemp-processing plants, and a variety of minerals, besides yielding much lumber from the forest of Servette.

Guigo II; Guigo III.—In 1057 Guigo I abdicated in favor of his son and went to live out his life as a monk at Cluny, where he died in the late 1070s. Of the son, Guigo II, little is known except that he extended the Grésivaudan holdings at the expense of three successive bishops of Grenoble and that he died at about the same time as his father. Under Guigo III, who ruled from 1080 to 1133, the struggle for Grésivaudan continued. Three times this Guigo III made war on Bishop Hugh of Grenoble, better known as Saint Hugh of Châteauneuf, even to driving the saint into exile. All three times—twice under excommunication—he renounced his Grésivaudan claims under pressure from the Archbishop of Vienne, his spiritual and temporal overlord. The entire Grésivaudan matter is made difficult of assessment by the fact that its whole evolution, from 1050 to 1133, must be deduced from Saint Hugh's contentious brief against Guigo III: no other relevant documents exist.

Guigo IV.—New wars against Saint/Bishop Hugh, still over Grésivaudan claims, were fought by the next-succeeding Count, Guigo IV, who had the second baptismal name of *Dalfinus*. In the course of his nine-year reign, 1133 to 1142, he went so far as to expel ecclesiastics who supported their bishop and in one case to burn a town, but for these deeds he made a pilgrimage of atonement to the shrine of Saint James of Compostela in Spain. Since his Countess, Margaret of Burgundy, was a descendant of Burgundian King Rudolf "Do-nothing" and therefore claimed the city of Vienne as her inheritance, Guigo IV *Dalfinus* also made war—unsuccessfully—on the Archbishop of Vienne, his spiritual and temporal overlord. Finally, in 1140, he was drawn into a border dispute with Count Amédée of Savoy, the husband of his sister, but he had the worst of it. In the siege of Montmélian he was ambushed by Amédée and died of wounds a few days later, on June 28, 1142.

In the course of the 1130s, however, Guigo IV *Dalfinus* apparently made his claim upon Graisivaudan secure once and for all. We may, then, define Graisivaudan as the most valuable territory among a heterogeneous collection of territories ruled by the Counts of Albon. It was a rural area, with no capital city, and its urban center was the politically detached city of Grenoble. Moreover, the heterogeneous territories ruled by the Counts of Albon had no collective name at all and no fixed governmental capital. If by any chance such a title as *Fürst von Graswaldan* was in use at the German Imperial court, it would have designated, not quite correctly, the Counts of Albon after 1135 or so. It is primarily with this Count Guigo IV *Dalfinus* that we would connect Schionatulander, but it may have been a blend of this ruler with his son which created the tradition upon which the literary figure depends.

Guigo V.—While his widow acted as Regent after the death of Guigo IV, *Dalfinus,* the young son of this couple was growing up, a fighter from the time he could grasp a sword and obsessed with revenge for his father's death. Around 1155 this son assumed rule as Count Guigo V, to which title some, but not all, documents add the name of *Dalfinus.* As soon as possible he reopened warfare against his uncle-by-marriage, Amédée of Savoy, again besieging Montmélian, but he had no more success than his father, and peace was arranged by the Archbishop of Vienne.

There were, however, compensatory gains. As early as 1155 Guigo V (*Dalfinus*) journeyed to Italy where Emperor Frederick Barbarossa was holding court. Just then the Emperor's main concern was reestablishment of Imperial power over the Rhone valley, and in this spirited young warrior he discerned an ally worth fostering. He personally knighted Guigo, bestowed an Imperial relative, Beatrice of Montferrat, upon him as bride, and granted him a silver mine recently discovered in the Alps, together with the right of independent coinage. By indirect means he also contrived to give him the city of Vienne, and thus the youthful ruler achieved peaceably what his parents had not been able to achieve by warfare. Yet these glories were only briefly enjoyed. In 1162 Guigo V (*Dalfinus*) died in his fortress at Vizille, survived only by a daughter, Beatrice of Albon, to inherit his lands. So ended "the first line"—*la première race*—of the Counts of Albon.

About the continuation of the line we shall speak in a moment; meanwhile we pause to consider how the baptismal name of *Dalfinus* evolved into the title, "the Dauphin."

Talfîn

Abruptly and without precedent in the ancestral line of the Guigos, the name Dalfinus first occurs in a still-preserved Latin document of October 31, 1110, where it designates the son and future successor of Count Guigo III as "Guigo *dalfinus*." At a guess, this boy with the double name of "Guy Dolfin" was born around 1100 and was therefore about ten years old when the document included him as co-giver, along with his parents, in an ecclesiastical donation. For the remaining years of his father's reign (to 1133) and from his own reign (1133–1142), his name appears in sixteen documents to a total of twenty-three times: five times as plain Guigo, eighteen times as "Guigo *dalfinus*," in spellings with *Dal-*, *Del-*, *Delph-*, and *Dalph-*.

In parallel case was his father's half-brother Guigo Raymund who died in 1079: *Guigo cognomento Raimundi* in the Latin records. *That* second baptismal name was apparently given by the mother in honor of *her* father, Raymund (*Ramón*) Berenguer, Count of Barcelona, i.e., Count of Catalonia. For these Counts of Barcelona/Catalonia see the List of Proper Names under item "Katelangen" below.

Such double names were not extraordinary in medieval times, and even triple names are recorded. King Louis VII of France (1137–1180) was baptized Louis-Flour; his son and successor, King Philip II (1180–1223), was baptized Philippe-Adéodat and

later came to be known as Philip Augustus. Under items "Ka-
telangen" and "Kiot" in the List of Proper Names we summarize
the history of Catalonian rulers and under "Kiot" we speak of
that great-grandfather of Eleanor of Aquitaine who was chris-
tened Guido (Guy), chose to be called Guido Gaufredus (Guy
Geoffrey), and took the regnal name of Duke William VIII of
Aquitaine; in 1063 he was a "Duke Kiot" *in*, but not *of*, Catalonia.

From the reign of the warrior Count Guigo V, ca. 1155 to 1162,
eight preserved documents give his name four times as plain
Guigo and four times as Guigo *Dalfinus*. Here the second com-
ponent is likely to have been his own unofficial addition out of
fervent admiration for his slain father.

With the untimely death of Guigo V in 1162 ended, as we
have mentioned, the first line—*la première race*—of the Counts
of Albon.

The surviving daughter of Guigo V, Beatrice of Albon, married
three times and by her second husband, Duke Hugh of Ber-
gundy, had a son Andrew who became the next ruling Count
of Albon. The preference for his mother's title over his father's
suggests the growing prestige of the state he ruled. Through
the early years of his long reign, 1184–1237, documents drawn
in his mother's name speak of him as: *Delphini filii nostri* (1184),
filius meus qui dicitur Delphinus (1190–92), and *filius meus Dalfinus*
(1194), but in 1202 as *filii mei Andree*. In these instances it is hard
to say whether *Dalfinus* is a second baptismal name, or a fond
nickname, or a title. Still ambiguous is the wording of May 1215:
dominum comitem Delfinum, but as of August 15, 1222, we read:
ego Andreas, Delphinus et comes Albionis, which plainly means: "I,
Andrew, Dauphin and Count of Albon." Thus no later than
1222, and probably three decades earlier, the personal name had
developed into a title: the ruling Count of Albon was "the Dau-
phin."

From Count Andreas Dalfinus of 1184–1237 the second line—
la deuxième race—of the Counts of Albon extended only to the
death of Andrew's grandson in 1282. Then, once again through
an only surviving daughter, the *troisième race* of Counts ruled
until the sale of Dauphiné to the French crown in 1349 to pay

for the astronomical debts of the last Dauphin. By that date the consolidated territories of the Counts of Albon were ten times the size of the original land grants of 1029/1030. When this state first came to be known as Dauphiné is a matter of guesswork: no preserved document uses the term *Dalphinatus* prior to 1293.

With the sale of 1349 it was stipulated that the title of "Dauphin" should be borne by the eldest son of each successive King of France from his birth until his coronation as King, parallel to the English title "the Prince of Wales." The custom was honored until 1830. From 1349 until 1790 Dauphiné was a *gouvernement* of the Kingdom of France, a valued province on the east bank of the Rhone, with Burgundy to its north and Provence to its south. In 1790 this province was subdivided into its present-day *départements* of L'Isère, La Drôme, and Les Hautes-Alpes, but the old name lingers on for reasons of sentiment and of tourism. Its urban center is, as it has always been, Grenoble.

Thus Schionatulander cannot have borne the *title* of *talfin* much earlier than the mid-1180s, more probably in the early 1190s. It is our notion that the title was borrowed, not by Wolfram himself but rather by an informant, and not in honor of reigning Count Andrew but rather in honor of the martyr-Count, Guigo IV *Dalfinus*, of 1133–1142, quite probably in a retrospective blending of that ruler with his warrior son, Guigo V (Dalfinus).

For the borrowing of the title we propose a date in, or soon after, 1193. From February 14, 1193, until February 4, 1194, German Emperor Henry VI was holding Richard Lion Heart for ransom, and in that period the wily captor proposed resuscitating the defunct Kingdom of Burgundy and installing Richard as its king. Shrewdly the Lion Heart avoided the lure, which would have made him a vassal of the German Empire. The Counts of Albon, we recall, had been Imperial vassals all along, and in the latter 1150s Guigo V (Dalfinus) had been the special protégé of the previous emperor, Frederick Barbarossa. With Guigo V's unexpectedly early death in 1162 the Imperial hopes failed and there would be no Imperial restructuring of the Rhone-valley states under that favored vassal. Now, a generation later, Emperor Henry VI was contemplating the abandoned project anew, casting the prestigious Lion Heart in the role of Guigo V (Dalfinus). In 1193 Rhone-valley politics was "in the news," especially among persons at the Imperial court, and the title of *talfîn* is likely to have been on many tongues.

The borrower of the title, however, erred in making the title retroactive to Schionatulander's father Gurzgri and to Schionatulander's mother, the *talfînette* Mahaute, because Count Guigo IV *Dalfinus* of 1133–1142 was the very first ruler in the area to bear the name *Dalfinus* in *any* sense. Significantly, the name of that ruler's Countess-mother *was* Mahaute, just as *talfîn* Schionatulander's mother has the name of Mahaute.

Mahaute

Latin documents spell the historical Countess's name, in the Nominative, as *Matildis, Matelda, Maelda, Maieuda,* and in the Genitive as *Mat(h)ildis, Maheldis, Maieudae,* and *Mahiot.* The forms without medial *t* reflect the "north-Provençal" pronunciation of Romance speech in Auvergne and Dauphiné. The English equivalent is Maud(e), and all forms represent the baptismal name "Mathilda"/"Matilda."

In 1105, when Count Guigo III was seriously ill, a church offering was made in his name and in the name of his wife "Maieuda," and also in the name of "all their sons, both living and deceased." Presumably, then, the couple had been married for a period of years. The identity of this lady, long a mystery, is a matter of some importance.

Bernard Bligny's *Histoire du Dauphiné,* p. 118, says:

> Guigues III épouse vers 1106 une certaine "reine Mathilde," fille très probablement du comte Roger de Sicile et veuve du roi Conrad d'Italie, le fils rebelle de l'empereur Henri IV, mère enfin de Guigues IV (1133–1142), auquel elle donna le surnom de "Dauphin" porté désormais par tous les comtes d'Albon.

In the document of 1105 already cited,[1] the phrase "all their sons, both living and deceased" reveals Bligny's *vers 1106* as an error; we doubt his evasive word *surnom* ("nickname," "pet name"); and his final *désormais par tous les comtes d'Albon* carries some false implications. Moreover, Bligny offers no reason for his identification of the Countess, nor does he bother to rebut the conclusions of Georges de Manteyer (1894; 1925), which are accepted, perhaps reluctantly, by F. Vernay: *Nouvelle Histoire du Dauphiné*, 1933, p. 37, and by Gaston Letellier: *Histoire du Dauphiné*, No. 228 of the *Que sais-je?* series, 1958, pp. 20–22.

Latin documents show that the lady was sometimes termed "Countess" (*comitessa*), as we would expect, and sometimes "Queen" (*Regina*),—and Manteyer is at pains (pp. 309 and 398–401) to make perfectly clear that she was not a Countess with the given name of "Regina." In the previously cited donation document of October 31, 1110 (Manteyer, p. 402), where the name of *Guigo dalfinus* first occurs, we find also: *Ego Guigo comes et uxor mea Regina, nomine Maheldis* . . . ; as of August 15, 1123, we find: *Guigo comes de Albione et uxor ejus, nomine Matildis, genere Regina* . . . (". . . by birth a queen"). Most startling of all is a document of 1106 which says: *Dominus Vuigo et uxor ejus Regina,*

---

[1] In this chapter all documents relative to the family of the Counts of Albon are cited either from the text (pp. 307–394) or from the notes (pp. 395–426) of Georges de Manteyer's *article* entitled *Les Origines du Dauphiné de Viennois* in the *Bulletin de la Société des Hautes-Alpes*, Series 5, Volume 44, 1925. On p. 394 Manteyer dates his article to 1894–5.

Gaston Letellier: *Histoire du Dauphiné*, 1958, p. 22, refers to a *two-volume work* by Manteyer, with the same title and publication date. So too does Bernard Bligny's *Histoire du Dauphiné* in the bibliography on p. 7, adding the subtitle: *La Première race des comtes d'Albon (843–1228)* and naming Gap as the city of publication. Since the *article* deals solely with the proveniences of the Countess Mathilda and of the name "Dauphin," it is presumably an extract from that two-volume work.

The *article* is to be found in the New York City Public Library and in the library of the Michigan State University at East Lansing, Michigan,—and perhaps elsewhere as well. But the Library of Congress mistakenly believes that the two-volume work is to be found in the East Lansing Library *only*. Apparently it exists nowhere in the United States. Moreover, in Zürich, Switzerland, as of late 1981, no library, bookdealer, or secondhand bookdealer was able to trace a copy of the two-volume work.

quae fuit de Anglia, ...''—"who was (formerly) of England," or possibly *". . . from* England." By birth, then, and necessarily by legitimate birth, the Countess Matilda was a Queen of England!

Matildas who were queens or princesses of England were numerous in the family of William the Conqueror, less numerous (despite Kolb, p. 11) in the Angevin line, and non-existent among the pre-1066 Anglo-Saxons. Under "Mahaute" in the List of Proper Names we list twelve historical Matildas, Norman or Angevin. Yet it is to the last Anglo-Saxon king of England that Manteyer would trace our Countess, supporting his claim by elaborate circumstantial evidence.

Our Countess, he claims, was the daughter of Edgar Aetheling, the elected but never-crowned King of England from latter October until early December of 1066. It is a well-known *fact* that Edgar's sister, Saint Margaret Aetheling, married Malcolm III, King of Scotland from 1058 to 1093; it is Manteyer's *belief* that Edgar himself married a sister of Gospatrick (Keltic *gos-*, "old," in the sense of "Senior"), Earl of Northumberland, of the junior branch of Scottish royalty, and that the Countess named her son *Dalfinus* in honor of one or another of her Scottish kinsmen, at least three of whom were named Dolfin. The likeliest candidate among the three, he thinks, is Gospatrick's illegitimate son, Dolfin, Earl of Cumberland and a nephew of the Countess's. Here, at one stroke, is offered a plausible explanation of the sudden appearance of the name Dolfin/*Dalfinus* in the family and in the region of the Counts of Albon. From Edgar Aetheling's nowhere-attested marriage Manteyer also finds a second daughter, Margaret, who married a Somersetshire landowner named William Lovel (d. 1155), and a son, "Edgar Adeling," who had dealings with the English treasury in 1158 and again in 1167.

Manteyer believes further that Edgar Aetheling named his first-born child Matilda in honor of William the Conqueror's queen; a daughter born in 1075 to the English royal couple (and who died in infancy) was named Agatha in honor of Edgar Aetheling's mother. The reciprocal show of good will between the reigning and the "deposed" kings would have been made in one of the periods when William and Edgar were amicably coexisting, notably the period 1074–1086. We submit the following chronology for our historical Countess:

—born ca. 1075 and christened Matilda in honor of William the Conqueror's queen;

—married "in the 1090s;" in February 1101 she was in Briançon as Guigo III's Countess: *ante dominum nostrum comitem et ante reginam uxorem suam . . .* (Manteyer, p. 345). Perhaps Edgar Aetheling himself brought her south on his way to Palestine and the Third Crusade; he was in Constantinople by early 1098;

—by 1105 she had borne an unspecified number of sons to Guigo III: ". . . all their sons, both living and deceased . . . ;"

—widowed by the death of Guigo III on December 21, 1133;

—bereaved of her illustrious son, Count Guigo IV *Dalfinus,* on June 28, 1142;

—died before October 17, 1144, when her eldest son Humbert, Bishop of Le Puy, was elevated as Archbishop of Vienne.

Under "dolphin" Ernest Weekley's *Etymological Dictionary* says: ". . . though not apparently recorded in Anglo-Saxon, (Dolfin) was a common personal name in the 11th century;" its commonest usage was in southern Scotland and northern England. Manteyer also cites English localities: Dolphingston, Dolphinholme, Dolphinsbarn, and, as of 1850, a vast estate of Dolphington in the region of Lanark, south of Glasgow. The marine mammal, the dolphin, was the emblem of the Dauphins. For more about the word and about the name see the item *"Talfîn"* listed alphabetically in the List of Proper Names below.

As for how Guigo's family could have been put in touch with Edgar Aetheling's family, Manteyer offers further circumstantial evidence to make Saint Anselm the intermediary. Born at Aosta, ca. 125 km/80 m NE of Briançon, Saint Anselm lived for a time at the important Norman monastery of Bec, became Archbishop of Canterbury in 1093, officiated on November 11, 1100, at the marriage of Henry I of England and Edgar Aetheling's niece,

Edith of Scotland (who changed her name to Matilda at that date), and in his multiple journeys had personal dealings with important personages from Scotland to Italy. There is, however, no documentary proof that he arranged the marriage of Edgar's daughter to Guigo III. In fact, neither record nor rumor cites *any* marriage of Edgar Aetheling himself.

Manteyer's web of circumstantial evidence is intricate but extremely well documented and the present writer is inclined to accept the claims made for the provenience of the title and of the mother of Guigo IV *Dalfinus*. The dates are appropriate. The origin of the name *Dalfinus*—a total mystery before Manteyer's writing—is plausibly explained. If, as contemporary records state, the *comitessa* also had the title of *Regina* and was *de Anglia*, alternate explanations are scarce. Bligny, as quoted on p. 108 above, simply ignored the available evidence. Let us note in passing how Wolfram, in *Willehalm*, emphasizes Giburc's title of "Queen," as former wife of pagan King Tibalt, even though she is Willehalm's *Countess* in the poem. On the other hand, *Parzival* 134 says that Jeschute renounced her title of "Queen" in becoming a Duchess by her marriage to Duke Orilus de La-lander.

The extraordinary rank of "Queen-though-Countess" for Guigo's mother is likely to have enhanced the glory of her son and of her son's legend, and perhaps that glory is reflected in the title of *talfinette* accorded to her literary counterpart. Significant too, we think, is the persistence of the historical lady's commonplace name of "Mahaute"—Maud—amid the fictional family consisting of: Gurnemanz, Schenteflurs, Lascoyt, Gurzgri, Liaze, Schionatulander, and Gandiluz.

For clarification of Manteyer's complex evidence we append to this chapter two genealogical charts and an outline life of Edgar Aetheling.

In summary: Schionatulander, (1) son of *talfinette* Mahaute, is (2) himself *talfin* and (3) ruling Prince of *Grâswaldân*, and (4) he is slain, apparently by treachery, in a joust. Both titles are fifty years and more before the historical title "Dauphin" existed.

Yet Schionatulander parallels Guigo IV *Dalfinus*, Count of Albon, 1133–1142, (1) whose mother's name was "Mahaute" (in variant forms); (2) who had *Dalfinus* as a second baptismal name, not as a title; (3) who ruled the territory of Grésivaudan—among other territories; and (4) who was mortally wounded in ambush. The *impression* of Schionatulander's youthful death may reflect the son of this martyr-Count, Count Guigo V, who seems also to have had *Dalfinus* as a second baptismal name and who died, not in battle, around age twenty, if not less, in 1162.

Addendum

A daughter of Guigo IV married Guilhem VII of Auvergne (ruled 1145–1168), and in the period while there was no ruling Count of Albon (see chart) the son of this pair assumed the name—or title?—of "Dauphin." As a vassal of Eleanor of Aquitaine, Guilhem VII came under control of Henry II of England, with disastrous results. Amid a family quarrel, Henry helped Guilhem VII's uncle, Guilhem VIII, to seize a fair portion of Auvergne. With the family quarrel still continuing, Philip II, Augustus, of France intervened in 1195, seized what territory was left, reorganized it as "La Terre d'Auvergne," and annexed it to the French crown.

The First Line (*La première race*) of the
COUNTS OF ALBON

GUIGO I, "the Old" (*Senex* or *Vetus*)
6th hereditary Lord (*Sire*) of Vion
1st Count of Albon
ruled ancestral estates + lands granted by the Archbishop of Vienne (the
southern *Viennois*) + Briançon (in direct fief from the German Emperor) +
portions of Grésivaudan (? taken by force of arms)
ruled 1029/30 to 1057; abdicated in 1057 to live
out his life as a monk at Cluny;
d. before 1080.

GUIGO II, "the Fat" (*Crassus* or *Pinguis*)
m. (1) 1050 Petronilla
m. (2) 1070 Agnes of Barcelona

Matilda/Maud (? 1097) —— GUIGO III, "the Count"
? daughter of
Edgar Aetheling
b. 1055/60
ruled 1080–1133
d. December 21, 1133

→ Guigo Raymund
(*cognomento Raimundi*)
d. 1079

Humbert
Bishop of Le Puy;
Archbishop of Vienne
from Oct. 17, 1144

GUIGO IV *Dalfinus*
b. ca. 1100
first documented Oct. 31,
1110 ruled 1133–1142
mortally wounded at the
siege of Montmélian
d. June 28, 1142

—m.–Margaret of
Burgundy

Matilda/Maud
m.
Count Amédée III
of Savoy
(ruled 1103–1148)

Margaret of Burgundy, Regent
1142–1155

GUIGO V (*Dalfinus*)
knighted by Emperor Frederick Barbarossa
acquired the added title of Count of Vienne
m. Beatrice of Montferrat, kinswoman of
Frederick Barbarossa
ruled 1155–1162

Margaret of Burgundy, Regent
1162–1164 (d. 1164)

Beatrice of Albon, daughter of Guigo V

Alberic Taillefer
of Toulouse
(no children)
(1)

(2)

(3) Hugh, Baron of Coligny
(two daughters)

Hugh III
Duke of Burgundy

ANDREAS *Dalfinus* first of the Second Line   (*deuxième race*)
ruled 1184–1237   of the Counts of Albon

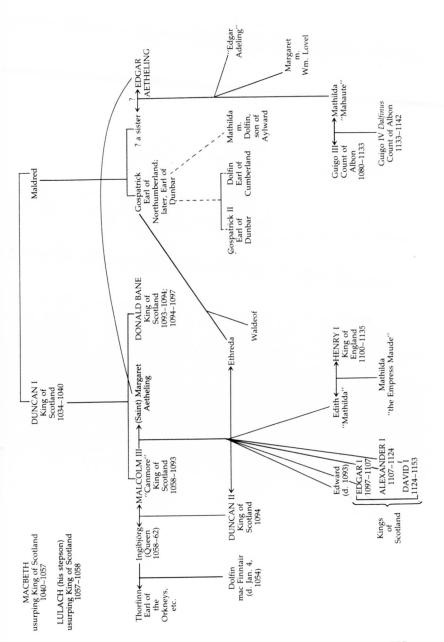

A Chronology for Edgar Aetheling

On January 5, 1066, Edward III, "the Confessor," King of England, died after a reign of twenty-four years. The following day witnessed his funeral and the election and coronation of his wife's brother, Harold, as King of England.

Harold's ten-month reign ended in death on the battlefield of Hastings on October 14th, when William, Duke of Normandy, became "the Conqueror" and the new King of England.

Within a week or so, certain north-of-England nobles elected as King of England the fifteen-or-sixteen-year-old Edgar Aetheling, last survivor of the Anglo-Saxon kings. His "reign" lasted about six weeks. In early December he "submitted" formally to the Conqueror, who was crowned on Christmas Day as King William I of England; ruled 1066–1087.

William treated the "deposed" Edgar well, giving him grants of land, but prudently took him along to Normandy when his own presence was needed there.

1068   From Normandy Edgar escaped, together with his mother Agatha, his sister Christine, and certain supporters, to Scotland, where his sister Margaret was the queen of Scottish King Malcolm III, "Canmore."

1069   Joint invasion of northern England by Malcolm and Edgar; the project failed and Malcolm eventually came to terms with William.

1072   Edgar was brought to Normandy, where William granted him a pound of silver a day for expenses.

1074   Edgar tried to flee to King Philip I of France but was shipwrecked and obliged to return to William's protection.

1074—1086   A period of apparent good will between Edgar and the Conqueror.

1086   Edgar led an expedition to the Norman lands of southern Italy but returned to Normandy.

1087   Death of William I, the Conqueror; accession of his *second* son, William "Rufus," as King William II of England; ruled 1087–1100.

1091   Edgar joined in a second unsuccessful invasion of northern England, from Scotland.

1093   Deaths of Malcolm III and Queen Margaret; accession of Malcolm's brother, Donald Bane (Shakespeare's Donalbaine), as King of Scotland; ruled 1093–1097.

1097   Edgar, at the instigation of William "Rufus," aided young Edgar of Scotland (his nephew and Malcolm's son) to seize the kingship from Donald Bane; Edgar of Scotland ruled 1097–1107.

1098   Edgar went to Palestine on the First Crusade, where he won high honors. With him was Robert Curthose, the Conqueror's eldest son, who was embittered at being merely Duke of Normandy while his *younger* brother, William "Rufus," was King of England.

1100   Death of William "Rufus" (August 2nd); before Robert Curthose could get home, the Conqueror's *third* son rushed to make himself King Henry I of England; ruled 1100–1135.

1106   A rebellion against Henry I by Robert Curthose and Edgar Aetheling was defeated in the battle of Tinchebray (September 28). Henry sent Robert—his own brother—to permanent imprisonment in Wales. Edgar was released, but lived in obscurity thereafter.

1127   Edgar was mentioned by a historian as being still alive, at about age eighty. The date of his death is unknown.

·V·

ANGEVINS AND IBERIANS
🕸 🕸 🕸

THE CORRRESPONDENCES between Schionatulander and the Delphinal family are too specific to be denied. Yet the facts are garbled—or else deliberately rearranged: his title is anachronistic, his parents' titles are historically impossible, *Grâswaldân* was never a country, and his death may quite possibly blend recollections of the battle-death of Guigo IV at age *circa* forty-two (1142) with the youthful death of Guigo V at age *circa* twenty (1162).

Too many resemblances to be coincidence, too many discrepancies to be history: with this notion as watchword, we proceed, as others before us have proceeded, to a comparison of the Angevins of history with the Angevins of *Parzival* and *Titurel*. Frequently anticipating basic data set forth in the List of Proper Names which follows this chapter, we begin with the complex figure of Gahmuret.

Gahmuret

The story of Gahmuret, as told in Books I and II of *Parzival* and in the First Fragment of *Titurel*, is a deliberate composite of experiences of three, possibly four, historical Angevins. Primarily Gahmuret represents Fulk V, "the Young," 1092–1143, Count of Anjou from 1109 to 1129; in one important aspect he represents that Count's European son by a first marriage, Geoffrey

V, "Plantagenet," Count of Anjou, 1129–1151; in a smaller aspect he reflects Fulk's "Oriental" son by a second marriage, Amalric I, King of Jerusalem, 1162–1174; and in one detail he may reflect Fulk's "Oriental" grandson, Baldwin IV, King of Jerusalem, 1174–1183. The fictional sequence of events disregards the historical sequence.

At age twenty-eight, in 1120, Fulk V made a journey to the Holy Land, where he was so impressed by the newly founded Order of Templars that upon his return home he instituted a "Templars tax" throughout his territories. In 1129 he made a second journey to the Holy Land under very different circumstances. As an eligible widower aged thirty-seven and reputed as an exceptionally able and admirable ruler, he had been suggested by the Pope as the best possible husband for the half-Armenian heiress to the Kingdom of Jerusalem, the Princess Melisende. Accordingly he abdicated his Countship of Anjou in favor of his son and took Melisende as second wife. At the death of his father-in-law, King Baldwin II of Jerusalem, he succeeded to the crown, being invested as King Fulk I of Jerusalem on September 14, 1131, and ruling until his own death on November 10, 1143.

Gahmuret likewise made two journeys to "the East," as detailed in "A Gahmuret Chronology" under item "Gahmuret" in the List of Proper Names below, and on the way home from his first journey won the love and country of a "pagan" Queen, Belacane.

Two sons of Fulk I and Melisende succeeded as Kings of Jerusalem: the childless Baldwin III, 1143–1162, and Amalric I, who during his reign from 1162 to 1174 made, not two, but five expeditions into Egypt, in 1163, 1164, 1167, 1168, and 1169. These forays were all undertaken with the active cooperation of the Caliph al-'Āḍid, who, from Cairo, ruled over an empire of sectarian Fāṭimid Moslems; see item "Baldac" below; the common enemy was the orthodox Sunnite Moslem force in Syria which was seeking the overthrow of a sectarian rival. The third of these expeditions, that of January–September 1167, included a conducted tour of the royal palace in Cairo (which dazzled the

Christians) as well as an unsuccessful attack upon Alexandria, which was held by the Sunnites under the command of the youthful Saladin. All five invasions failed in their objective, and on September 10, 1171, Saladin proclaimed orthodox Islam in conquered Egypt. Three days later Caliph al-'Āḍid died, the last ruler of the two-centuries-old Fāṭimid state.

Gahmuret, who on his first expedition in support of the Baruch Ahkarin of Baldac had ignominiously unhorsed Ipomidon "before Alexandria" (P 106), was treacherously slain by that same Ipomidon "before Baldac"—Cairo—on his second expedition in support of the Baruch. Amalric I, however, died in bed and of natural causes, to be followed as King of Jerusalem by his son Baldwin IV, 1174–1183.

Neither of King Fulk's sons had been "speckled"—like Feirefiz—in any sense, but this grandson of his, Baldwin IV, was indeed "spotted"—with leprosy. Despite heroic efforts, even to directing battle from a litter, his disease forced Baldwin IV's abdication in 1183; he died in 1185. Then followed the brief reign of his nephew, Baldwin V, 1185–86, the last of the Angevin kings of Jerusalem. Through females of the Angevin line the kingship passed to various husbands, one of whom, King Guy of Lusignan, acted as Regent 1183–86, before acquiring the title in his own right. In 1225 German Emperor Frederick II of Hohenstaufen acquired the title by his marriage to Isabella of Jerusalem.

The "Gahmuret correlatives" mentioned above regard the years 1120, 1129, 1131, 1167, and possibly, in the case of Baldwin IV, the period 1174–83. We now return to King Fulk I, formerly Count Fulk V of Anjou, to go backward from 1120.

The story-parents of Gahmuret do *not* correspond to the historical parents of Count Fulk V, though the real-life mother has, nevertheless, a counterpart in the Gahmuret story. The Gahmuret-Count was the son of Fulk IV, Count of Anjou 1067–1103 and again 1106–1109, and known as "the Surly" (*le réchin*), by a third wife, Bertrada of Montfort. This lady fled from the Surly Count to become the mistress of King Philip I of France (ruled 1060–1108), who subsequently married her—bigamously. Since the Surly Count's first wife had provided him with a son and heir (the future Geoffrey IV), the fleeing lady was allowed to take the infant Fulk V with her in her flight and to rear him at the French court.

The boy Gahmuret was reared, away from Anjou and away from his true parents, by "Amflise, Queen of France," while her unnamed spouse, "the King of France," was still alive (P 69,29). Upon the death of this unnamed King of France Amflise offers herself, her crown, and her land to Gahmuret (P 77,1-2)—in outright contradiction to actual French law, but the offer is rejected and Gahmuret marries Herzeloyde instead. Thus Gahmuret's boyhood rearing by "the Queen of France" corresponds to historical fact, and the fact is hardly surprising since in real life the two were mother and son. In the story Amflise becomes a youthful "lady" who fosters a squire in preparation for knighthood, but history forbids their having been "children together," as P 94,27 asserts, just as history forbids the offer of self, crown, and land, for reasons both moral and political.

In 1103 the Surly Count abdicated in favor of his son by his first wife, Geoffrey IV, who ruled Anjou 1103–06, until his early death in battle. The Surly Count then resumed rule from 1106 to his death in 1109, whereupon the seventeen-year-old Fulk V succeeded him.

In Wolfram's fictional account the *kingdom* of Anjou passed, upon the death of *King* Gandin, to Gahmuret's elder brother (not half-brother), Galoes (P 6),—whose name is surely a form of *Galois*, "Welsh(man),"—so that Gahmuret, as landless younger brother, is obliged to seek his fortune in knightly service to the Baruch of Baldac. But upon the premature death of Galoes in love service to Annore, Queen of *Averre* (Navarre), Gahmuret directly succeeds him as *King* of Anjou (P 80; 91–92; 134). The length of Galoes's reign cannot be precisely determined, but a span of three years would fit very well into the time-scheme of *Parzival* Books I and II.

As soon as the news of Galoes's death reaches Gahmuret, the latter discards the anchor emblem (P 14) which he has worn during his knightly service and adopts his father's (and his elder brother's) coat of arms (P 99,13), the panther (*pantel*, P 101,7). The heraldic device of the historical Counts of Anjou is usually said to have been the leopard, but the Medieval Latin word for "leopard" was *pantera*, and in any case the two animals were regarded as identical in the Middle Ages.[1]

In one supremely important detail Gahmuret represents, not Fulk V, but Fulk V's son, that Geoffrey V, surnamed "the Handsome" and "Plantagenet," who ruled as Count of Anjou from his father's abdication in 1129 until his own death in 1151. On August 22, 1127, at Rouen in Normandy, he—aged fifteen!—married the Anglo-Norman Princess Matilda, heiress to the two "lands" of England and Normandy. In the fictional account Gahmuret, by winning the Kanvoleiz "vesper games" on the eve of the tournament proper, gains in marriage the lady Herzeloyde, heiress to the two "lands" of Waleis and Norgals.

Before proceeding further we summarize the correspondences thus far established, following the story-order of events; note the mixed sequence of dates in the right-hand column.

1 King Gandin of Anjou dies, elder son Galoes succeeds him, and younger son Gahmuret makes a first journey to the East to serve the Baruch of Baldac.
Fulk V's first journey to the Latin Kingdom of Jerusalem, 1120.

---

[1] T. H. White: *The Bestiary*, New York, 1954; p. 13, fn 1, quotes the 1367 English translation of twelfth-century Bartholomaeus Anglicus: "The perde varieth not fro the pantera, but the pantera hath moo white speckes." The verbal confusion is age-old:

Greek *pánthēr, -eros*, "panther"	*párdos* (from Old Persian), "pard, leopard, panther"
Latin panthēra (f.), "panther"	*pardus*, "male panther"
Old French	*pard* (m.)/*parde* (f.), "*léopard, panthère*"
Mod. French *panthère* (f.)	*léopard*, "leopard, cheetah"

Greek *leópardos* meant a supposed hybrid of lion and pard. Henry II, upon becoming the first Angevin king of England (1154), changed the "leopard(s)" of his paternal ancestors into lions.

2 Gahmuret fights "before Alexandria," (recalled in P 106).

Fulk V's "Oriental" son, King Amalric I of Jerusalem, on a *third* expedition (of five), invades Egypt, 1167, and attacks Alexandria in the interests of the sectarian caliph of Cairo.

3 On his homeward journey Gahmuret marries "pagan" Queen Belacane, thereby becoming the King of Zazamanc.

Fulk V travels a second time, 1129, to the East, marries the half-Armenian Princess Melisende, thereby inheriting the Latin Kingdom of Jerusalem.

4 Gahmuret and black Queen Belacane have a black-and-white-speckled son, Feirefiz.

Fulk V's "Oriental" grandson, King Baldwin IV of Jerusalem, 1174–83, was "spotted" with leprosy.

5 Gahmuret, disregarding his "pagan" marriage to Belacane, marries Herzeloyde, the heiress to the two "lands" of Waleis and Norgals.

Fulk V's "European" son, Geoffrey V, surnamed "Plantagenet," marries, 1127, Matilda, the heiress to the two "lands" of England and Normandy.

6 Amflise, Queen of France, partially reared the lad Gahmuret at the French court. Now that "the King of France" has died (P 69,29), Amflise, as Gahmuret's first "lady," pleads prior claim to him, over Herzeloyde.

Fulk V's mother, Bertrada of Montfort, reared him till age 17 at the court of King Philip I of France, her second husband; King Philip I died in 1108, when Fulk V was age sixteen.

7 A "court of love" adjudges Gahmuret to Herzeloyde, rather than to Amflise.

(Eleanor of Aquitaine is said to have held "courts of love," perhaps in the 1170s.)

8 At the moment of winning Herzeloyde in marriage Gahmuret learns that his elder brother Galoes had died and that he himself is now *King* of Anjou.

Fulk V becomes Count of Anjou, 1109, at age 17, upon the death of his *half*-brother, Count Geoffrey IV, 1103–06, *and* the death of his father, the Surly Count, in 1109.

9 Gahmuret at once adopts the panther (*pantel*), the heraldic device of the "Kings" of Anjou, as his own.

The heraldic device of the historical Counts of Anjou was the *pantera,* usually translated as "leopard," but to medievals panther and leopard were identical animals.

10 Gahmuret is killed "before Baldac" (i.e., Cairo) on his second expedition in support of the Baruch of Baldac.

Fulk V's "Oriental" son, Amalric I, on his 1167 invasion of Egypt in support of the sectarian caliph of Cairo, fights near Cairo, amicably visits the royal palace in that city, but dies, in 1174, of natural causes, in Palestine.

N.B.—In the fictional reorganization of the historical data Fulk V's first marriage is ignored; his second marriage, 1129, to Melisende and his son's marriage, 1127, to Matilda, the heiress to the two "lands," become two successive marriages of Gahmuret, to Belacane and to Herzeloyde. Fulk's two Eastern journeys, 1120 and 1129, become two Eastern journeys of Gahmuret, about three years apart, both in service to the Baruch in reflection of Amalric I's Egyptian invasions.

The Gahmuret narrative is focussed upon the two marriages, historically 1127 and 1129; otherwise the historical era is 1106 to some point between 1174 and 1183. All the historical correspondences have, in our opinion, been superimposed upon a figure derived from Keltic story. That figure is dimly perceptible in the "King Bans/Braus of Gomoret" in Chrétien's "Perceval;" see item "Gahmuret" below. In *The Mabinogion* that figure is King Bran the Blessèd, who was ultimately, in all probability, a "prehistoric" Keltic god of waters.

A second group of Angevin-related correspondence centers upon Herzeloyde.

Herzeloyde

King Henry I of England, 1100–1135, son of William the Conqueror, intended to bequeath his "two lands" of England and Normandy to William, his only legitimate son,—he had about twenty *il*legitimate sons,—but when William perished in a shipwreck of 1120, it was daughter Matilda who was designated heiress to the "two lands."

Born in 1102, Matilda was betrothed at age eight (1110) to German Emperor Henry V and married to him at age twelve (1114). Through eleven years of marriage these two singularly ill-tempered persons produced no children. In 1125 the Emperor died at age forty-four and Matilda, aged twenty-three, returned to England, where she was commonly known as "the Empress Maude." Two years later (1127) she married Geoffrey V, "Plantagenet," Count of Anjou, to whom she bore, in 1133, a son, Henry, often termed "Henry Fitz-Empress." Her Wolframian counterpart is Herzeloyde, "the virgin widow" (*Titurel* 27 and 35) of King Castis/Kastis, who wooed and won her at Munsalvaesche but who died on the homeward journey, leaving the marriage unconsummated but bequeathing to her his two "lands" of Waleis and Norgals.

At her father's death in 1135 "the Empress Maude" claimed her inheritance in vain. The kingship of England was "wrested" from her by her first cousin, who ruled 1135–1154 as King Stephen I of England. Through those nineteen years civil war divided the country, with Matilda maintaining precarious control over southwestern England with the support of her illegitimate half-brother, Duke Robert of Gloucester. Meanwhile husband Geoffrey "Plantagenet" held Normandy in her name until he died in 1151. In 1141–42 Matilda met defeats from Stephen's armies, narrowly escaping with her life on one occasion, but after 1148 she lived continuously at Rouen in Normandy until her death in 1167. The back-and-forth battles of those nineteen years are not reflected in *Parzival* and *Titurel*, but, significantly, Waleis and Norgals were "wrested" away from Herzeloyde soon after Parzival's birth (P 128) and at the end of the story their reconquest lies still further into the future (P 803,21–23). Between their loss and recapture an interval of nineteen years would be consistent within the time analysis of *Parzival*.

Henry Fitz-Empress first came to England (at Bristol) at the age of nine (1142), and he came again in 1144 and 1149, but most of his boyhood and youth were spent on the continent, in Normandy or Anjou. The lady Herzeloyde, however, withdrew from her capital cities soon after Parzival's birth and took her infant "to a forest, to the clearing in Soltane," there to rear him in ignorance of knights and warfare, (P 117 and ff.). For about sixteen years, by our estimate, the boy was continuously in "Soltane," but then he encountered knights anyway and eagerly left home for adventure. Herzeloyde died of grief to see him go. Before his departure she informed him (P 128) that "the proud, bold Lehelin wrested two countries away from your nobles, . . . Waleis and Norgals;" (Anjou is not mentioned). The historical equivalent of these words could well have been spoken by "the Empress Maude" to the nine-year-old Henry Fitz-Empress at Bristol in 1142. Thus Parzival *as a boy* corresponds to Henry Fitz-Empress *as a boy*; subsequent parallels between the two will be discussed later. A glance at lines 416–483 of Chrétien's "Perceval" will reveal upon what a simple, folkloristic base the Angevin political features have been superimposed.

Usurping King Stephen I (1097–1154) was the son of William the Conqueror's granddaughter Adela by Count Stephen of Blois, and for generations the House of Blois had been the foe of the House of Anjou. Moreover, Stephen's elder brother Theobald, Count of Blois 1102–1152 and Count of Champagne 1125–1152, was the father of that Adelicia/Adela/Alice whom Louis VII of France took as his third wife after consenting to divorce Eleanor of Aquitaine, that very Eleanor who hastened from her divorce to remarry with Henry Fitz-Empress in 1152. Thus both brothers from Blois had double reasons for being anti-Angevin, and it is not surprising that Theobald, from the continent, supported Stephen's usurpation of England.

According to *Parzival* 128, it was Lehelin alone who "wrested" Waleis and Norgals away from infant Parzival's nobles; but in *Parzival* 152 and elsewhere Lehelin is the brother of Duke Orilus de Lalander, so that the story, like the history, has a pair of brothers who are (anti-Angevin) villains. Wolfram, however, makes little of the brothers-motif, and, averse as usual to portraying villainous conduct, he leaves the villainy-motif vague: he has Orilus "turn to the good" (apparently) and allows Lehelin's "evil" to be reported by other characters. (Curiously, "The Later Titurel" stresses both the brothership and the villainy.)

In 1894 Jessie L. Weston (in Notes to her *Parzival* translation, Vol. I, p. 293) remarked:

> Though Stephen was the principal aggressor, it must not be forgotten that Theobald, the elder brother, was invited by the Normans to become their Duke on the death of Henry I (1135); but on arriving in Normandy, and finding that Stephen had already seized the crown of England, Theobald resigned his claim to the Duchy and threw in his lot with that of Stephen.

An *English* writer, she adds, would probably have overlooked Theobald's part in the business, whereas an *Angevin* would have remembered *both* brothers. We concur; but we have in mind, not an Angevin history-writer, but a pro-Angevin oral informant. To this point we shall speak later, as we shall also speak later about the extra "layer of meaning" in the *name* "Lehelin." In setting Stephen and Theobald parallel to the villain-brothers Lehelin and Orilus, let us note that Chrétien's "Perceval" has no equivalent to Lehelin, indeed no political "plot" at all, except for the vague and folkloristic "usurpation" of the hero's lands, and that his Orilus-equivalent, inherited from Keltic tradition, is also allowed to "turn to the good" (apparently). For the complex matter of a "vengeance quest" one must turn to other Perceval tales, as Loomis explains in pp. 394–414.

Continuing our summary of correspondences:

11 Herzeloyde is "the virgin widow" of King Castis/Kastis.

Matilda is the childless widow of German Emperor Henry V, as of 1125–1127.

12 Herzeloyde, heiress to the two "lands" of Waleis and Norgals, marries Gahmuret, the youthful *heir* to Anjou.

Matilda/"the Empress Maude," heiress to the two "lands" of England and Normandy, marries the fifteen-year-old *heir* (in 1127!) to Anjou.

13 Lehelin usurps Waleis and Norgals (but not Anjou) from Herzeloyde and her infant son Parzival.	Stephen, Matilda's first cousin, usurps England (1135) from her and her infant son Henry Fitz-Empress.
14 "Villain" Orilus de Lalander is the brother of "villain" Lehelin.	Stephen's brother Theobald attempts to usurp Normandy and also supports Stephen's usurpation of England.
15 The *boy* Parzival, living with his mother in a remote "forest," learns from her (P 128) about Lehelin's usurpations.	The *boy* Henry Fitz-Empress, sometimes living with his mother, could well have learned from her about Stephen's usurpations, particularly at age nine, in 1142.

Points 11–15, like points 1–10, focus on the marriage of 1127, but this time with regard to the political consequences of that marriage. The smaller time-span begins with Matilda/Maude's widowing in 1125 and continues to some date in the 1140s when the boy Henry Fitz-Empress could understand the usurpation of his "land(s)" and the civil war resulting therefrom. The subject matter is *English* history as viewed by a continental pro-Angevin partisan.

Further Angevin Correspondences

To find parallels for the parents of Galoes and Gahmuret, whom Wolfram calls King Gandin and Queen Schoette, we must look to Angevins prior to Fulk IV, the Surly Count, whom we disallowed and whose reign began in 1067.

Under item "Angevin" in the List of Proper Names below we mention that Anjou was ruled from *circa* 900 until 1151 by a series of Counts named either Fulk or Geoffrey. Until 1060 the rulership passed in father-to-son succession, but when Geoffrey II, "the Hammer" (*Martel*), died childless in 1060 the title passed, by way of a sister, to a nephew, Geoffrey III. Records give the name of this sister as either Hermengard or Adela, and the name of her husband, who was a Count of Gâtinais, as either Geoffrey or Alberic. The territory of Gâtinais, east of Anjou and near Orléans, came under Angevin control through this husband of alternate names, though neither he nor his heiress-wife ever ruled Anjou. Rather, the title passed directly to their elder son, the late Count's nephew, Geoffrey III, "the Bearded," who governed incompetently, 1060–67. In 1067 he was deposed by his younger brother, the Surly Count Fulk IV, who kept him in prison for twenty-eight years (!) while he himself ruled still more incompetently, 1067–1103, and then again, 1106–1109. In the three-year interval, 1103–06, it was the gracious Geoffrey IV (Galoes) who was Count of Anjou until he died from a poisoned arrow in battle. The Surly Count then resumed rulership, 1106–09, until, at his own death, the inheritance passed to the admirable Fulk V (Gahmuret).

In one generation, two brothers, Geoffrey III and Fulk IV; and in the next generation, two half-brothers, Geoffrey IV and Fulk V: we suspect that the fictional genealogy fused these two generations into one, so that the Count of Gâtinais and his Angevin-heiress wife, both of uncertain name, are the counterparts of "King" Gandin and "Queen" Schoette. In the territorial name "Gâtinais" we tend to see the origin of the perplexing name "Gandin;" see item "Gandin" in the List of Proper Names below. If we are correct about this equivalency, Wolfram's fictional Angevins have historical parallels back only to 1060 and that "jog" in the family line.

Yet Wolfram continues the line back from Gandin: to Addanz (who was a *Bertûn* and brother to Utepandragun), to Lazaliez, to an "ultimate" Mazadan,[2] whereas history attests five Angevin Counts, all named either Fulk or Geoffrey, from 1060 back to nearly 900, all in direct descent from an Ingelger, who was the son of a half-legendary "Tortulf the Forester." None of these was "British" in any sense of that term.

---

[2] Possibly "Addanz" = Old French *Adan-s*, "Adam," but it seems unlikely that "Mazadan" should be half-Keltic, half-French *Mac Adam*, "son of Adam," though Bartsch suggested both of these interpretations. "Adam" in Welsh is *Adda*. Unlikely too is any connection with the cave-dwelling monster, the Addanc, slain by the hero of *Peredur*.

Gahmuret himself lists these pre-1060 forebears of his (P 56,6–21) in his farewell letter to Belacane, where he also states that Mazadan was carried away by a fairy (*feie*) named Terdelaschoye (*Terre de la Joie*) "into *Feimurgân*," which is to say "into Morgain le Fay!" "Land of Joy" surely betokens one of the variant names for the Keltic Afterworld, but the reversal of personal name and place name is startling.[3] In P 400,5–9 King Vergulaht (son of Gahmuret's sister Fluradamurs) is also derived from Mazadan "out of the mountain (*berc*) in *Fâmorgân*, and his race was of the fairy."

In this supernatural ancestress we see a benevolent counterpart of the "Demon Countess" associated with Fulk III, "the Black" (*Nerra*), Count of Anjou, 987–1040. Legend had it that this nameless Countess could not endure Holy Mass and that when she was one day detained in church by force she flew away and disappeared forever. Richard Lion Heart is credited with the remark: "What wonder if we (Angevins) lack the natural affections of mankind, we who come from the devil and must needs go back to the devil?"

Yet the Middle English verse romance, translated from a Norman-French original of *circa* 1250—a mere fifty years after the death of Eleanor of Aquitaine (1204)—refers this legend (in lines 164–230) to Richard Lion Heart's mother![4]

> Her name is Cassadorien. She and her father, King Corbarin of Antioch, arrive by magic ship, "King Henry" marries her that very day, and at next morning's Mass she swoons at the elevation of the Host. This event is overlooked and for fifteen happy years she lives as "King Henry's Queen," bearing him sons Richard and John and a daughter named Topyas. One day, as advised by "an earl," Henry forcibly detains her in church. At the Consecration she flies out through the church roof carrying John and Topyas with her; John falls and

---

[3] To explain the reversal, Bartsch (p. 134) went so far as to "reconstruct" a pair of lines from the text of Kyot the Provençal (!) which Wolfram "misconstrued:" *en la terre Morgain la fee,/ceo fut la terre de la joie.*

[4] See B. B. Broughton: *Richard the Lion-Hearted* (and other works), Dutton paperback, New York, 1966.

breaks his thigh, but the mother and daughter were never seen again. Richard, at age fifteen—historically at age thirty-two!—becomes King.

The legend must, then, have a been a floating one and not connected solely with Fulk III and the years 987–1040. The conversion of evil-into-benevolent is an extreme case with Wolfram.

With surprise we note that the Norman-French original of this romance should, as early as *circa* 1250, recall Henry II as having only two sons, Richard and John. Apparently, popular memory, even in England, had forgotten sons Henry, "the young King" who died in 1182, and Geoffrey, who died in 1186. At the death of Henry himself in 1189, to be sure, there were only two sons *left*, and even in the 1190s it could have seemed to an enthusiastic pro-Angevin observer *from the continent* that Henry had only two sons. Let us note in passing that, given the partial equivalency of Henry II and Parzival, the two surviving sons of 1189, Richard and John, would, in the fictional genealogy, be paralleled by Parzival's twin sons Loherangrin and Kardeiz-2, who appear, aged about five years, at the end of the story.

Continuing our summary of correspondences:

16 *Gandin* and Schoette are the parents of Galoes and Gahmuret.	The Count of *Gâtinais* and his Angevin-heiress wife (both of uncertain names) were the *grand*parents of Geoffrey IV (Galoes) and Fulk V (Gahmuret). The intervening generation, with Geoffrey III and Fulk IV, was telescoped together with its successor generation.
17 The benevolent fairy Terdelaschoye, spouse of the ultimate Angevin ancestor, brought "fairy blood" into her descendants, (P 400,5–9).	The "Demon Countess" of Fulk III, 987–1040, was thought by Richard Lion Heart himself to have brought devil-characteristics into the whole Angevin family.
18 Parzival, at the end of the story, discovers that he is the	Popular tradition *in England* around 1250 seems to have re-

father of *twin* sons, Loheran-grin and Kardeiz-2.

membered Henry II as having only two sons, Richard and John, i.e., the sons who actually succeeded him as Kings of England.

Our points 9 (panther) and 17 (fairy), as listed above, were claimed by Friedrich Panzer in 1939 and summarized in a 1949 article by J. H. Scholte,[5] along with five other points with which we cannot agree. Of six points summarized by Scholte from Willem Snelleman (1941), we concur with point 6: that Trevrizent's itinerary in P 496–499 parallels that of the fleeing Richard Lion Heart in December of 1192; this matter will be discussed here presently. Snelleman's point 5 is also attractive: that the brothers Pompeius and Ipomidon, as opponents of both Gahmuret and the Baruch, correspond to the brothers whom Europeans called "Saladin" and "Saphadin." At age thirty, Saladin (an-Nāṣir Ṣalāh-ad-Dīn Yūsuf ibn-Aiyūb) met Amalric I of Jerusalem in mutually courteous exchange at Alexandria (1167); despite victories over the Crusaders, including the permanent capture of Jerusalem in 1187, he passed into Christian legend as a paragon of knighthood and of uprightness; Dante (*Inferno* 4,129) places him in Limbo with the noblest Romans and Greeks; he died in March of 1193, after thwarting Richard Lion Heart's attempt to recapture Jerusalem. His brother Saphadin (al-'Ādil Saif-ad-Dīn Abū-Bakr ibn-Aiyūb) often acted as his loyal lieutenant, as did other relatives, but came into prominence only in 1200, when he became Sultan of Egypt and Syria; he died in 1218. Thus certain disparities of dates and other circumstances render suspect the purely literary "twinning" of these two as the brothers Pompeius and Ipomidon, not to mention the fact that Ipomidon's treachery is alien to both. We reject Snelleman's other four points.

Our disagreements focus on Panzer's claim: *Gahmuret ist ein idealisierter Löwenherz.* In our opinion Gahmuret is nothing of the sort. Enthusiasm *for* Richard Lion Heart, we believe, was indeed

[5] J. H. Scholte: *Kyot von Katelangen,* in *Neophilologus* XXXIII (1949), pp. 23–36.

the motivation of conjoining Angevin history with the basic Par-zival story of Keltic-French origins in the first place, as we shall presently explain, but the factors involved lie, not in a "hori-zontal" time plane centered on Richard, but in a "vertical" time plane of Angevin history from 1060 to 1195. From evidence thus far adduced we consider "the life of Gahmuret" to be a mosaic of data relative to Richard's great-grandfather, Count Fulk V of Anjou and subsequently King Fulk I of Jerusalem, combined with data relevant to that ruler's "Oriental" son (Amalric I) and grandson (Baldwin IV), plus the important factor of the marriage of his "European" son, Geoffrey V, "Plantagenet," to the heiress of two "lands." Let us press the issue of the "Angevin-ness" of these persons:

> —Count Fulk V of Anjou and King Fulk I of Jerusalem were one and the same person, and Richard's great-grand-father;
> —Geoffrey V, "Plantagenet," and Amalric I of Jerusalem (he of the Egyptian expeditions) were half-brothers; to Ri-chard, grandfather and great-uncle, respectively;
> —Henry II, the first Angevin King of England, and Baldwin IV, the leper King of Jerusalem, were first cousins; to Richard, father and cousin, respectively.

Otherwise stated, there were two closely related branches of the Angevin family, one ruling in Jerusalem from 1131, the other ruling in London from 1154.

Kings of Jerusalem and Kings of the Grail

It was no random choice on the part of King Baldwin II of Je-rusalem (a non-Angevin) when he invited Count Fulk V of Anjou to marry his daughter and eventually succeed him in his "holy" office. The Latin Kingdom of Jerusalem, established a mere thirty years before, had great need of an able administra-tor, a political and military strategist, and a man of justice and honor. Various candidates were considered, and at the recom-mendation of the Pope the choice fell upon Fulk of Anjou. In

1128, when the invitation was issued, Fulk was a widower, aged thirty-six, and with a son already prestigiously married the year before to the heiress of England and Normandy. Fulk came in 1129, married Melisende, and in 1131 succeeded as King Fulk I of Jerusalem. He reigned prosperously until his own death in 1143.

With these facts in mind, we look anew at P 455. Kyot the Provençal (so Trevrizent tells Parzival) set about discovering more about the Grail than what he read in heathen Flegetanis:

> Kyot, the wise master, set about to trace this tale in Latin books, to see where there ever had been a people dedicated to purity and worthy of caring for the Grail. He read the chronicles of the lands, in Britain and elsewhere, in France and in Ireland, and *in Anjou he found the tale.* (Italics ours.) There he read the true story of Mazadan, and the exact record of all his family was written there, and further how Titurel and his son Frimutel bequeathed the Grail to Anfortas, whose sister Herzeloyde was. By her Gahmuret had a child who is the hero of this story. . . .[6]

No such Latin chronicle of Anjou could have existed. Wolfram's Angevins are six in number, in five generations: Mazadan, Lazaliez, Addanz, Gandin, Galoes, and Gahmuret, and all bear names alien to Anjou, whereas history, from the early 900s to 1151, lists ten Angevin Counts, all named either Fulk or Geoffrey, in eight generations. Few of these were conspicuous for "purity" (*kiusche*). Yet the quoted passage declares the fictional Angevins to be warranted, by their "purity," as keepers of the Grail, but the Grail becomes Parzival's only through his non-Angevin mother, Herzeloyde. What, then, qualified Titurel, Frimutel, and Anfortas to be keepers of the Grail? Moreover, Wolfram regularly terms his hero "a Waleis;" the Angevins in *Par-*

---

[6] By its allusion to the Gahmuret-Herzeloyde marriage the date of this alleged Latin document would need to be later than the historical marriage of 1127. Jessie L. Weston (Vol. I, p. 294) shrewdly notes that *Ireland* would hardly have been listed in P 455 until it had "come into the news" with Henry II's "conquest" of 1172.

zival are primarily Gahmuret and Feirefiz, each of whom is so designated sixteen times in the text.

In our opinion, Kyot's search and discovery of the Latin *tale* is a literary device that corresponds to Baldwin II's and Pope Honorius II's search and "discovery" of Fulk V of Anjou as the worthy successor to the Latin Kingdom of Jerusalem.

The Angevins of *Parzival* and *Titurel* represent, as we have shown, idealized Angevins of Europe and of Palestine, with biographical elements reorganized and coordinated with peripheral portions of the old Keltic-French scenario, but the Grail dynasty has been changed from Angevin—the historical fact—to something unexplained and unexplainable, something semi-supernatural, out of time and out of history. Doubters may claim that poetic privilege allowed the creation of a purely imaginary Grail dynasty, but we cling to our conviction that Wolfram's unique Grail dynasty is the idealized counterpart of the uniquely "holy" Latin Kingdom of Jerusalem, whose rulers from 1131 to 1183 (or 1186) were Angevins.

The members of Wolfram's Grail family, however, do *not* correspond to historical Angevins, either of Europe or of Palestine, for two cogent reasons: (1) most of them are figures inherited, beyond the possibility of major alteration, from Keltic-French tradition, and (2) the Jerusalem Angevins had, in historical fact, become notoriously "unworthy."

Under Fulk's son Baldwin III, King of Jerusalem, 1143–1163, military reverses occasioned the Second Crusade, which accomplished little. Fulk's second son, Amalric I, 1163–1174, for all his efforts, barely maintained the status quo. The leper King, Baldwin IV, 1174–1183, had all the qualities for leadership except adequate health. Until he died in 1185, and during the nominal reign of his nephew Baldwin V (a minor), 1185–1186, another nephew, Guy of Lusignan, acted as Regent and then became King in his own right. The very next year, 1187, witnessed major disaster for the Christian kingdom in Saladin's capture of Jerusalem. Then out went anguished appeals for the Third Crusade, to which the most conspicuous help was brought by Richard Lion Heart—King Guy's second cousin. Through the

1190s the kingdom-without-its capital was either claimed or actually ruled by the second, third, and fourth husbands of Amalric I's daughter Isabella. The dismal theory of palace intrigues and of general decline of the Latin Kingdom may be read in Volume I (1958) of the five-volume *History of the Crusades* still in course of publication by the University of Pennsylvania Press.

None of these persons has a counterpart among the members of Wolfram's Grail family. Anfortas, Trevrizent, Herzeloyde, and Repanse de Schoye (along with Cundrie *la sorcière*), all bearing names first assigned by Wolfram, are derivatives from Keltic story placed in a position analogous to an idealized form of the Jerusalem Kingdom as of, approximately, 1131 and following. Only in the "sickness" of the two dynasties might a dubious correspondence be claimed. Anfortas is still "the maimed king," Trevrizent is still "the hermit uncle" of the hero, Herzeloyde is still "the widow lady" with the heroic son; Repanse de Schoye, as Grail Bearer, still retains the function of the goddess Eriu—"Ireland in summer"—who served the Keltic gods from her food-and-drink-multiplying platter at divine banquets,—and Cundrie *la sorcière* still has traits of the same goddess in her hideous aspect as "Ireland in winter." The figure of Titurel, in our opinion, is introduced from a different Keltic-French source, and the figure of Loherangrin from yet another such source. We cannot account for the figure of Frimutel, unless, perhaps, he is a "doublet" of Titurel, functioning primarily as a symbol for Titurel's abnormally prolonged life.

Particular importance seems to attach to the notion of "the five—not four—children of Frimutel." *Titurel* stanzas 9–10 enumerate them, Trevrizent traces their stories for Parzival in a passage culminating in P 476–477, and in P 823,11–12 Wolfram tells his audience: "The true story has now come to you of the five children of Frimutel." Among the five, eldest daughter Schoysiane differs from the four others by having no counterpart in Keltic-French tradition. Nor is she an Angevin. Her role is slight: she marries "Duke Kiot of Katelangen" and dies in giving birth to his daughter Sigune. Schoysiane's true function is to link both the Grail family and the fictional Angevins with a group of characters out of Iberian history who are *Angevin-related* through Eleanor of Aquitaine.

Iberian Characters in Parzival *and* Titurel

"Katelangen" is surely Catalonia, that area of northeastern Spain ruled by a succession of Counts, first called "of Barcelona," then "of Catalonia," throughout its long history as an independent state; see item "Katelangen" in the List of Proper Names below. None of these Counts was named *Kiot/Kyot* (French *Guiot*), nor was Catalonia ever ruled by a Duke. With Herbert Kolb (*Munsalvaesche*, pp. 16–24), however, we agree that the name recalls an actual and very famous Duke *in* Catalonia for the conquest of Moslem Barbastro in 1063; see items "Kiot" and "Berbester" below. Baptized "Guy" (*Guido*), this Duke later chose, for reasons unknown, to call himself "Guy Geoffrey," but when he came to rule adopted the regnal name of Duke William VIII of Aquitaine and Count William VI of Poitou. He was the great-grandfather of Eleanor of Aquitaine. We stress that Wolfram's fictional Duke has *only the name* of this illustrious ancestor of Eleanor's.

Adjoining Catalonia on the west lay the still small Kingdom of Aragon,[7] which, beginning in 1094, was ruled by three brothers in succession. Kings Pedro I, 1094–1104, and Alfonso I, 1104–1134, both died childless, while the third brother, Ramiro, had lived as a monk since 1093 at an abbey in Narbonne. When on July 17, 1134, Alfonso I was killed in battle and the kingdom was

[7] The independent Kingdom of Aragon was created outright in 1035 when King Sancho III of Navarre divided his territories among his sons, bestowing upon one of them the small Pyrenean area centered on the town of Jaca on the River Aragon. Long after Wolfram's time Aragon was to become an extensive Mediterranean empire.

In *Parzival* a King Schafillor of Aragon fights at the Kanvoleiz tournament on the side of "the outer army" along with certain unsympathetic characters (including Lehelin) (67). He unhorses Utepandragun of Britain (74) but is unhorsed and taken captive by Gahmuret (78). Aragon is not mentioned in *Willehalm* or in the *Titurel* Fragments.

left without an heir, the monk, absolved from his vows by Pope Innocent II, came out of his monastery, assumed government of Aragon as King Ramiro II, married and begot an heiress-daughter, and then, in 1137, returned to his monastery for the rest of his life; he died in 1147. His wife was Agnes of Poitiers—also called Mahaut!—seven years the childless widow of a certain Viscount of Thouars, and a paternal aunt of Eleanor of Aquitaine.

The heiress-daughter, born 1136, was named Petronilla.[8] She was a first cousin to Eleanor of Aquitaine and, upon her father's abdication she became at once, in the first year of her life, Queen of Aragon. In that same first year of her life her father betrothed her (August 11, 1137) to Count Ramón Berenguer IV of Catalonia, who married her in 1150. In her name the Count ruled her kingdom with the title of "King *in* Aragon" until his death in 1162. The son of this couple succeeded automatically in 1162 to the three titles of: King Alfonso II of Aragon, Count Alfonso I of Catalonia, and Count Alfonso I of (southern) Provence;[9] he was commonly called the King of Aragon. This Alfonso II was, then, a second cousin to Richard Lion Heart and, as adults, they became close friends.

In both *Parzival* and *Titurel* Wolfram's fictional account speaks of three brothers:

1. King Tampunteire of Brubarz (capital city Pelrapeire), in whose name we discern *d'Ampunteire**/*d'Ampunterre** from the Catalonian port city of Ampurias, or from the district of Ampurdan, both in the extreme northeast of Catalonia; see item "Tampunteire" below;
2. Duke Kiot, who holds the *duchy* of "Katelangen" in fief from his brother Tampunteire; see item "Kiot" below;
3. Duke Manfilot, of unspecified territory; see item "Manfilot" below.

[8] The Introduction to Martin's *Kommentar* (to *Parzival* and *Titurel*; 1903), p. XLIII, notes elements of Ramiro II's life parallel to the story of Duke Kiot and Sigune but does not cite the connections with Eleanor of Aquitaine and Richard Lion Heart and draws no inferences.

[9] For the political dependency of southern Provence upon Catalonia see note 10 below.

When Duke Kiot married Grail Princess Schoysiane, his brother and overlord King Tampunteire came to Katelangen for the wedding. Later, when Schoysiane died in childbirth, the grief-stricken Kiot entrusted his infant daughter Sigune to Tampunteire and renounced knighthood to live as a hermit in a mountain glen not far from Pelrapeire. From sympathetic grief Duke Manfilot likewise abjured knighthood and joined his brother as fellow-hermit. At her father's abdication Sigune, at age one, became Duchess of Katelangen. Five years later, upon the closely successive deaths of her uncle King Tampunteire and his son King Kardeiz-1, little Sigune was sent to be reared in Waleis by her maternal aunt Herzeloyde, Parzival's mother.

Admitted non-parallels here between fact and fiction are, in our opinion, outweighed by parallels:

1 Catalonia
   Katelangen
2 three brothers: Pedro I, Alfonso I, and Ramiro II
   three brothers: Tampunteire, Kiot, and Manfilot
3 two kings die (*before* the main episode): Pedro I and his
      brother Alfonso I
   two kings die (*after* the main episode): Tampunteire and his
      son Kardeiz-1
4 withdrawal of Ramiro II to a monastery
   withdrawal of Kiot and Manfilot as hermits
5 Ramiro II, Agnes of Poitiers, and their infant daughter
      Petronilla
   Kiot, Schoysiane, and their infant daughter Sigune
6 Petronilla declared Queen of Aragon at age one and later
      removed to Catalonia
   Sigune declared Duchess of Katelangen at age one and later
      removed to Waleis
   Agnes of Poitiers did not, apparently, die in childbirth like
   Schoysiane, but we have been unable to ascertain the date
   of Agnes's death.

Too many resemblances to be coincidence, too many discrepancies to be history. The historical facts are less likely here, we think, to have been garbled than to have been deliberately rearranged.

We believe that Schoysiane, who had no Keltic-French pro-
totype to connect her with the Grail "family," was consciously
made one of "the five children of Frimutel" (when there should
have been only four) by Wolfram's oral informant. That infor-
mant may have been a subject of the ruler of Catalonia-Aragon-
(southern) Provence motivated by loyalty to the governing fam-
ily. Or he may have felt such religious awe for the self-sacrifices
of Ramiro II and Agnes of Poitiers that he invented a Grail-family
connection for them. We recall that the *riconquista* of Spain was,
in the view of the Papacy and of much of Christendom, deemed
a crusade and quite as "holy" a cause as the expulsion of the
"infidel" from the Holy Land. But we think that the informant's
basis for so proceeding with the Schoysiane character was the
Angevin connection of Agnes of Poitiers, through Eleanor of
Aquitaine.

Henry II, by his marriage to Eleanor in 1152 (two years before
becoming King of England), had come into control of Eleanor's
native Aquitaine, and both spouses hoped to expand their hold-
ings in what is now southwestern France. A prime objective was
the County of Toulouse, and, as it chanced, that objective suited
the purposes of Ramón Berenguer IV and Petronilla. In 1159 it
was the Catalonians who proposed to fortify their alliance with
the Angevins by marrying their infant daughter Berengaria to
the future Lion Heart, who was then two years old. That these
children were second cousins to each other was an obstacle that
might be dealt with when the time came. Again the Introduction
to Martin's *Kommentar* takes note of this proposal but draws no
inferences from it. Actually, nothing came of the matter.

The two families were together again in February of 1173 when
the Angevins held court at Limoges, and the future Lion Heart,
then fifteen-and-a-half, there formed a friendship with the fu-
ture Alfonso II, another second cousin from Catalonia. Present
also, among many guests, was King Sancho VI of Navarre, father
of a different Berengaria, the Princess Berengaria of Navarre,
whom Richard did marry in 1191. We can only wonder whether
Wolfram's oral informant confused the two Berengarias delib-
erately or accidentally.

Before the year's end, however, the perennially rebellious Aquitainian barons were once more in revolt: Having always withstood real (as opposed to theoretical) control by their nominal overlords, the kings of France, they were now resisting absorption into Henry II's expanding Angevin empire. It was Eleanor's wish to establish Richard, her favorite son, as ruler of Aquitaine, but, though her subjects were perfectly willing to accept *her*, they opposed her son just as they opposed her husband. In 1175, at age eighteen, Richard undertook a personal conquest of the region. In the eighth successive year of his "war" he found himself, at age twenty-six, fighting side by side with his Catalonian second cousin, now King Alfonso II, as they besieged the anti-Angevin warrior-troubadour Bertrand de Born in the latter's castle of Hautefort. (Defeated and then forgiven by Henry II, Bertrand turned pro-Angevin!) In 1185 Eleanor was obliged to resume personal rule of Aquitaine, but in 1186 Richard started his war anew.

Thus the Angevin-Catalonian alliance of the 1150s still endured in the 1180s, largely sustained by the personal friendship of Richard and Alfonso II. A new Angevin ally was won in 1190 when Eleanor arranged the marriage of the Princess Berengaria of Navarre to Richard. The aging Queen herself escorted the bride to Messina, Sicily, the staging area for the Lion Heart's crusade to Palestine, and the marriage took place on May 12, 1191, on the island of Cyprus,—which Richard interrupted his voyage long enough to conquer. Meanwhile a third Angevin ally had been made in Iberia back in 1170, when Henry and Eleanor married their nine-year-old daughter, Eleanor Plantagenet, to Alfonso VIII, King of Castile 1158–1214. Thus ever-rebellious Aquitaine had to its north the block of Angevin states comprising Anjou, Maine and Normandy, to its northwest Angevin Brittany and England, and three pro-Angevin states across the Pyrenees to its south; and in the Norman Kingdom of Sicily (and southern Italy) the Lion Heart's sister, Joan Plantagenet, was the wife of Norman King William II, though Joan became a widow in November of 1189.

Mentioned more than twenty times in Books I and II of *Parzival* is Gahmuret's kinsman and loyal friend Kaylet of Hoskurast, "the King of 'Spain' (*Spâne*)" or "the Spaniard (*Spânôl*)," with capital city at Toledo (*Dôlet*). Unmistakably, then, he is a King of Castile, despite his fictitious name, for Toledo was the capital of Castile. (Since its Christian capture in 1085 Toledo's kings were named either Alfonso or Sancho.) Kaylet's Queen, mentioned only in P 84,10, is Rischoyde, a maternal cousin of Herzeloyde.

The name *Rischoyde* is a form of Germanic *Rîhhilt/Richilde*, and Herbert Kolb (p. 11, fn 10) finds that a lady named Richilde was married in 1153, as second wife, to Alfonso VII of Castile (ruled 1126–1157). This Alfonso VII was the grandfather and close predecessor of Alfonso VIII, who in 1170 married Eleanor Plantagenet. Discrepancy of generations precludes any equivalency of Queen Rischoyde with Eleanor Plantagenet, yet the cousin-ship of Rischoyde and Herzeloyde, as well as the close friend-ship of Kaylet with Gahmuret, seems to betoken awareness of an Angevin-Castilian alliance. Under item "Herzeloyde" below it is explained that the two *names*, Herzeloyde and Rischoyde, in different forms, are paired in various literary works and assigned to two female characters of varying relationships.

To continue our summary:

19 The Grail kingdom is a "sacred kingdom," fictitious, out of time and out of history, intended to represent the *ideal* of the Latin Kingdom of Jerusalem.

The Latin Kingdom of Jerusalem, founded in 1099–1100, was a "sacred kingdom." Its dynastic crisis was resolved in 1131 by the accession of Count Fulk V of Anjou as King Fulk I of Jerusalem, and Angevin males followed him in direct descent until 1183 (or 1186).

P 455 starts to say that its rulers were Angevins but awkwardly turns in mid-sentence to speak of Parzival, the nephew of sinning Grail King Anfortas.

At the end of the poem Parzival is the "redeemer" of the Grail kingdom.

In our opinion, the total poem of *Parzival implies* that Richard Lion Heart *will be* the "redeemer"

20 Grail Princess Schoysiane was deliberately made one of "the five children of Frimutel" in order to link the Grail family with the ruling families of Catalonia and Aragon, with particular reference to the years 1134–1137.

(The story of the *adult* Sigune is elaborated, in *Parzival* and in *Titurel*, from the heroine of the (lost) French *lai* of *Li Joenet de la Lande*.)

of the despiritualized Latin Kingdom of Jerusalem.

Ramiro II, King of Aragon 1134–1137, was the adapted model for Duke Kiot of Katelangen.

His Queen, Agnes of Poitiers, was the adapted model for Schoysiane; she was *Angevin-related* by being a paternal aunt of Eleanor of Aquitaine.

Their infant daughter Petronilla was the adapted model for the infant Sigune.

See page 139 above for further parallels.

21 The historical Angevins had personal and political alliances in the Iberian peninsula:

    a) with the ruling family of Catalonia-Aragon-(southern) Provence from the 1150s, first with Eleanor and Petronilla as first cousins, and then with Richard and Alfonso II as second cousins;

    b) with the ruling house of Castile from 1170 with Eleanor Plantagenet as wife of Alfonso VIII of Castile; but *Parzival* Books I and II represents a cordial Anjou-Castile friendship and kinship in the previous generation; the basis for this is not satisfactorily accounted for;

    c) with the ruling house of Navarre by Richard Lion Heart's marriage in 1191 to the Princess of Navarre.

Homage to Eleanor of Aquitaine

The Iberian characters in *Parzival* and *Titurel* are, as we have said, linked to Wolfram's Angevins by Eleanor of Aquitaine, but Eleanor herself is not represented among those Iberians. She does appear "in her own right," we believe, in other aspects of *Parzival* (but not in *Titurel*), and in two of these aspects it is not so much the lady herself that is in question, but the "legend" about her.

Galoes, Parzival's paternal uncle and "an Angevin," perished in love service to *Annôre* (P 346,16), "Queen" of Navarre (*Averre*; P 91,23). Despite dislocation of story time from historical time, as in other cases mentioned, the allusion to a "beloved lady" from Navarre may be taken as an allusion to Richard's bride from Navarre, but *Annôre,* as a by-form of "Eleanor," may well represent a compliment to Richard's mother as "legend" portrayed her in her youth.

> Back in the early 1150s Eleanor had been lavishly praised in the poems of Bernart of Ventadour, who may actually have been in love with her. At least, young Henry II thought it prudent to put safe distances between his wife and her troubadour. It may be mentioned in passing that as of their wedding day in 1152 the bride was nearly thirty and the mother of two daughters by Louis VII of France, whereas Henry, the bridegroom, was aged nineteen. We fancy that the bride's allegedly irresistible charms were, at least in part, due to troubadour convention.
>
> Let us note, however, a five-line lyric in Middle High German, beginning *Waer diu werlt alliu mïn,* in which the unidentified poet says he would give the world entire "if but the Queen of England lay in (his) arms." If the poem's date is unknown, Eleanor was Queen of England for thirty-five years, 1154–1189,—and the revered Queen Mother for fifteen more years after that.

History does not record, but tradition has steadfastly maintained, that Eleanor held "courts of love" and presided in judgment over trials in which the rights and wrongs of lovers were in dispute. The 1170s may have been the time, Poitiers may have been the place. In our opinion, the gallant practice is recalled in the name of Parzival's wife Condwiramurs. Under item "Kondwiramurs" below we note that all twenty-three occurrences of the name in *Parzival* show a division into two parts: *Condwîr âmûrs,* and that in two cases *Condwîr* is inflected, in the Accusative, as *Condwîr(e)n,* as if it were a verbal noun taking *âmûrs* as its own Direct Object in the Accusative plural. Thus the bizarre name means "To conduct loves." Moreover, the name is a conspicuous substitute for the *Blancheflor* of Chrétien's "Perceval." Note also the "court of love" actually held late in Book II of *Parzival*, "point 7" above.

Our interpretation fits precisely with the two genealogical tables, of the fictional and of the historical Angevins. Our "point 15" above places the *boy* Parzival parallel to the *boy* Henry Fitz-Empress (as of around 1142). The adulthoods of these two boys are radically divergent, yet Parzival marries "To Conduct Loves" as Henry married Eleanor who "conducted courts of love."

Further: as Condwiramurs keeps the land of Brubarz safe during Parzival's "five years" away from home and restores it to him intact at the end of the story, so Eleanor kept England safe for Richard through his "five years" of absence, on Crusade and in captivity, 1190–1194. And finally ("point 18" above), Condwiramurs, at the end of the story, appears as the mother of five-year-old twin sons, somewhat as Eleanor in 1194 gazed, as a widow, on two sons left to her, Richard and John.

Thus *Parzival* and *Titurel* pay homage to Eleanor of Aquitaine in various ways, which we summarize as follows:

22 Duke *Kiot* of Katelangen is named for Eleanor's paternal great-grandfather, the illustrious Duke *Guiot* Geoffrey William VIII of Aquitaine, who in 1063 won Barbastro ("Berbester") with an army *in*, but not *of*, Catalonia.

23 Duke Kiot's wife Schoysiane is the genealogical counterpart of Eleanor's paternal aunt, Agnes of Poitiers.

24 The infancy of Kiot's and Schoysiane's daughter Sigune parallels the extraordinary experiences and circumstances of the infant Petronilla, Queen of Aragon, Eleanor's first cousin.

25 These kinships of Eleanor's are also the basis for introducing the *role* of Duke Kiot as bereaved widower and subsequent hermit and for introducing further characters into the story: Tampunteire, Manfilot, and perhaps Kardeiz-1.

26 Eleanor and Petronilla were first cousins, as are Condwiramurs and Sigune, but where the fictional pair are represented as being of the same age, Eleanor was born (probably) in 1122, Petronilla in 1136.

27 The *name* of *Annôre* (P 346,16), as a by-form of "Eleanor," may allude to the "legend" of the young Eleanor of Aquitaine as a lady of irresistible charms.

28 The *name* of Condwiramurs, meaning "To Conduct Loves," alludes to Eleanor's conducting of "courts of love."

29 In the two genealogical tables Condwiramurs, as the wife of Parzival, stands parallel to Eleanor, as the wife of Henry II.

30 At the end of the poem Condwiramurs brings Parzival his small twin sons, both future kings; she has also kept her kingdom of Brubarz safe for Parzival. Eleanor, in 1194, was left with two (grown) sons: Richard, who was already a king, and John, who (unfortunately) was a king-to-be; she had also kept the Angevin empire safe for Richard.

Wolfram's Informant

Not for a moment do we suggest that central-European Wolfram personally assembled all the historical data we have adduced, or that he alone determined all these equivalencies and combinations. We believe—though forbidden to do so—in an oral informant called "Kyot the Provençal."

Kyot's name, representing French *Guiot* and not Provençal *Guizot*, may betoken a Frenchman with unexplained affiliation with Provence. He may have been an Angevin, since in Angevin family tradition *Guiot* was commonly the name for a second or third son, after the requisite "Fulk" or "Geoffrey," in which case family pride may have motivated his glorification of Angevins. But we do not think so. Or, again, he may have been a Provençal subject of the Counts of Catalonia after 1112.[10]

---

[10] In 1112 Ramón Berenguer III, Count of Barcelona (see item "Katelangen" below), married Dulce (or Douce), heiress to Provence, which was both a Marquisate and a County, and in the following year, 1113, assumed control of the whole area, with the dual title of Marquis *and* Count of Provence.

In 1125, however, Provence north of the River Durance was detached and called the Marquisate in order to provide a portion for Dulce's younger sister Stephanie. South of the Durance the *County* of Provence was retained by Ramón Berenguer III.

At his death in 1131 Provence passed to his younger son, but when that son

Frenchman or Provençal, Kyot will have been a Templar associated with Richard Lion Heart during the Third Crusade, perhaps from the mustering of forces at Lyon on July 10, 1190, or from the embarkation at Marseille on August 7th, or from the reembarkation at Messina, Sicily, on April 10, 1191, but surely in Palestine after June 7th or so. He will surely have been one of the small company that sailed with Richard from Palestine on October 9, 1192. After reversing voyage (to avoid waylaying of Richard by enemies), Kyot was surely one of the twenty-one persons who survived shipwreck off Ragusa (Dubrovnik) in what is now Yugoslavia, and he must have been one of the survivors of the second shipwreck at the north end of the Adriatic in early December.

Somewhere near Aquileia the party procured horses. Count Mainard of Gorizia granted safe-conduct through his territories after receiving a ruby ring from "the merchant Hugh," but he replied that *King Richard* might pass unharmed, as might also (according to an eyewitness who informed the chronicler Coggeshall): Baldwin of Béthune, *Magister Philippus regis clericus atque Anselmus capellanus,*—and *quidam fratres Templi.* But the perfidious Count pursued anyway and captured eight of the group. The rest escaped, by way of Friuli, to Freisach in Carinthia, whence, after being recognized anew, Richard fled on with only two companions. Three days and three nights they were

---

died in 1144 title and territory reverted to the elder son, Ramón Berenguer IV, 1131–1162, Count of Barcelona, or, as he was now beginning to style himself, Count of Catalonia, and by betrothal and subsequent marriage to Petronilla of Aragon, "acting King" in Aragon.

From 1162 to 1196 the son of this pair succeeded to the triple title: King Alfonso II of Aragon, Count Alfonso I of Barcelona/Catalonia, and Count Alfonso I of Provence.

In 1196 son Pedro became King Pedro II of Aragon and Count Pedro I of Catalonia, with younger son Alfonso as Count of Provence. At the latter's death in 1209 Provence again reverted to the elder brother, Pedro, who then ruled it until his own death in 1213.

Thus from 1112 to 1213 the *County,* or southern half, of Provence was continuously ruled by Counts of Catalonia, and continued to be so ruled past the time of Wolfram's death. Hence Wolfram's *Katelangen* may well have included Wolfram's *Provenz.*

without food. On December 20th or 21st Richard himself was captured *in domu despecta* (a poor inn?) near Vienna,—some think in Wiener Neustadt. Duke Leopold of Austria, whom Richard had gravely offended at Acre back in June of 1191, was the gloating captor of this invaluable prisoner.

The Aquileia-to-Vienna itinerary is only partially known, but it may, in fairness, be eked out from *Parzival* 496–9 (as Willem Snelleman recognized in 1941), where Trevrizent, describing travels of *his*, names Aquileia, Friuli, Cilli, "the Rohas," and that village grossly magnified into "vast Gandine" at the junction of the small stream of the Greian with the River Drave in the "land" of Styria. Written records of that journey of December 1192 could hardly have reached Wolfram: he *must* have heard of it through oral report.

By February of 1193 Duke Leopold was obliged to sell the prisoner to his overlord, German Emperor Henry VI of Hohenstaufen, to whom the prisoner was even more invaluable. Leopold (who was excommunicated for kidnapping a Crusader) took Richard up the Danube to Regensburg, then back down as far as Dürrenstein, where Emperor Henry took custody of him on February 14, 1193. By unknown overland stages the prisoner was then sent west.

Two English abbots, who were searching for him, came upon him at Ochsenfurt in Bavaria. To him they reported that brother John was fomenting treason in England and that all Aquitaine was in revolt. Perhaps they also reported that Llewlyn ap Iorwerth, soon to be called "the Great" by his countrymen, was trying to "wrest" all of Wales from Richard's control. This was *brand new* news. In "usurper" Llewlyn we see the origin of the *name* "Lehelin;" the *role* of Lehelin, as said in "point 13" above, depends, in *Parzival*, upon the genuine usurper, King Stephen I of England, 1135–1154. But there was the comfort that Queen Eleanor was thwarting brother John's plots in England, while the Aquitanian barons were being checked, at least temporarily, by the loyal seneschal of Gascony and by Richard's brother-in-law, the young King of Navarre.

April brought the captive to Castle Trifels, west of the Rhine and north of Alsace, and there he remained some nine months. If Kyot was not with Richard up to the capture near Vienna, he may have followed the captive's trail; as a Templar he could easily have done so. Or he may have had access to Richard at Trifels. He may well have learned that Emperor Henry was offering inducements to his prisoner to assume the role in Rhone-valley politics envisaged half a lifetime ago for Guigo V (*Dalfinus*) of Albon. The semi-legendary features of Schionatulander, however, would more plausibly come from the literary man Kyot than from German courtiers or jailers. In proclaiming, in December 1193, the forthcoming release of his royal captive, Emperor Henry also set a date in March of 1194 for Richard's coronation as "King of Provence,"—which would have made him an Angevin vassal of the German Empire. The scheme came to naught, but Henry did obtain "a king's ransom" from England—and with it he financed his conquest of the Norman Kingdom of Sicily, Richard's ally.

Richard was released on February 4, 1194, to be met by his seventy-two-year-old mother, who had come to fetch him home and to bring down-payment on the ransom. Mother and son then sailed leisurely down the Rhine, meeting with potential German allies for any future war against France. On March 13th Richard touched English soil at Sandwich. On the 16th he made his triumphal entry into London. On the octave of Easter he "wore the crown" again in the old Saxon capital of Winchester so all his people might see that England had *not* become a vassal of the German Empire. By May he was already back fighting Aquitanian barons.

In Aquitaine he remained until April 6, 1199, when he died of an infected arrow-wound, at age forty-one-and-a-half. Then brother John, at age thirty-three, succeeded to the whole Angevin empire. Four years later almost nothing of that empire remained to him except England. The rest was lost to his enemies. In 1204 Queen Eleanor, at age eighty-two, died amid the empire's collapse.

Between 1190 and 1194—before, during, or following the Third Crusade,—Kyot, we believe, heard from Richard himself extended tales from Angevin history, in which he discerned— in all sincerity—striking parallels with the scenario of the Perceval story in Chrétien's or some other (lost) version. As a literary man (of some sort) he elaborated further "parallels." To him we attribute the whole Iberian block of story and characters. His objective was the glorification of Richard Lion Heart and of Eleanor of Aquitaine; his dream was of a resuscitated "sacred kingdom" which should include Jerusalem and Europe and a Christianized "East," to be accomplished, perhaps by Richard, perhaps by Richard's future offspring. Angevin politics, as such, concerned him only as the instrument for achieving World Christendom.

In 1193, or 1194, or 1195, Kyot, we think, met Wolfram personally, found him engaged in a first, Chrétien-based, version of *Parzival*, beginning where Book III now begins, and advised him as to "needed" modifications and as to the story's missing conclusion. In the epilogue to *Parzival* (P 827,1–11) Wolfram says precisely that:

> If Master Chrétien de Troyes did not do justice to this story, that may well vex Kyot, who furnished us the right story. The Provençal correctly tells how Herzeloyde's child won the Grail. . . . From Provence to Germany the true facts were sent to us, as well as this adventure's final conclusion.

"Were sent" (*sint gesant*) does not, admittedly, suggest a personal interview, but P 416,28: "Whatever he told of it (the story) in French" (*swaz er en franzoys dâ von gesprach*) seems to imply oral recitation, in Wolfram's presence, of a literary work by Kyot himself. The word *gesprach* probably means "recited" rather than "told." And P 453,6 says, oddly, that Kyot requested him to "conceal" certain information about the Grail: *mich bat ez helen Kyôt*. Possibly P 455 reflects such "concealment," but the Grail is shrouded in multiple mysteries and any number of such could have been intended for being kept secret.

Place Names in Parzival *and* Titurel

Not all the European place names in these two poems need to have come from Kyot, yet, viewed in their aggregate, their distribution has its own significance.

Kyot was no central European. The dozen German place names occur in Wolfram's personal asides and are extrinsic to the story. Northward, "Denmark" (P 605; a horse from there) is insignificant, and "Norway" (8 x) is the "Arthurian" name for Gawan's homeland. Southward, Italy is a geographical blank save for two incidental allusions to Rome; the Italian-Sicilian terms clustered in P 656–7 belong to the Clinschor story, which we regard as from a *French* source other than Kyot. That all of them fall within the Norman Kingdom suggests that the French source work was political and satirical; it could not have been composed earlier than 1195; see the "Note on Anagrammed Names" under item "Sigune" below. Eastward, Slavdom is represented only by the misplaced Wends (*windisch diet*) of Trevrizent's itinerary,[11] yet the Aquileia-to-Syria itinerary, unfamiliar in Arthurian tales, is represented by 8 or 9 names, reinforcing our impression that it depends on oral report of the Lion Heart's journey of December 1192.

Disallowing "Arthurian" names from the British Isles as transmitted only by "poetry," we are left with one "Ireland," an ambiguous "Scotland," and two city names: London and "Sinzester" (doubtless Winchester), a hat from the first (P 313,10), a twice-mentioned hat from the second (P 605,8; 722,18). "England" itself, always in the German form *Engellant*, is the source of a certain harp (663), a possession of Arthur's (735), and in 761 one in a list of *terres*: *Löver* (which = Welsh *Lloegr*, "England"), *Bertâne*, *Engellant*, and the stretch from Paris to Wissant (!).—Apparently Kyot never set foot in the British Isles.

---

[11] The inconclusive crusade against the Wends was fought in 1147 along the lower Elbe and the coast of the Baltic Sea. Possibly some of Richard's party recognized South Slavic speech as akin to Wendish. (Upper and Lower Wendish are still spoken by about 150,000 persons in two adjacent linguistic islands southeast of Berlin.)

By contrast, we count 20 French place names north of the Loire, 15 of them north of the Seine, and 4 of these in "Belgium"—but in 1200 within the German Empire: "France" (meaning the royal domain), 6 major fiefs, plus "Belgian" Brabant and Hainaut and "Belgian" cities Antwerp and Ghent. Few of these would be plausible places of origin for so ardent a pro-Angevin as Kyot,—unless he was himself an Angevin, and that possibility remains.

Surprisingly, only 6 places south of the Loire: the fiefs Gascony and Poitou, both Angevin-controlled from 1154; politically fictional Graswaldan and politically ambiguous Provence (see footnote 10 above); Arles (an area or a city?), and an unexpected Lunel.

From Iberia, on the other hand, we find 11 items: the 6 regions of Aragon, Catalonia, Galicia, Navarre, "Spain" (in the sense of Castile), and Portugal; 4 Christian cities: Toledo, Barbastro, Tudela, and a hostilely mentioned "Vedrun," presumably Pontevedra in hostilely mentioned Galicia; and Moslem Seville, with concomitant awareness of sailing routes from there to Morocco; see item "Seville" and item "Spain" below.

The Historical Time of Parzival and Titurel

Angevin history, as reflected in *Parzival,* may begin at 1060 or even earlier, but clear equivalencies start at 1092 or so, when infant Fulk V was taken from Anjou to the French court, and extend to about 1142. The Iberian parallels in both poems regard primarily the years 1134–37. The focal events are the two marriages of 1127 and 1129, with the reign of Geoffrey IV (Galoes), 1103–1106, brought forward, and the 1167 Egyptian expedition of Amalric I brought backward, into the era. Reckoning from Petronilla's (Sigune's) birth in 1136, a fourteen-year-old Sigune would be reading the jeweled hound's-leash in 1150, but by making Sigune the same age as Condwiramurs the episode needs to be dated fourteen years after 1122, the probable year of Eleanor's (Condwiramurs's) birth. Even the reign of Guigo

IV *Dalfinus*, 1133–1142, has been transposed backwards a trifle to make a sixteen-year-old Schionatulander capture the dog Gardeviaz. Let us note also that, in Schionatulander, Count Guigo IV has been put in the stead of Count Ramón Berenguer IV, and that these two may have been cousins to each other; see the genealogical table of the Counts of Albon on page 114.

The dates have been freely manipulated, to be sure, but there is a sparseness of historical parallels after 1150, until we come upon the parallels of the 1190s, notably that Aquileia-to-Syria itinerary of December 1192. These late parallels have also been removed backwards to the primary era of the 1120s and 1130s. We suspect that Kyot was middle-aged in the 1190s and that, for him, "the glorious time" was in his father's generation.

Conclusions

Wolfram could hardly have received these transformed historical data before 1195. Then, we think, he set about the composition of Books I and II of *Parzival*, which, to a significant degree, represent a story of Kyot's conjointure. Beginning at Book III, he reworked "the *Urparzival*," superimposing upon it the new features gained from Kyot. In time, his draft of "Titurel" was similarly revised as the Second Fragment, and a new "First" Fragment was composed and coordinated with the Kyot material; in it the Iberians and Dauphins predominate.[12] By now we are past 1200 and into the reign of John I of England, 1199–1216.

In terming the Gahmuret story (in both poems) "of Kyot's conjointure" we disclaim any servile imitation of Kyot by Wol-

---

[12] Of 51 occurrences of "Anjou" and "Angevin" (taken together) in *Parzival*, 23 fall in Books I and II; 17 in Books XV and XVI, where the strands of story are being collected; 4 in Book IX, where the hero is apprised of his ancestry; the rest are scattered, often for purposes of "recall."

"Angevin" occurs 4 x in *Titurel*, always relative to Gahmuret, and 2 x in *Willehalm* (45 and 54), in recollections of Feirefiz.

"The Later Titurel" merely echoes the "Anjou"/"Angevin" of Wolfram, as does the anonymous *Lohengrin* late in the 13th century.

fram as we disclaim any notion that the passages in question are a mere collage of historical data. Rather, the data have been astutely related to a traditional literary figure derived from King Bran the Blessèd in *The Mabinogion*, traits of whom are discernible in Gahmuret's lavish hospitality, in his retinue of youths (P 63), in his exuberance, and in his battle-death in an alien land; see Loomis, p. 350. Poetic coordination of all factors was Wolfram's achievement, as well as the lively portrayal of a young husband who must forever be joyously adventuring and whose "anchor," repeatedly cast, nowhere holds firm.

Ironically, the definitive *Parzival* and the "final" version of the *Titurel* Fragments were realized in the reign of John, that cruel, petty, libidinous, treacherous, vacillating monarch who began by letting the Angevin empire collapse (while he scarcely bestirred himself), and proceeded, by way of excommunication (1209) and military disaster (1214), to the last indignity of being captured by his own nobles and forced to sign the Magna Charta of rights (1215). Anjou, the home territory of the family, was annexed to the French crown in 1203. Meanwhile the Jerusalem Angevins were being absorbed into other families while their kingdom deteriorated. Wolfram, then, could not conceivably be preaching pro-Angevin politics.[13] To him, as to his audiences, these Angevins and Catalonians and Dauphins-of-old were glamorous exoticisms appropriate to literature, and he set their lives and deeds in the long-past time of King Arthur and in an imaginary landscape of his own poetic contriving.

A Note on "the Kyot Problem"

About all six allusions to "Kyot the Provençal" in *Parzival* there is something odd. The first, at 416, is startlingly abrupt; 453 and

[13] To us it seems out of the question that Wolfram should be propagandizing for the luckless German Emperor Otto IV, the half-Angevin nephew of John of England. Otto's reign was only partially effectual from 1208 to 1212, and after 1212 he was crowded off the political stage by the rival Emperor Frederick II of Hohenstaufen. Wolfram's sole allusion to Otto, in *Willehalm* 393, likens a heathen warrior's gorgeous battle-dress to the attire worn by Otto at his Roman coronation on October 4, 1209. We take the allusion to be sardonic, and it is our guess that the remark was made upon hearing of Otto's death in 1218.

455 are earnest-sounding but mysterious; 827 (quoted on page 150 above) seems forthrightly stated. But in 431 Kyot is cited as the authority for what Gawan said after breakfast, and in 776 for festive coiffures and ladies' make-up. Since we find the Gawan sections of the poem devoid of Kyot-influence, these last serve merely to keep Kyot in evidence.

The Romantic era believed Kyot to be a real but lost poet until, in 1857, Karl Simrock, in the preface to the third, revised edition of his *Parzival* translation into modern German, suddenly expressed doubts: Kyot, he now felt, was a figment of Wolfram's imagination, invented to cover up his radical alterations of the old story. Yet Simrock ventured to guess that the false name stood for the historical twelfth-century poet, Guiot of Provins,—Provins being a town southeast of Paris on the road to Troyes.

This Guiot existed, and he knew all the right people: Louis VII of France, Henry II of England, Alfonso II of Aragon-Catalonia, even the Lion Heart himself. His only large work, however, is *La Bible (Guiot)*, a caustic review of the shams and corruptions in the various professions and social classes. The mentality behind that work shows no affinity at all with either the matter or manner of *Parzival*. In the early twentieth century the Guiot of Provins issue was sidetracked amid a scholars' quarrel about the respective literary merits of Wolfram and Chrétien de Troyes and about whether Wolfram had "belittled" Chrétien. For this rancorous episode see Kolb's *Munsalvaesche*, pp. 179–208.

In 1959 Henry and Renée Kahane identified Kyot with one "Master William," a bourgeois poet known as "Guillot," from Tudela, in Navarre. The proposal has found few supporters.

Kolb himself, 1963, without pronouncing judgment, offers for reconsideration, on p. 199, a set of twenty-two lines by an anonymous twelfth-century French poet in praise of one *Guios* or *Wiot*, who composed poems about miracles of the Virgin. Praised also are: Gautier of Arras, Chrétien, *li Kievres*, and Benoit de Sainte Maure—famous poets all, as well as an obscure Rogiers de Lisaïs. The era, 1150–1200, is appropriate. A *Guios/Wiot* may well have composed miracle-poems in that period, but he does not sound like the Kyot we are searching for.

From the Simrock of 1857 a scholarly lineage still extends. In 1950 the *Parzival* translator Wilhelm Stapel declared that "there is simply nothing to be done with persons who still believe in the existence of 'Kyot the Provençal.'"

In the present book we confidently profess belief in Kyot's existence, aware—in Horace's phrase—that we "proceed through fires beneath treacherous crust of ashes."

·VI·

LIST OF 57 PROPER NAMES IN WOLFRAM'S TITUREL

including entries on *talfîn*, on "Templars and templars," and, under item "Sigune," a Note on Anagrammed Names.

🎎 🎎 🎎

L = Albert Leitzmann's text of *Titurel* as described on page 8₁ above (fn)

LT = "The Later Titurel" (*Der Jüngere Titurel*): edition by K. A. Hahn, 1842; and partial edition by Werner Wolf: Volume I, 1955, and Volume II, 1964; as described on pp. 36–37 above.

M = Marta Marti's re-edition of Karl Bartsch's text of *Titurel* as described on page 8 above (fn)

MHG = Middle High German

OF = Old French

P = *Parzival*

T = Wolfram's *Titurel* Fragments

W = *Willehalm*

* = a reconstructed word-form

Bartsch = Karl Bartsch: *Die Eigennamen in Wolframs 'Parzival' und 'Titurel,'* in *Germanistische Studien, Supplement zur Germania,* Volume 2, Vienna, 1875; pp. 114–159. (Author's date: December 1870.)

Diu Crône = A MHG Arthurian romance, "The Crown (of Stories)," 30,041 lines, by Heinrich von dem Türlin, ca. 1220; edited by G. H. F. Scholl, Stuttgart, 1852, on the basis of: (a) the only complete manuscript (P), faulty, on paper, dated 1479; (b) a better manuscript on parchment, dated to ca. 1375, but containing only the first 12,281 lines (or ca. 40% of the poem); and (c) a late medieval fragment of 136 lines.

Flutre = Louis-Fernand Flutre: *Table des noms propres avec toutes les variantes figurant dans les romans du moyen âge écrits en français ou en provençal et actuellement publiés ou analysés;* Poitiers, 1962.

Fourquet = Jean Fourquet: *Les noms propres du Parzival,* in *Mélanges de philologie romane et de littérature médiévale offerts à Ernest Hoepffner,* Paris, 1949; pp. 245–260.

Kolb = Herbert Kolb: *Munsalvaesche,* Munich, 1963.

Langlois = Ernest Langlois: *TABLE DES NOMS PROPRES de toute nature compris dans les chansons de geste imprimées,* Paris, 1904.

Martin = Ernst Martin: *Kommentar* (Volume II of his edition of *Parzival* and *Titurel*), Halle, 1903.

West = G. D. West: *An Index of Proper Names in French Arthurian Verse Romances 1150–1300,* University of Toronto Press, 1969.

Weston = Jessie L. Weston: *Parzival* (translation), London, 1894: Appendices and Notes to Volume I, pp. 291–329; Appendices and Notes to Volume II, pp. 189–224.

For a more extensive listing of sources and of variant spellings of Wolframian names in the manuscripts, and for other information, see Werner Schröder: *Die Namen im 'Parzival' und im 'Titurel' Wolframs von Eschenbach,* Walter De Gruyter, Berlin/New York, 1982.

AGREMUNTIN (-*în*)—121,2 ". . . such heat . . . as the mountain of Agremuntin imparts to the worm salamander."

4 x in P.—Trevrizent (496), as a *Frauenritter* in his youth, jousted in Europe, Asia, and Africa, "before Gaurioun," "at the mountain of Famorgan" (= Etna), and

"before the mountain of Agremontin. If you seek combat on one side of the mountain, fiery men come riding out; on the other side (the jousters) do not burn."

Feirefiz's surcoat (*wapenroc*) (735) was woven by salamander worms in the hot fire of Agremuntin; his salamander gambeson (*kursît*) (812) saved him from a fiery knight there. 770,7, however, implies a *country*: "Duke Lippidins of Agremuntin."

2 x in W.—Poidwiz of Rabes (421) won his horse *vor dem berge zAgremuntin.* King Matusales ("Methuselah") rules (349) from Hippopotiticun to Agremuntin.

Martin: Agrimonte, east of Salerno, in the Basilicata; *or* (?) Etna. Schröder: (?) Etna, from a nearby Acremont. I have yet to find a map with either of these places. No volcano of this name is listed in Michael Scot's treatise on natural phenomena, written in 1227–1235 for Frederick II. (J. K. Wright: *The Geographical Lore of the Time of the Crusades,* 1926; Dover reprint 1965; p. 222.)

Salamanders, until the 18th century, were believed to live in fire. By confusion with the cocoons spun by silkworms, they were thought to weave the thread-like mineral asbestos; see Wright, p. 285. For the allusion in the "Letter of Prester John," composed between 1165 and 1177, see Zarncke: *Der Priester Johannes,* p. 915.

The silkworms/salamanders must be Asiatic; all P, T, and W allusions suggest Asia or Africa; LT, H-6132 locates Agremonte in "India," near the Earthly Paradise. We believe that Agremuntin is neither Italian nor a volcano, but a mythical mountain in Asia; its apparently Latin name indicates a Christian myth.

AHKARIN (L *Akarîn*)—40,2 Schionatulander accompanied Gahmuret "across into heathendom to the Baruch Ahkarin."

= the *unnamed* Baruch of Baldac (P 13), who is "the pagan Pope," i.e., Caliph. In his service Gahmuret perished (P 101–2 and 107–8). In retelling these passages, LT, H-780–984, calls him Akerin.

W 45 recalls him *by name* as *der bâruc Akerîn,* in fame second only to Feirefiz the Angevin. W 73 identifies Akerin, King of Morocco, as "of the family (*geslehte*) of the Baruch who buried Gahmuret at Baldac with Christian rites."

In W 96 this King of Morocco corresponds to the *Acarin* of *Aliscans* 1428, the sole occurrence and without variants in the MSS; presumably = OF *acerin/aceri/aceré,* "(made of) steel;" (but the *Eserê* of W 77 = the *Aceré* of *Aliscans* 1171 + 33).

Arabist Paul Kunitzsch says "Ahkarin" is not Arabic at all; he also rules out any Arabic source for *bâruc,* insisting on Hebrew *bârûk,* "blessèd," only; (*Die Arabica im 'Parzival' Wolframs von Eschenbach,* in *Wolfram-Studien II,* Berlin, 1974; p. 18; also in a personal letter). Note the Old Testament book of *Baruch* (Vulgate Bible: *Prophetia Baruch*), where "Baruch" is the author of the book.

ANFORTAS—9,3 Mentioned first of the five children of Frimutel.

38 x in P, (A*m*- in 455, 617).—(455) Titurel's grandson; (478) eldest son of Frimutel and third King of the Grail, until (796) succeeded by Parzival.—(478) Contrary to Grail vows, he became a *Frauenritter*, in love service (616) to Orgeluse, Duchess of Logrois, and in jousting against an unnamed heathen (479) he was pierced through the testicles by a poisoned spear. The wound festered, all remedies failed, but because (480–3) the sight of the Grail was forced upon him once a week, he could not die. (Cf LT H-6177.) He will be healed if a visitor knight asks, unprompted, a certain question (484), but will no longer be King. Parzival comes (224–240), beholds Anfortas's agony, but asks no question. At his second coming (796) he inquires: *Oeheim, waz wirret dir?* ("Uncle, what is it that troubles you?"), and instantly Anfortas is healed.

4 x in W, all allusions to P: (99) to his tendance; (167 A*m*-) to his suffering; (283) to his cure; (279) to his love service to Orgeluse.

In Chrétien's "Perceval" 3495 (Roach edition) he is called *le riche Roi Pescheor*, "the rich Fisher King," to whom no other name is given, though in other Grail romances his analogue may be Bron, Pellinor, or even Joseph of Arimathea (Loomis, p. 371), to say nothing of his Keltic analogues.

Wolfram (and LT) alone call him "Anfortas." Bartsch: from Provençal *enfermas/-atz*, (not OF *enfertes/-tez*), from Latin *infirmatus*, via a Vulgar Latin *infirmitatus*,* meaning "the sick/infirm man." Schröder lists further discussions.

ANGEVIN (*Anschevîn*)—40,1; 54,3; 94,1; 111,3—all as "the Angevin," meaning Gahmuret, King of Anjou,—though 40,1 and 54,3 refer to story-time *before* his kingship, as if readers knew about his succession to Galoes in P 80, 91–92, and 134.

16 x in P referring to Gahmuret, 16 x referring to Feirefiz, and once (746) referring to both. (Another case of Wolfram's astonishing "literary arithmetic.")

2 x in W (45 and 54) referring to Feirefiz. In the one allusion to Parzival (271) the term is *not* used.

Neither T nor W mentions "Anjou" (*Anschouwe*), but P mentions it 17 x as a *kingdom* of unspecified location, capital city *Bêâlzenân*. Bartsch: Provençal *beal-z*, "fair, beautiful," + Provençal *enan(s)*, "jutting rock;" of Italian *di-nan-zi*. Martin: ? the town of Baugé/? the town of Beaugency. In Roman times the "capital" was *Juliomagus*, "Julius

(Caesar's) Field" (or "Market"). Ever thereafter it has been "Angers," in one linguistic form or another, from the Keltic tribe of the Andes/Andecavi.

The Anjou of history was never a kingdom; it was not even a duchy until 1360. As the territory of the Keltic Andes/Andecavi it was conquered by a lieutenant of Julius Caesar's in 57 B.C. and Roman-ruled for 400 years as the *Civitas Andegavensis.* From ca. 900 until 1151 it was ruled by *Counts* alternately named Fulk or Geoffrey, who supported the French kings against the Normans. Last of that line was Count Geoffrey V, "Plantagenet," who, by marrying Matilda—"the Empress Maude"—heiress of England and Normandy on August 22, 1127, became the father of Henry II, King of England (1154–1189), the grandfather of Richard Lion Heart, and the progenitor of the Angevin line of English kings down to 1485.

In Palestine Count Fulk V (father of Geoffrey "Plantagenet") became King of Jerusalem in 1131, originating a line of male Angevin Kings of Jerusalem until 1183 (and nominally until 1186); thereafter the husbands of female Angevins ruled.

In 1203 Anjou was seized from John I of England and annexed to the French crown. In 1266 Saint King Louis IX of France, who had made his brother Charles the Count of Anjou, allowed Charles to accept the kingship of Sicily, and in 1277 Charles purchased the *claim* to the kingship of Jerusalem. This later Angevin line is unrelated to the previous one.

ANPHLISE (*-îse*)—38,1; 39,1; 92,4; 96,2; 100,3; 122,2; 123,4.—(122) "the Queen of the French" (*der Franzoyser künigin*) and Gahmuret's first "lady." (38,96) she reared Schionatulander (124) "from the time he was weaned." (39) she sponsored Gahmuret's knighting and on that occasion (39, 92, 96) "lent" (*lech*) him Schionatulander, who was her page; (96) she is still fond of the lad. Herzeloyde (122–123) fears Anphlise has prompted Sigune's passion for Schionatulander for "revenge," i.e., to take Sigune away from Herzeloyde as Herzeloyde took Gahmuret away from Anphlise.

7 x in P (5 x *Ampflise,* 2 x *Amph-*).—Ampflise, *rêgîn de Franze,* now widowed (69,29), sends a deputation (76–78) to Gahmuret to offer him "a crown, a scepter, and a country" rather than to marry Herzeloyde, whom Gahmuret has "won" in the Kanvoleiz tournament, but a "court of love" (95–98) supports Herzeloyde's claim. This is the "theft" referred to in T 122–123. The gist of the matter is repeated by Cundrie at Arthur's court in 325. In 406 Antikonie fends off Gawan's amorous advances by saying that she is treating him no less

kindly than Ampflise "treated my uncle Gahmuret, without going to bed together" (*âne bî ligen*).

Bartsch: from Provençal *afflicha*, with intrusive *n/m*, (NOT from OF *afflis*), though both are from Latin *afflicta*, "the injured/unfortunate woman." Martin, to P 76,7, sees the name as borrowed from an "Anfelise" in certain *chansons de geste*, but (to T 38,1) sees it as borrowed from the Latin text of Andreas Capellanus's *Art of Courtly Love* (1174), where a lady of the court is named *Amphelix**—in the text, Ablative: *Amphelice*. Fourquet prefers the latter explanation.

Martin also notes, without comment, the Grail maiden Ampflise in P 806,22. Kolb, pp. 12–13, noting a second Grail maiden, Clarissanz, finds "Saracen" princesses Anfelis and Clarissanz in *La Mort Aimeri de Narbonne*, a *chanson de geste* of ca. 1180. Thus Grail maiden Ampflise would derive from the *chanson de geste*, leaving French Queen Ampflise to be, presumably, derived from Andreas Capellanus.

Flutre lists *Angelise/En-* for two romances, *La Prise de Defur* and *Galeran de Bretagne*.

The matter is perplexing. Kolb may well be right in finding different sources for the two Ampflises; if the Grail maiden takes her name from the *chansons de geste*, the French Queen's name would seem to be "Arthurian," to judge by Flutre and Andreas Capellanus. A derivation of the latter from Latin *infelice-m*, "the unfortunate woman," seems rather more plausible than Bartsch's "*afflicha* with intrusive *n/m*." Perhaps there is a "reflection" of the Welsh feminine name *Angharad*, "unbeloved," related to Welsh *câr*, "friend," *cariad*, "love; lover," etc., cognates of Latin *carus*. In the Welsh *Peredur* the hero seeks the love of Angharad Golden-hand.

AZAGOUC—80,1 (L 79,1) Gahmuret, on his second expedition to the East, is furnished with "jewels of Azagouc."

12 x in P.—Gahmuret, returning from his first expedition to the East, arrives (P 16–17) by storm-driven ship at Patelamunt, capital of Zazamanc, where the people are "pagan" and black *Moere und Moerinne* (19). To the *west* (P 25,23) lies the adjacent kingdom of Azagouc, of similar population. In a war between these two kingdoms, Isenhart, the black king of Azagouc, is supported by white knights from Normandy, Spain, and Champagne, as well as by Fridebrant the Scotsman (*Schotte*, 25), who has temporarily sailed off to Scotland (*Schotten*, 16, 58, 70), taking with him his troops from Greenland (*Gruonlant*, 48) and Morholt (49) of Ireland (*Yrlant*, 67). Gahmuret

defeats these foes of Queen Belacane of Zazamanc, marries the black queen, inherits both kingdoms, and sires the black-and-white-speckled Feirefiz, older half-brother to Parzival.

2 x in W.—"Black folk of Azagouc" fight in the first battle of Alischanz under their king, Rubiun (27, 46), and under another leader in the second battle (350, 392).

In P 234 Grail maidens wear garments of green samite from Azagouc. Stanza 439 of the *Nibelungenlied* mentions "silk from Azagouc," stanza 362 mentions "silk from Zazamanc, as green as clover;" 7 lines further these are equated with the best silks from Morocco and Libya. Almost certainly the *Nibelungenlied* borrowed these place names from *Parzival*.

Martin and Schröder: Zazamanc = *Garamentae*, Azagouc = *Azachaei*, both from the geography of Caius Julius Solinus (3rd or 4th century).

As proposed in our *Willehalm*, p. 327, we see "Azagouc" as a garble of Arabic *az-zuqaq*, "The Strait (of Gibraltar)." We now suggest that Patelamunt, port city of capital of Zazamanc, = the Mediterranean port city of Ceuta (classical *Septa,* Arabic *Sabtah*) and that the *adjacent* kingdom of Azagouc to the *west* = Tangier (classical *Tingis,* Arabic *Ṭanjah,* French *Tanger*), facing onto the Atlantic and providing easy access for the ships of King Isenhart's European allies.

In making this suggestion we would connect these names with Seville (see item "Seville" below); with the *Katus Erkules* of W 141 and 359, understanding *Gades Herculis* in the sense of "Cadiz;" with the "Morocco" of P and W, and particularly with Gahmuret's sea voyages; also with Schionatulander's voyage in LT, H-2524–2628 as described on p. 60 above.

BALDAC—73,2; 81,4 (L 80,4) The Baruch's capital, besieged by Pompeius and Ipomidon; Gahmuret was slain there by Ipomidon.

11 x in P.—Gahmuret, as a landless younger brother, journeys to Baldac (13–15) and wins fame in the service of the Baruch (Ahkarin). During his second tour of service to the Baruch (102) he is slain "on the plain before Baldac" (105) and buried inside the city (106; 108). His death there is mourned by Trevrizent (496), reported by Parzival to Feirefiz (751), and recalled by the poet in W 73.

6 x in W.—(73); in 96, 413, 434, 439, and 466 Terramer is "the ruler of Baldac."

Flutre lists *Baudac* and variants for 16 OF romances but for *no* work of Chrétien. Variant "Baldac" only in *Les Prophécies de Merlin*.

Martin: = OF *Baudas,* seat of the Caliphs; no examples.

The meaning hovers between Baghdad in Mesopotamia and Cairo in Egypt.

1. Etymologically, *Baldac* = BAGHDAD: built new in 762 on the E bank of the middle Tigris and the seat of the Sunni (orthodox) Caliphs until its total destruction by the Mongols in 1258. Accompanying names in P 13–14 and 101–2 support the Mesopotamian location: Babylonia, Nabuchodonosor (Nebuchadnezzar), Ninus, and Nineveh. All these names, except Nineveh, occur in the first two Books of Orosius's *Seven Books of History against the Pagans,* ca. 418 A.D. For more on this point see under "Pompeius" below.

"Ninus" is not in the Bible at all, and we believe Wolfram's "Nineveh" comes only indirectly from the Bible. Nineveh, the *Assyrian* city on the *upper* Tigris, was permanently destroyed in 612 B.C., but medieval Christians applied the name to Mosul (Arabic *al-Maw-ṣil*), located just across the river on the *west* bank. Beginning June 28, 1098, the Crusaders had long to do with the powerful armies out of Mosul.

In the OF prose romance, *Le Petit Jehan de Saintré,* 1456,—see under "Beuframunt" below—we read of

> . . . *Mesopatine, ou est le grant cité de Ninivee, qui a III journees de long, qui ores est dicte Babillone; et la est le commencement de la merveilleuse tour de Babel, qui a III^m pas de large, et la sont les provinces de Caldee, de Arabie, de Sabba et de Tarssie;* . . .

(Compare P 629,22: ". . . Thasmê, larger still than Nineveh . . .")

2. *Baldac* = CAIRO. Flutre lists more than 40 OF romances in which "Babylon" = Cairo, (often represented as a port city).

William of Malmsbury's *Gesta regum,* ca. 1125, reflects Strabo, the Greek geographer of Augustus's time, by speaking of Babylon as "not the city built by Nimrod and enlarged by Semiramis and now said to be deserted, but that which Cambyses, son of Cyrus, built in Egypt . . .," (in 525 B.C. and colonized from Mesopotamian Babylon). On the (? 4th-century) *Tabula Peutingeriana* 800 years later *this* Babylon is shown with two towers to indicate a medium-size city. On its northern edge the invading Arabs of 640 A.D. built Fustat, and in 969 Cairo, just to the N of Fustat. A European map of 1339 shows Egypt itself as "Babilonja."

From Cairo the Caliphs of the sectarian Fatimids ruled, 973–1171, over Egypt, North Africa, Sicily, and Syria. With these sectarians Amalric I, the third *Angevin* King of Jerusalem, 1163–1174, made an alliance against the orthodox Sunnis and staged an "invasion" of Egypt in 1167. The "invaders" were escorted through the Caliphal palace in Cairo and were dazzled by its splendors. They also conducted an unsuccessful siege of Alexandria, where the youthful Saladin was in command of the Sunni forces. See pp. 119–120 above.

That "Baldac" = Cairo in P and T is likely: (a) from the mention of *Alexandrîe* in P 18, 21, and 106; (b) from the implication that Gahmuret arrives there by ship; and (c) from the Angevin connections with both cities in 1167.

In W, however, "Baldac" is more plausibly Baghdad.

BELACANE (*-âne*)—37,1 "How Gahmuret left Belacane, . . ."

8 x in P (6 x in *-kâne*).—The black and "pagan" Queen of Zazamanc whom Gahmuret (16–58) delivers from her foes from Azagouc, marries, and abandons. Despite love-sorrow for her (90), he marries Herzeloyde,—the "pagan" marriage being regarded as null and void. The poet praises her (337), and Parzival (758), introducing Feirefiz to Gawan, says: "My father by his fame won the love of Belacane, who bore this knight."

Bartsch: from Provençal *bela cana*, "fair reed,"—though the Meyer-Lübke dictionary, p. 1597, shows "fair chain" and "fair throat" as possible alternates.

Not in Flutre.

Martin: "doubtless refers to Balkis, the Queen of Sheba." More properly, Arabic *Bilqis.* Schröder omits all reference to this far-fetched derivation.

BERBESTER—42,2 Schionatulander's maternal uncle, Ehkunat, the Count Palatine, "was known as 'from strong Berbester.'"

Not in P.

3 x in W (303, 329, 380) as the city ruled by Willehalm's brother, Bertram-1, probably reflecting *Aliscans* 5134, where "Barbastre!" is the war cry of William's brother Bueve. Ehkunat's title of "Count Palatine" may have been taken over from Willehalm's nephew, Bertram-2. The confusion is sorted out in the List of 434 Proper Names in *Willehalm*, in our translation of that poem, under items: Berbester, Bertram-1, Bertram-2, and Komarzi; also in pp. 288–289 of the same work.

Berbester = the city of Barbastro in NE Spain (classical *Labitolosa*, Arabic *Barbashtru*), taken in 1064 from the Moslems by a French army under command of Duke William VIII of Aquitaine, great-grandfather of Eleanor of Aquitaine; see under "Kiot" below. Lost again, it was retaken in 1102, but it was the conquest of 1064 that formed the basis for the *chanson de geste* of "the William cycle" called *Le Siège de Barbastre* (7,392 12-syllable lines grouped in 203 *laisses,* from the last third of the 12th century), with a wholly different William substituted as hero. The French poem sheds no light on the role of Ehkunat.

Flutre lists "Barbastre"—as a river-name! = only for *Perceforest.*

BEUFRAMUNT—150,3 Maiden Queen Clauditte of Kanedic "summoned a court (*einen hof*) at Beuframunt" so her vassals might select a suitable husband for her.

Not in P or W.

Flutre lists it as "Beffremont" (with 5 variant spellings) for three late, post-Wolframian romances and defines it as *Bauffremont,* in the *département* Vosges, *arrondissement* Neufchâteau, (near Joan of Arc's native village of Domrémy). Martin adds: "near the Maas river." In Wolfram's time this would have been in the Duchy of Upper Lorraine, within the German empire.

> *Le Roman de Ham,* in pp. 213–384 of F. Michel's 1840 anthology, is largely a versified roll call of actual French nobles who, in 1278, participated in a tournament at Compiègne (or at Creel), including (p. 358) Pieron de Bueffremont, who = *cil de Beffremont* (p. 359).
>
> *Le Tournois de Chauvenci,* 1285, is another such versified rollcall for a tournament held at Chauvency, *département* Meuse, ca. 5 miles from the present Belgian border and ca. 35 miles from Luxembourg City. Lines 361 and 2172 list participant Perrars/Pieres of *Berfroment,* doubtless the same individual who jousted at Ham.
>
> *Le Petit Jehan de Saintré,* 1456, is a long prose romance about a thirteen-year-old boy who is devoted to the noblewoman who fostered him; after a long separation he seeks her in extensive travels and finds her at last in a convent—where she is the mistress of a monk. Incidentally mentioned twice, pp. 277–278, is a lord of *Bauffremont.*

In T 150,3 realistic Beuframunt is probably a residence-castle-and-town, rather than the capital city of the "Arthurian" and wholly nonrealistic kingdom of Kanedic (q.v.).

BRITON—147,2 (*Britûn*)—King Arthur's son is "Ilinot the Briton."

The spelling is unique in T.—P has *Bertûn* 27 x, W 2 x, corresponding to OF *Breton/-un/-oun,* (rarely *Berton*). *Berteneis/-eys,* 20 x in P, may be Wolfram's "pseudo-Old-French,"—like his *Burgunjois* for regular OF *borgenon.*

The country, not mentioned in T, is *Bertâne* 10 x in P, *Bretâne* in P

701, and *Britâne* in P 455, corresponding to OF *Bretagne*, occasionally *Ber-*. Wolfram nowhere uses the OF qualifiers: *la Grant*, for Britain, or *la Petite*, for Brittany.

Wolfram's *Bertâne* includes: Nantes, 12 x as capital city; *Prizljân/ Brizljân* (P 129, 206, 253, 271), i.e., the Forest of Broceliande in Brittany, SW of Rennes; *Karidoel* (P 280, 281, 336, 401), which linguistically = English Carlisle at the Scottish border; and *Schamilôt* (P 822), which ought to be "Camelot," somewhere in SW England. This "land" is distinct from *Engellant* (P 735), from both *Engellant* and *Löver* (P 761), from *Curnewâls* (P 429), and from *Waleis, Norgals*, and *Logrois*. (*Löver* and *Logrois* both = Welsh *Lloegr*, "England.") Nowhere does Wolfram mention Caerleon-on-Usk, Arthur's capital city according to Geoffrey of Monmouth, and even in rehearsing the story of *Erec* in P 401 he substitutes *Karidoel* for the Welsh town of Cardigan, named by both Hartman and Chrétien. (The Welsh themselves call "Cardigan" *Aber Teivi*, "mouth of the river Teivi.")

Clearly Wolfram did not distinguish "Britain" from "Brittany," and if he seems to ignore the very existence of the English Channel, the French romances often ignored it. In short, "the kingdom of *Bertâne*" is medieval Brittany enlarged and diversified at the poet's caprice.

BRUBARZ (*Brû-*)—28,2; 29,2. A kingdom ruled, in succession, by King Tampunteire, his son Kardeiz-1, and his daughter Kondwiramurs. Its capital and port city is Pelrapeire. There the orphaned Sigune lived until age five, when she was removed to Waleis and the care of her maternal aunt Herzeloyde.

5 x in P, all as *Brô-*, (in MS G all as *Briu-*, so Schröder reports): 180, 214, 224, 781, 799. Almost all of Book IV takes place in Brobarz, where Parzival rescues, then marries, Kondwiramurs.

Bartsch: from Provençal/OF *brus*, (modern Fr. *brousse*), "underbrush," "wilderness;" no suggestion about the second component. Martin: nothing. Fourquet, in a non-committal list of terms on p. 254, notes a resemblance to *Briébraz* (= *au court bras*), the epithet for Karadues in Chrétien's *Erec*. (West lists more variants of *Briébraz*.) We find all these proposals forlorn.

The first component, we submit, is the noun *bro*, "region, country, district," common to the Welsh, Cornish, and Breton languages. Note modern Breton *Bro-Alamayn*, "Germany;" *Bro-Hall*, "France," ("Gaul-land"); *Bro-Skos*, "Scotland;" and *Bro-Zaoz*, "England," ("Saxon-land"). See pp. 211–212 below.

The second component, which grammatically *must* be a noun or adjective attributive to the first element, is less sure. Moreover, the final -z may be the OF Nom. sing. ending and not part of the Keltic word. With Welsh *bardd*, Cornish *barth*, or Breton *barz*, all meaning "bard, poet," the compound might = "bard's country." With Breton *porz* it might = "harbor country." We do not venture a decision.

Compare, however, the "lake" of *Brumbâne* in P 261, 340, 473, 491, corresponding in Chrétien's "Perceval" 2986 (Roach ed.) to *une riviere*: we see this name as a garble of Welsh or Breton *Bro-Bran*, "the region of Bran."

This region is NE Wales (Denbighshire and the valley of the River Dee), containing the hilltop ruins of *Dinas Bran*, "the fortress of Bran" and "the original of the Grail Castle;" (compare Chrétien's *Disnadaron* and Wolfram's *Dīanazdrûn*, both "castles" of Arthur's); *Gorsedd Fran*, "the throne of Bran;" *Llyn Bran*, "the lake of Bran;" *Cadair Fronwen*, "the seat of Branwen (Bran's sister);" and *Nant Manawyd*, "the valley of Manawyd (Bran's brother);"—all formations of nature with names assigned by folk tradition, not by literary authors.

See: Helaine Newstead: *Bran the Blessed in Arthurian Romance*, Columbia University Press, 1939; 1966 reprint by AMS Press, New York; p. 23.

CLAUDITTE-3 (L *Kl-*)—149,2 This Queen of Kanedic is in *Titurel* only; Clauditte-1, 4 x in P Book VII, is the girl-playmate of little Obilot; Clauditte-2, 2 x in P, is an Oriental queen loved by Feirefiz.

Summoning her vassals to "a court" at Beuframunt so as to select a husband for her, she found the choice left to her own discretion; she chose her *ami, duc* Ehkunat, though he was of lower rank than she. Her message to Ehkunat is spelled out in jewels on the leash of the dog Gardeviaz; stanzas 149–153.

The name must = modern French "Claudette," ultimately from Latin *Claudia*, but it is odd that Wolfram should assign it to three different characters; still more odd is the fact that Flutre does not list it for the entire body of French and Provençal romances.

EHKUNAT—42,1; 151,1 (M *-aht*; L *Ekju-*); 151,4; 157,1 (M *Ehcunaht*). "Translated into German," 152,4, as *Ehcunaver* (L *Ehk-*).

3 x in P.—178,19: "(Mahaute's) haughty (*stolzer*) brother Ehkunat;" 413,15: "the proud (*stolze*) Ehkunat," and not Gawan, treacherously murdered King Kingrisin; 503,16: "Count (*der grâve*) Ehkunat" was guilty of that evil deed. Neither T nor LT alludes to the murder.

In T 42 Schionatulander's mother Mahaute is "a sister of Ehkunat, the rich Count Palatine (*phalenzgrâven*), who was known as 'from strong Berbester.'"

LT, H-671, (in the position of T 42) repeats this statement, terming Ehkunat *voit einer pfalzen guter,   benant vil rich zer starken Perbester*. (*voit*, modern *Vogt*, "governor, prefect;" *Pfalz*, from Latin *palatium*, = a territory whose ruler enjoyed royal privileges.)

We feel that the title of "Count Palatine" in T has been "superimposed" upon the title of "Count" in P 503, and that the title of "Count Palatine" and the association with Barbastro in NE Spain have both been brought over into T from *Willehalm*, ultimately from *Aliscans*. Patient readers may work out this complex matter for themselves by consulting pp. 288–9 of our *Willehalm*, plus the following items in the List of Proper Names to that work: Bertram-1, Willehalm's brother, "of Berbester;" Bertram-2, *der phalenzgrâve* (Willehalm's nephew, who corresponds to *Bertrant li palazins* in *Aliscans*); and Willehalm's brother Buov(on) of Komarzi, who corresponds to Bueve of Commarci in *Aliscans*, whose battle cry was "Barbastre!"

In T 151 Queen Clauditte selected as her husband "*le duc* Ehkunat de Salvasch Florie," (M: *Duc Ehkunahten de Salvâsch flôrîen*; L: *duc Ekjunaten de Salvâsche Flôrîen*), "(whose) heart counted for more than her crown," (153,3), i.e., despite his being a mere Duke whereas she was a Queen.

Wolfram himself then volunteers (T 152,4) to "translate this name into German."

> —M: *der herzoge Ehcunaver von bluomediuwilde*, "Duke Ehcunaver of Flowering Wildwood," by reading *bluomediuwilde* as *bluomendiu wilde*; Marti's note is abstruse in the extreme.
>
> —L: *duc Ehkunaver von Bluome-   der wilde*, emending *diu* to *der*, "Flower of the Wild." LT attempts *no* translation of the name, "into German" or any other language, but H-1382 has *Der von den blumen wilde* (OR *Von denn plumen der wilde*); H-1399 has *der wilde florie Ehkunat*; and H-1839, in the jeweled text, Clauditte addresses him as *uber alle man ein blume*.

Because of the Count/Duke discrepancy Marti's Names List (III,263) lists two different characters named Ehkunat; and Martin, to both P 178 and T 151, also says the two "seem" to be distinct. Albrecht, however, has only one Ehkunat and terms him either *fürste*, "ruling prince," H-1399, or *voit einer pfalzen*, H-671, as mentioned above.

The discrepancies regard more than the title, however, as we suggest on pp. 80–81 above, and we have no explanation for them. We wonder whether "Duke of the Flowering Wildwood" may have been an *appelation précieuse* either in some select circle of courtiers or in the private love-language of Clauditte and "the Count Palatine of Berbester"?

Fourquet, p. 257, equates the name "Ehkunat" with the Arthurian knight "Equinot, son of Count Haterel" in Hartman's *Erec* 1669, and on pp. 81–82 above we explain why we think "Equinot" is a form of (*Hell*)*equin-ot*.

FLORIE (*Flôrîe*)—147,1; 148,1. The Queen of Kanedic who died of grief when her *ami*, Ilinot, perished in love service to her; she was succeeded by her sister, Clauditte-3.

1 x in P.—Florie of Kanadic (586) reared Ilinot from childhood, imposed too stringent a love service upon him, and thereby caused his death. (Passage quoted under "Ilinot" below.)

Grail maiden *Flôrîe de Lûnel*, in P 806, is an entirely different character.

Flutre lists characters named Florie for eleven romances, as well as variants of the name for many more romances. All forms mean "flower" or "flowering," and are assigned to both male and female personages.

FRENCH—*Franzoisinne*, "Frenchwoman," in 37,3; 38,1; 99,2; (and P 88) all refer to French Queen Anphlise; likewise 54,2 and 122,2: "Queen of the French," (as in P 94,17).

Wolfram's *franzois/-oys/-eys* always applies to persons living in the royal domain. Inhabitants of the great fiefs were *Champenois, Borgenons, Picards*, etc. W 15 speaks of "Provençaux, . . . Burgundians, and true Frenchmen (*rehten Franzoise*)."

FRIMUTEL—7,2; 12,3; 27,4; 35,1. From his infirm, aged, and abdicating father Titurel, Frimutel (7) receives "the Grail's crown and the Grail," which (12) he possessed worthily.

9 x in P.—Only 474 is substantive: Trevrizent says Frimutel wore the dove emblem on his shield as his father Titurel had done before him; that he lost his life in a joust; that he "loved his wife as never another man had loved a woman . . . in true faithfulness;" and that Parzival resembles him in looks. His sword was engraved (643) by Trebuchet, (the wizard smith of the OF Perceval romances).

Nowhere does Wolfram name Frimutel's mother, wife, or slayer, but LT, H-418 says his mother was Richaude-1, daughter of a Frimutel in Spain; H-434 reports that, as one of twelve children, he married, H-449, a Spanish princess named Clarisse; and H-5712–3 report his death in love service to a Princess Floramie, daughter of King Flordibintze and Queen Albaflore, rulers of the land of Flordibale.

The name "Frimutel" is unexplained. Flutre lists no name resembling it. Bartsch suggested a basis in Germanic *Frimunt*. Kolb, p. 29, thinks that a statistical count based on Langlois: *Table des noms propres* . . . would show 3-syllable personal names ending in -*el*, -*as*, and -*ent*/-*ant* to be Oriental, but Kolb's own discussion in pp. 26–34 results in exceptions—beginning with "Titurel."

The important problem is not Frimutel's name but the literary justification for his slight and forgettable role.

GAHMURET—27,2; 37,1; 39,1; 47,1; 55,2; 74,1; 79,1 (L 78,1); 88,2; 90,1; 92.1. Also 4 x as "the Angevin;" see under "Angevin" above.

Ca. 65 x in Books I and II of *Parzival* plus 23 recollections of him through the rest of the poem.

2 x in W.—W 73 recalls his funeral at Baldac from P 107–8; W 243 recalls, from P 7, 27, that his inheritance from his father consisted of nothing but his armor.

A Gahmuret Chronology

Before P 5:
—At some early point in his life he was sent from his native Anjou to Amflise, Queen of France, presumably to be her page; the King of France was then still alive (P 69,29).
—His education in chivalry came from Amflise (P 94), though the two were "children together" (P 94).
—Amflise sponsored his knighting (T 39); gave him revenues (P 95); and "loaned" (*lech*) him Schionatulander (T 96), whom she had reared (T 38) "from the time he was weaned" (T 124).
—She "often enough brought Gahmuret into great peril by her love" (P 69–70), i.e., by sending him out as her knight to dangerous jousts.
—Gahmuret "took to Anjou the training in chivalry fostered by her counsel" (P 94).
—He had "already traveled a bit" (P 8,9) and had seen knightly action with his elder brother Galoes (P 8,17).

P 5–8:
—*Then* his father, King Gandin of Anjou, died in knightly combat (P 5) and Galoes succeeded to the kingship of Anjou (P 6), leaving Gahmuret, as landless younger brother, to seek his fortune as best he might (P 7–8).

P 13 to P 101:
—He made a *first expedition* to the East, distinguishing himself in service to the Baruch of Baldac (P 13–14), and after ad-

ventures in Zazamanc and Azagouc (all the rest of Book I) arrived for the first time in Waleis (P 59).

—T 40 and footnote 11: he brought Schionatulander (unmentioned in P) with him to Waleis.

—At the death of Galoes (in love service) (P 80, 91–92, 134), Gahmuret becomes King of Anjou and, properly for the first time, "the Angevin."

—He marries Herzeloyde (P 100), who for a number of years had had the rearing of Sigune (T 29, 32; P 477).

—For a period of time not clearly indicated in P 101,7–20 he lived with Herzeloyde in Waleis, presumably at Kanvoleiz, with Schionatulander and Sigune as members of the household; in that period he was frequently away on knightly expeditions—apparently 18 of them (P 101,14). (18 = 18 *weeks*, since tournaments were permitted by the church only on Mondays, Tuesdays, and Wednesdays.)

P 101,21 to P 113:

—Learning that the Baruch of Baldac was under attack, Gahmuret set out on a *second expedition* to the East (P 101–2), taking Schionatulander with him, presumably as his squire (T 79–81). On the outward journey he holds his colloquy with Schionatulander (T 92–107).

—Before Baldac he was slain in a joust with Ipomidon (T 74; P 105–108) and buried, with Christian rites, inside the city.

The *name* "Gahmuret," (with otiose *h*, as in "E*h*kunat" and "A*h*karin"), is generally agreed to = *Gomeret* (and variants), properly the name of a *kingdom:*

Hartman's *Erec* 1977 *künec Bêals von Gomoret,* corresponding to

Chrétien's *Erec,* F 1975, *li rois Bans de Gomeret;* R 1923, . . . *de Ganieret.*

Chrétien's "Perceval" 467 *roi Ban* (variant *Braus*) *de Gomorret.*

Loomis, p. 349: "Gomeret represents a natural misreading of (OF) *Goiñet,* the *in* being mistaken for *m,* and the stroke over the *n,* representing a second *n,* being mistaken for the sign for *er.*" First thus noted by F. Lot in *Romania,* XXIV (1895), p. 335.

Goiñet, properly read as *Goinnet,* was Old French for *Gwynedd,* "northwest Wales." See further under "Waleis" below.

The *personage* Gahmuret derives, ultimately and retaining only residual features, from Bran, son of Llyr, perhaps a sea god once, but in the *mabinogi* of *Branwen, Daughter of Llyr,* King Bran the Blessèd, who holds court either at Harlech (on the NW coast of Wales) or at

Aberffraw (on the island of Anglesea). See Loomis, pp. 347–355 and the extensive demonstrations in Helaine Newstead's *Bran the Blessed in Arthurian Romance.*

GANDIN (*-în*)—82,2 (Gahmuret) "this son of bold (*genendegen*) Gandin."

14 x in P.—Gandin, King of Anjou, (5, 6, 410, 499), died in knightly combat (5, 56) and was succeeded by his elder son Galoes (80, 134). He was the husband of Queen Schoette (92), maternal uncle of King Kaylet of Spain (59), grandfather of Parzival and of Feirefiz (56), and, by daughter Flurdamurs, Queen of Ascalun, (420) grandfather of King Vergulaht of Ascalun. His emblem was the panther (*pantel*, 101); to medievals, panther and leopard were identical animals, and the leopard was the emblem of the historical Counts of Anjou.

P 498–9 claims that Gandin took his name from the "vast (*wîten*) *Gandîne*," a city located "just where the Grajena (*diu Greian*) flows into the Drave (*die Trâ*), . . . and the kingdom (*lant*) is called Styria (*Stîre*)."

Historical Styria, a part of Bavaria for more than two centuries, was detached from Bavaria in 1180, elevated to a duchy, and conferred upon the Duke of Austria; it so remained until 1246. It was never a kingdom. The modern *village* of Haidin, at the location described, was called Candin in medieval documents.

We regard this fanciful etymology as misinformation sincerely accepted by Wolfram.

The name remains unaccounted for, but we note: (a) an extended episode in Gotfried's *Tristan* 13,101–13,454 about an Irish baron named Gandin who tricks King Mark into surrendering Isolde to him; and (b) a Gandein listed by Flutre for *Floire et Blancheflor*.

It is tempting to see the name as a mistaken form of Gaudin, listed by Flutre for nine romances and the name of one of Willehalm's nephews, (*Aliscans: Gaudins*, elsewhere in OF as *Gualdin*). As a common noun OF *gaudine* and MHG *gaudîn(e)* meant "a copse, a small stand of trees." These words clearly depend on a Germanic *wald-*.

GARDEVIAZ (*-vîaz*)—143,4; 155,3; 156,4; 159,4; 166,4. The name of the dog dispatched, with a message spelled out in jewels on its collar and leash, by Clauditte to Ehkunat. In 143 Wolfram translates the name as *Hüete der verte*, "Watch (thy) way(s)!" There is general agreement that "Gardeviaz" = Provençal *garda vias* (an imperative).

Discussion in pp. 71–73 and 89–93 above.

GRASWALDAN (*Grâswaldân*) In 83,2 Schionatulander is "the young (ruling) prince from Graswaldan," in 92,2 "the young Dauphin from Graswaldan."

= Grésivaudan/Graisivaudan, a fertile agricultural area NE of Grenoble along the west bank of the Isère River. Claimed by the Counts of Albon from at least 1050, it may not have been securely held by them until ca. 1140. At no time in history was it an independent political unit.

Discussion in pp. 101–105 above.

GURNEMANZ OF GRAHARZ—41,2 *von Grâharz Gurnemanz* is the father of Gurzgri and the grandfather of Schionatulander.

17 x in P, (7 of them Gurna-).—Gurnemanz *de* Graharz unofficially rides the first joust (68) in the Kanvoleis tournament and fights, like Gahmuret, on the side of the "friendly" Inner Army.

In P 162–179 young Parzival comes, by chance, to Graharz, where during a 14-day stay Gurnemanz instructs him in knighthood and *wordly* wisdom. His wisdom supersedes the simple instructions of Herzeloyde in P 127 and is superseded in turn by the *spiritual* teachings of Trevrizent in Book IX. His precept: "Do not ask too many questions," (171,17), motivates Parzival's silence (239) at the Grail ceremony. He names his three sons slain in knightly combat and his surviving daughter Liaze, but does not mention that his third slain son, Gurzgri, is Schionatulander's father. He *appears* only in 162–179, but is recalled with decreasing frequency as far as 486.

Chrétien's "Perceval" 1352–1698 (Roach ed.) mentions no children of *Gornemans de Gorhaut*, Perceval stays only overnight, and the precepts in 1639–70 are more concise than in P 170–3; the particular injunction of 1648–56 is against excessive talk and gossiping. (In neither poem does he have the long-windedness of Wagner's Gurnemanz in *Parsifal*.)

Hartman's *Erec* 1632 lists *Gornemanz von Groharz* fourth (after Gawein, Erec, and Lancelot) in the roll call of Arthurian knights, parallel to Chrétien's *Erec* (F 1695/R 1675):

Gornemanz de Gohort. Also:

>   *Gornomans,* a "wise prince," no land or city, in Ulrich's *Lanzelet* 2630;
>
>   *Gornomanz Côorz* jousts at Arthur's court, *Diu Crône* 607; *von Cornomant Gôorz,* 856;
>
>   *Goorz von Gornomant* is recalled, 25,935, as advising Parzival against too many questions;
>
>   *Gornuman de Grohaut* and other variants are listed by Flutre.

Equally futile are (a) Bartsch's derivation from a Romance *guerneman,* from a Germanic *warinman,* "one who warns;" and (b) Martin's association, by sound, of "Graharz" with the town of Greierz (French Gruyère) in canton Fribourg, Switzerland. Loomis, p. 484, says: "Origin unknown, unless the combination Gornemant de Gohort is a corruption of Gwrnach Gawr in *Kuhlwch* (the 7th story in *The Mabinogion*), Gawr meaning 'giant.'" The multiple occurrences of the name suggest a figure once prominent in Welsh lore but remembered only as the counselor of the young hero in the Perceval romances.

In the Welsh prose tale of *Peredur* (before 1225) he has no name at all, has two unnamed sons instruct the hero in fighting, and he declares himself to be Peredur's maternal uncle.

Graharz

7 x in P.—Riding less than a full day's time from "Nantes," young Parzival arrives (162) toward evening at Graharz, approaching by a road and through a green meadow up to a broad linden tree beneath which Gurnemanz is sitting alone. Coming away from "Graharz the town" (*die stat*, 177), Parzival comes in one day's riding "through wild, high mountains" to the port city of Pelrapeire in the kingdom of Brobarz.

Chrétien's Perceval arrives (839) from Cardoeil—linguistically "Carlisle" on the English-Scotch border. Emerging from a forest, he rides across a plain to a wide, deep river, swifter than the Loire. Unable to cross, he follows the stream bank down to where the river empties into a bay of the sea. Along the opposite bank a rugged cliff extends, sloping eventually to the sea, and on the slope stands a square castle—presumably "Gohort"—with four low corner-towers and a great central donjon. Gornemans, with two squires, is strolling on the drawbridge, over which he presently admits the visitor.

Wolfram, we believe, deliberately transformed this description into an isolated inland place symbolizing the lonely isolation of Gurnemanz himself. By the same device he made only Pelrapeire a seaside place, whereas Chrétien's "Gohort" and "Beaurepaire" are both port cities. Under "Waleis" below (p. 209) we speculate on the "original" geography involved.

GURZGRI (*-grî*)—41,2; 43,1; 84,4; 127,2; 158,4.

Gurzgri is the son of Gurnemanz of Graharz, 41; *talfîn*, 127, and husband of *talfînette* Mahaute, 126; father of Schionatulander, 41, 158; of lineage less noble than the Grail family's, 43; died a painful death at the hands of Mabonagrin, 84, in the adventure called "Schoydelacurte," 41.

2 x in P.—Third son of Gurnemanz, husband of Mahaute, and slain by Mabonagrin (177–8), but *not* said to be the father of Schionatulander. Father of *duc Gandilûz*, a young squire of Gawan's, mentioned only in P 429,20–21.

Since Wolfram alone attributes children to Gurnemanz of Graharz, the personage of Gurzgri cannot be traced. The name is unexplained. (We greatly doubt Bartsch's: *gurz* = Germanic *wurz,* or the given name Warzo/Werzo, + Provençal *gri*/OF *grin,* as in Isengri(n).)

HERZELOYDE—10,3; 26,2 (*-oide*); 27,1 (*-oide*); 29,1 (*-oide*); dubious stanza 34,1 (*-oüde*). L has *-oide* in all cases. "Frimutel's daughter," 35; called "the Queen" in 109–131.

Listed second of Frimutel's three daughters, 10; wedded at Muntsalvatsch to King Kastis, who bequeathed to her the cities of Kanvoleiz and Kingrivals, 26–27; "a virgin widow" at her marriage to Gahmuret, 27, 35.

She brought her five-year-old niece Sigune to live with her, 29. This statement is confirmed in P 477 but contradicted in P 805.

34 x in P, all in *-oyde*; Schröder says MS G has 32 of these in *-oide.* First in P 60 as the maiden Queen of Waleis; "the queen" (61, 62); "the woman of Waleis" (*Wâleisin*) (81, 83); first called Herzeloyde (84) after Gahmuret has won the tournament.

87–100 describe how she overcame Gahmuret's objections to marrying her, but the marriage itself is not mentioned; an unspecified period of wifehood, 101,7–20; while Gahmuret is away in the East, 102, she rules the *three* kingdoms: Waleis, Norgals, and Anjou. In her 18th week of pregnancy she learns of Gahmuret's death, 109; two weeks later (112) she bears the infant Parzival, but remains grief-distraught (113–4).

At the beginning of Book III (116) she has fled with her infant son to the forest of Soltane. When the boy discovers knights by chance and tells her of it, she faints (125). She allows him to venture into the world, but in fool's garments (127); after giving him rudimentary precepts (128), she tells him that "the proud, bold Lehelin" has seized Waleis and Norgals—no mention of Anjou. As the lad rides away, she falls to the ground, "where grief stabbed her until she died" (128).

Only P 116–128 is paralleled in Chrétien's "Perceival," lines 69–634. There she is "the widow woman (lady)/of the lonely forest" (*la veve fame (dame)/de la gaste forest soutaine*), 74–75; Chrétien assigns her no personal name at all.

Bartsch (p. 143): from south-French *Herceleude/-laude,* from Germanic *Harchehildis*; parallel to her cousin "Rischoyde" (P 84,10), from south-French *Richaude*, from Germanic *Richildis*. Martin grants the latter but finds "Herzel-" mysterious.

Rischoyde is the wife of King Kaylet of Spain (Castile), and Kolb, p. 11, fn 10, says that Alfonso VII of Castile, 1126–57, married, as a second wife, Richilde in 1153.

In the 216-line Provençal *Ensenhamen*, lines 208 and 210 name *Riqueut* and *Arselot* as characters whose stories ought to be in a reciter's repertory; the allusion is probably to an OF *Fabliau de Richeut*, ca. 1159, in which Richeut is a panderess and Herselot is her serving woman. Thomas's *Tristan*, episode "Brengevein's Revenge," chides Ysolt for being "a Richolt." Henry and Renée Kahane, reluctant to believe that Wolfram named two noble ladies after a pair of comic bawds, suggest (ZfdA 89, 1958–9) that he must have taken the names from a *lost serious* poem of which the *Fabliau* was a burlesque. Note also that in the "beast epic" the wife of Isengrin the wolf is *Hersent*, the wife of the fox is *Richent* (or *Hermeline*).

Weston (I,306) cites Bartsch's derivation from *Herceleude* but names the character *Herzeleide* in her translation, because "it is poetically right." But Weston was here influenced by Wagner, who, late in Act II of *Parsifal*, has Kundry say: *ihr brach das Leid das Herz/und—Herzeleide—starb* ("Sorrow broke her heart,/and—Heart's Sorrow—died"). Some people believe Wolfram so punned on *Herceleude*.

Other people point to the 800-line "Bliocadran Prologue" (to Chrétien's "Perceval"), where the hero's father is named Bliocadran, and where the hero's mother is Bliocadran's "wife of sorrowful heart" (*cuer dolent*, line 153). Moreover, in the *Vulgate Lancelot* the widow of King Ban is *la roine as grans dolors* (Loomis, p. 348, fn 6).

Marti, to P 140,18, would relate the first component of *Herzeloyde* to OF *herce* (modern *herse*), "a harrow, a drag-plow," since the line reads: *grôz liebe ier solhe herzen furch*, "Such a furrow did great love plow in (your mother's) heart;" the previous line "interprets" the name "Parzival" as "right through the middle" (*mitten durch*). Chrétien's line 300, moreover, has the boy Perceval say to the knights: "Over there are my mother's harrow-men (*herceor*);" line 306 specifies that they are harrowing (*hercent*) the (field of) oats. But possibly both poets may have had in mind Luke 2:35: "Yea, a sword shall pierce through thy own soul also."

Special pleading seems required for the "Heart's Sorrow" interpretation as for the interpretation based on "harrow," whereas

Bartsch's double etymology of *Herceleude* and *Richaude* is cogent, especially when those two names are repeatedly associated in different medieval texts.

I̲L̲I̲N̲O̲T̲ (*-ôt*)—147,2. Ilinot the Briton, reared from childhood by Queen Florie of Kanedic, became her *ami* and perished in love service to her.

3 x in P (383; 575 *Ily-*; 585 *Ily-*).—The poet begs Lady Love (585) not to slay Gawan as she slew Gawan's cousin (*neven*) Ilinot: "As a child (Ilinot) had left his father's land, and Queen Florie had reared him. In Britain (*ze Bertâne*) he was a stranger. Florie so burdened him with her love that she drove him from the land. In her service he was found dead. . . ."

In 383 certain captive Britons (*Berteneis*) continue to wear the *gampilûn* ("a dragon-like beast"), "for that was Ilinot's coat of arms, who was Arthur's noble son." Gawan (575) wears "two *gampiluns* made of sable fur, such as Ilinot the Briton once wore. . . ."

"Britons" inherit the dragon device from Uther Pendragon. Rachel Bromwich: *The Welsh Triads*, 1961, pp. 93–95 and 520–1, explains that in the oldest Welsh poetry *draig/dragon* meant "fighting man, hero, leader" and that "Pendragon" meant "foremost leader;" but Geoffrey of Monmouth (VIII, 17) took the term literally as "dragon's head," apparently in the Medieval Latin sense of a military standard with a dragon's head as emblem.

The *name*:—Bromwich, pp. 416–8, believes that Llacheu son of Arthur (*Llacheu mab Arthur*) belonged, with Kei and Bedwyr, to the oldest stratum of Arthurian tradition in Wales. First in French as *Loholz, li fiz le roi Artu*, Chrétien's *Erec* (F 1732/R 1700); echoed by Hartman's *Erec* 1664: *Lohut fil roi Artus*. Flutre lists 3 more romances with variants: *Loholt, -hoot, -hos, -hot(h)*, and *hoz*. Ulrich's *Lanzelet* 6891 has *Lont/Lant*, which Webster-Loomis emend to *Loüt* (two syllables). *Perlesvaus* has *Lohot*.

Loomis, pp. 486–7, sees Chrétien's *Loholz* as "probably a corruption of Welsh Llacheu," but Bromwich considers it Breton-French and points to Joseph Loth's discovery of an actual landowner named *Loholt* in 12th-century Cornwall. Bromwich finds it unlikely (p. 417) that "there is any genuine early association between the names and characters of *Llacheu* and *Loho(l)t*."

Wolfram's unique form *Ilinot/Ilynot* may have acquired its initial letter by mistaking some scribal flourish for capital *I*. (Compare Wolfram's Jofreit son of *Îdoel* with Chrétien's Gifflés son of *Do* and Hartman's *fil Dou Giloles*, where the Welsh original was Gilfaethwy son

of the *goddess Don*.) This notion implies a *French* manuscript unknown
to us.

The *personage*:—At least two Welsh poems speak of *Llacheu* as dying
in battle. *Perlesvaus* (= "The High History of the Holy Grail"), Branch
XV, Title VIII, has *Lohut* murdered in his sleep by Kay. Ulrich's *Lan-
zelet* has *Loüt* ("*Lont/Lant*") vanish with Arthur until "a second com-
ing." Wolfram, in both P and T, has *Ilinot* perish in love service to
a lady—from an immediate French source surely, and perhaps from
the *lai* of *Li Joenet de la Lande*.

IPOMIDON (-*ôn*)—73,4; 74,4. The heathen knight who slew Gahmuret at
Baldac.

5 x in P.—"Ipomidon of Nineveh, that proud Babylonian" (111)
and his brother Pompeius were maternal nephews of Nabuchodo-
nosor and descendants of Ninus (who founded Nineveh before Baldac
ever existed) (102). Gahmuret, on his first expedition to the East, (13–
14), unhorsed Ipomidon in a joust, apparently at Alexandria; in re-
venge, Ipomidon slew Gahmuret in a joust before Baldac (106,7–11)
during the latter's second expedition to the East; apparently he
poured he-goat's blood over Gahmuret's impregnable helmet so it
"became softer than a sponge" (105). The joust is recalled in 751. (See
under "Pompeius" below.)

"Ipomidon" is ultimately classical Greek *Hippomedon*, "horse-
ruler," from the story of the "Seven against Thebes," known to me-
dievals through the Latin account by Statius. Wolfram may have bor-
rowed it from the *Ypomedon* of Heinrich von Veldeke's *Eneit* 3315 (as
Martin claims), or from the verse romance *Ipomedon*, between 1174
and 1191, by the Anglo-Norman Hue de Rotelande (Hugh of Rut-
land). The same poet's romance of *Prothesilaus* may have yielded Wol-
fram's Duke *Prothizilas* in P 27 and 52.

KANEDIC (M: Kana-; L Kane-)—147,1. The land ruled in succession by
the two sisters Queen Florie and Queen Clauditte, and where Florie
reared Ilinot.

3 x in P (2 in -*e*-, 1 in -*a*-)—From 586 the lines about Florie and
Ilinot are quoted under "Ilinot" above.

Orilus won the lady Jeschute (135) "at the joust for the sparrow
hawk at Kanedic." In 277, Arthur, in receiving Jeschute at court, con-
firms that the sparrow hawk prize was won at Kanedic.

Yet this location contradicts: (a) Chrétien's *Erec* 342–1084, which
sets the sparrow hawk contest in an unnamed town belatedly called
Lalut(*h*), lines 6197, 6199, and 6268, which is said to be near *Caradigan*;

(b) Hartman's *Erec* 174–1098, which sets the contest at *Tulmein* (*Erec* 175), scarcely seven miles from *Karadigân* (*Erec* 1093); and (c) Wolfram's own recollection of Hartman's account in P 401, where *Tulmeyn* (P 401,17) is again the scene of the contest. (French "Caradigan" = modern Cardigan/Welsh Aber Teivi on the west coast of Wales.)

The sparrow hawk contest "at Kanedic" (P 135 and 277) implies a *city*, while P 586 and T 147,1 imply that "Kanedic" is the *country* of Queens Florie and Clauditte. Perhaps the country and its capital city were both called Kanedic; but then what was Beuframunt? A castle in the city of Kanedic? or a residence-castle elsewhere in the country of Kanedic? And Beuframunt (q.v.) is an identifiable town in Lorraine.

The name itself is a puzzle. Chrétien's *Erec* (F 1722; R 1692) has *li fiz au roi Quenedic*, "the son of King Quenedic;" Hartman's *Erec* 1655 has *des küneges sun von Ganedic*, (? "the king's son from Ganedic," or ? "the son of King Ganedic"). Loomis, p. 489, lists variants *Quinedic* and *Quinodinc*, adding: "Origin unknown." In a list of Arthur's knights in *Diu Crône* there is a *fil le rois Quinedinch* (line 2312).

With the name *Quenedic* we compare the *forest* of *Quinqueroi/Kinkerloi/Kinkenroi* in Chrétien's "Perceval" 951 and 4127 (Loomis, p. 489), and, in the third "Perceval" Continuation (Manessier) 35,196, a *castle Quigagrant/Quikagrant/Quinqueran*, listed by Flutre, suggesting alternate possibilities for the first component in these names: Welsh *gwig*, "forest," or Breton *gwik*, "town," (from Latin *vicus*, and found as *-wick/-wich* in English place names), the Welsh term being the more likely of the two.

KANVOLEIZ and KINGRIVALS, capital cities of Waleis and Norgals, respectively.

—KANVOLEIZ—26,3; 35,4; 45,3; 46,1. Bequeathed by King Kastis to Herzeloyde, 26, who was won by Gahmuret in the tournament there, 35; "renowned afar and in many languages . . . (and) termed the capital city (*houbetstat*) of loyalty," 45; there began the love of Schionatulander and Sigune, 46.

16 x in P (6 x in *-eis*).—First in 59 as Gahmuret arrives there for the tournament; the tournament itself, 68–82, and recalled in 145, 325, 400, and 796; Parzival was born there (140, 749, 755); usurped by Lehelin (128, 141), but destined for future rule by Parzival's small son, Kardeiz-2 (803).

Martin: = *Camp Valois*,—which Martin himself admitted he could not find. Under "Waleis" below we note that Wales *had* no capital city.

Might the name depend on Welsh *canol*, "middle, center"? *Canoldir* = "midland."

—KINGRIVALS—26,4; 79,1 (= L 78,1 K*o*-). Bequeathed by King Kastis to Herzeloyde, 26; Gahmuret, with Schionatulander, set off secretly from there, 79 (78).

5 x in P.—Bequeathed by King Castis to Herzeloyde (494); her capital while Gahmuret was in the East (103); Sigune foretells that Parzival will rule there (140); the future seat of Kardeiz-2 (803); Gawan hails Parzival as "kinsman from Kingrivals" (759).

Bartsch, though aware that *Norgals* = Gwynedd, claimed *Kingrivals* = OF *Guin(gre)* + *vals*, "valley," and identified it with Guinkirchen/ Wingersthal in Lorraine. Martin compared *Kin-* with Breton place names Guingamp, Guinguené, and Quimper. (This last is Breton *kember*, "river junction.") We think the *Kin-* likely to be identical with the *Quin-* discussed under item "Kanedic" above. But *Kanvoleiz* and *Kingrivals* both remain unexplained.

KARDEIZ-1—28,1. Son of King Tampunteire of Brubarz and older brother of Kondwiramurs. P 293 reports that he perished in love service (to an unspecified lady). (Named for him is Parzival's son, Kardeiz-2, P 803, twin brother of Loherangrin, and P 781 implies that he will some day rule his mother's kingdom of Brobarz.)

Bartsch (p. 144) implausibly thought: from Burgundian dialect *cordeiz/cordez*, "stout-hearted." Fourquet is more shrewdly advised in suggesting (p. 254) *Karadués Briebraz* (Chrétien's *Erec*, F 1719, R 1689), who is *Garedeas von Brebas* in Hartman's *Erec* 1652 and *Karidobrebaz* in *Diu Crône* 12,548; all of these are surely the Welsh Hero Caradawc, whose Welsh epithet was *Breichbras*: Welsh *braich*, "arm," + *bras*, "large,"—Loomis, p. 50, says "Arm-strong"—misunderstood as French *Brief-bras*, "short-arm(ed)."

KASTIS—26,1; 27,1. "Kastis died, who had wooed the fair Herzeloyde at Muntsalvatsch," 26, and bequeathed to her his capital cities of Kanvoleiz and Kingrivals, 27.

P 494 recalls the marriage and the bequest of the two cities, "but (Castis) was not to enjoy (Herzeloyde's) love. . . . It was on his homeward journey (from Munsalvaesche) that he lay down to die." Thus in T 27 Herzeloyde is a virgin-widow.

Bartsch (p. 143): from OF *li caste-s/li chaste-s*, "the chaste one," in allusion to the unconsummated marriage.

KATELANGE(n)—14,1; 15,2; 58,1; 105,2; 109,1; 165,2,—all Datives in *-n*; dubious stanza 31,2 has the Accusative in *-n*.

Kiot "of" (*ûz*), 14; ruling prince of (*der fürste ûz*), 105; married Schoysiane there, 15; Sigune heiress to, 31, 109, *Duchess* "from" (*Ducisse ûz*), 58; she would give her whole country of Katelangen, 165, to have the precious dog leash back.

3 x in P (186, 477, 799)—all "Duke Kiot of Katelangen."

Surely connected with, but not necessarily taken from, Hartman's *Erec* 1679: *Malivliôt von Katelange* (no final *n*), with *Malivliot* = to "Manfilot" (q.v. below) and with transfer of *Katelange* to Manfilot's brother Kiot.

= Catalonia, the NE area of Spain now comprising the three Mediterranean provinces of Gerona, Barcelona, and Tarragona, plus inland Lérida. Flutre lists *Catheloigne* for only one late romance, but Langlois (p. 87) lists *Cateloigne/-oingne/-ongne* for various *chansons de geste*. Modern French *Catalogne*; Spanish *Cataluña*; Catalan *Catalunya*.

Catalonia

Conquered by Visigoths in 419 A.D., the area, after 507, formed part of Visigothic Spain, capital at Toledo. Moslem-conquered by 719. Partially retaken by Charlemagne (Gerona 785, Barcelona 801) and incorporated into his Spanish March (*Marca Hispanica*). The western half became, first, the Kingdom of Navarre, then, in subdivision, the two kingdoms of Navarre and Aragon; the eastern half was ruled by Frankish "Counts of Barcelona" in father-to-son succession after 878, with independence won from the Franks before 992. From 1018 to 1162 these independent Counts bore, in alternation, the names Berenguer Ramón and Ramón Berenguer. In 1112 the whole of Provence was acquired by marriage, but after 1125 only the southern half of it was retained, as "the County of Provence;" see Chapter V, footnote 10, pp. 146–47. With Ramón Berenguer IV, 1131–1162, the title "Count of Barcelona" began to be superseded by "Count of Catalonia;" ("Count of Provence" was a second, adjunct title).

In 1137 this Count Ramón Berenguer IV, at age 22, was betrothed to infant Queen Petronilla of Aragon, whom he married in 1150; he ruled in Aragon also, but with the title of "King *in* Aragon."

His son by Petronilla ruled, 1162–1196, as King Alfonso II of Aragon *and* as Count Alfonso I of Catalonia. The joint dominion—with Catalonia predominant—continued under Pedro II, 1196–1213, under Jaime I, 1213–1276, and on down to 1410, when the male line of the Counts of Catalonia ended.

Aragon

Meanwhile Aragon had been ruled by three brothers as successive kings: Pedro I, 1094–1104; Alfonso I, "the Warrior," 1104–1134; and

Ramiro II, 1134–1137. This Ramiro had become a monk in 1093, but when Aragon was left without an heir in 1134, he left his monastery (with monastic vows absolved by Pope Innocent II), married Agnes of Poitiers, a paternal aunt of Eleanor of Aquitaine and a childless widow since 1127, begot a daughter Petronilla, betrothed her as an infant to Count Ramón Berenguer IV of Catalonia, and then, with kingdom and succession in trusted hands, returned to his monastery for the rest of his life; he died in 1147.

On page 139 above we list significant parallels between these historical facts and the matter of *Parzival* and of the *Titurel* Fragments. See further under "Kiot" and under "Manfilot" below.

KINGRIVALS—See under KANVOLEIZ and KINGRIVALS above.

KIOT (Kîot)—14,1; 16,1; 24,2; 25,2; 32,1; 104,4; 105,1; 108,3.

Kiot "of" (*ûz*) Katelangen, 14; warrior and ruling prince (*fürste*), 105; "the country's lord" (*des landes hêrre*), 16; married Schoysiane, eldest of Grail King Frimutel's three daughters, 14; his brother, King Tampunteire of Brubarz, from whom Kiot held Katelangen in fief, 22, came to Katelangen for the wedding, 15; when Schoysiane died in giving birth to Sigune, Kiot entrusted land and infant daughter to Tampunteire, 22, kissed the child farewell, 25, and renounced knighthood, 22; his brother Manfilot, from sympathetic grief, renounced knighthood also, 23.

11 x in P (all as *Kyôt*).—When, in 186, Parzival first meets Condwiramurs,

> Kyot of (*von*) Katelangen and noble Manpfilyot, dukes both, led forth their brother's (Tampenteire's) child, the queen of (Brobarz). They, for the love of God, had renounced their swords. And now these noble princes (*fürsten*), gray-haired and comely, with great courtesy escorted the lady. . . .

This corresponds to Chrétien's "Perceval" 1788–94 (Roach edition):

> Two noblemen (*preudome*) and a maiden advanced to meet (Perceval). The noblemen were gray (*chenu*) but not completely white-haired and would have been in the flower of their beauty and vigor if they had not been suffering privation and hardship.

In P 477 Trevrizent tells Parzival:

> "My sister Schoysiane bore a child, but of that birth she died. Her husband was Duke Kyot of (*von*) Katelangen, who after that renounced all joy. Sigune, his little daughter, was given into your mother's (Herzeloyde's) care."

Duke Kyot leads the escort party (P 797, 799, 800, 801) that fetches Condwiramurs from Brobarz to the Grail. In P 805 he is the kinsman-tutor (*magezoge*) of little Kardeiz-2.

"Kiot"/"Kyot" = OF *Gui* or *Guiot*, oblique case *Guion*; diminutives *Guielin, Guiet*; ultimately from Germanic *Wido*, Latinized as *Guido*; Provençal *Guizot*; English *Guy*.

NOTE: all rulers of historical Catalonia were Counts, not Dukes. None of them was named Guido or Manfilot/Manpfilyot; nor did any king of Aragon bear either of these names.

But, though there never was a historical "Duke Guiot of Catalonia," there was, in 1063, a famous Duke Guiot *in* Catalonia, (Kolb, pp. 16–24). His given name was "Guiot" (*Guido dictus in baptismo*); for reasons unknown he called himself "Guy Geoffrey": (*Gaufredum . . . et Wido vocatus est*); he ruled 1058–1086 as Duke William VIII (*Guillelmus cognomine*) of Aquitaine and as Count William VI of Poitou. He was the great-grandfather of Eleanor of Aquitaine. At the invitation of Count Ramón Berenguer II he entered Catalonia in 1063 with an army and conquered Moslem-held Barbastro—see under "Berbester" above—on the Aragon-Catalonia frontier. A century or so later this feat was celebrated in *Le Siège de Barbastre*—the hero of which is that other William whom Wolfram calls Willehalm.

KONDWIRAMURS (*Kondwîrâmûrs*)—25,3; 29,3. When King Tampunteire brought infant Sigune into his household in Pelrapeirè, "Kondwiramurs (his daughter) was also an infant at the breast," 25; when Sigune was taken away, after Tampunteire's death, Kondwiramurs wept at losing her cousin and playmate, 29.

23 x in P, all with initial C, 4 of them as C*u*-).—First mentioned (177) by Gurnemanz as resisting all importunate suitors; first appearance (186) as the maiden queen of Brobarz escorted by her uncles, Kyot of Katelangen and Manpfilyot. The night she spends in Parzival's bed (192–5) is chaste, as is not the case with Chrétien's "Perceval" 1945–2069.

Absent from the reader's sight from 196 to 800, her memory is evoked by the three blood-drops in the snow (282–3); Parzival in his wanderings recalls her (333), and remembrance of her "comes across four kingdoms" (781) to give him his victory over Feirefiz. She is more beautiful than Jeschute, Enite, Cunneware de Lalant, and "both Is*a*ldes," (187), than Orgeluse (508), than Repanse de Schoye (811).

Mysterious writing on the Grail (781) proclaims her Queen of the Grail; Kyot of Katelangen escorts her (796) from Brobarz to the Grail

Castle, bringing with her Parzival's twin sons Loherangrin and Kardeiz-2.

Her name is Wolfram's substitute for Chrétien's *Blancheflor* ("Perceval" 2417, 2912).

Bartsch took the name as *coin de voire amors*, "ideal of true love." (OF *coin*, yielding English *coign* and *coin*, = "die-stamp, perfect model;" OF *voire/veire*, from Latin *verus*, "true;" OF *amor/amur/amour*, "love;" the terminal *-s* would be OF Nom. Sing. ending.)

But all 23 occurrences in P are in two words: 16 x *Condwîr âmûrs*; 2 x (P 327 and 508) with the first component in the Accusative: *Condwîren âmûrs*, *âne Condwîrn âmûrs*, as if *condwîren* were an inflected verbal noun. MHG *co-/cundwieren*, from OF *conduire*, is used as an unexceptional verb in P 155,18; 495,22; 511,28; 696,18; in 401,13 and 741,15 *ein condewier* means "a safe-conduct;" in 920,29 Anfortas accompanies Feirefiz *durch condwieren*, "as a guide." W 391,1 *mit grôzem kundewiers* means "with vast supporting forces." Martin, to P 177,30, lists further usages.

We understand *Condwîr âmûrs*, in its multiple forms, to mean "To Conduct Loves" or "Conducting Loves," with the terminal *-s* as OF *Acc. pl.* ending,—bizarre as such a name would be—and connect it with those "courts of love" which tradition says were held by Eleanor of Aquitaine and her daughter Marie de Champagne, probably in the 1170s. (Note also the "court of love" held in P 95–96.) Specifically, we take *Condwîr âmûrs* as Eleanor of Aquitaine herself in the genealogical table of Wolfram's Angevins.

MABONAGRIN (*Mâbonagrîn*; L *Mabô-*)—84,4. Gurzgri, Schionatulander's father, died a painful death "at the hands of" (*vor*) Mabonagrin.

3 x in P.—Gurzgri "rode to (*nâch*) Schoydelakurt" where "Mabonagrin slew him" (178); King Clamidê says (220): "My uncle's son Mabonagrin also endured long suffering (in love)" for Condwiramurs; in a list of perils (583) the poet recalls what Erec faced "when he won Schoydelakurt away from Mabonagrin."

Mabonagrin is the giant-tall knight in red armor and riding a fiery-red horse in the concluding adventure of Hartman's *Erec*, 7808–9970, and (as *Mabonagrain-s*) in the corresponding section of Chrétien's *Erec*, 5367–6509. In the Welsh prose tale, *Gereint, Son of Erbin* (the last story in *The Mabinogion*) this knight is left nameless. In Malory's *The Tale of Sir Gareth of Orkeney* he is "the Rede Knyght of the Rede Laundys;" Tennyson, in *Geraint and Enid*, omits the episode altogether.

"Mabon-" = the Keltic god *Maponus*. Joshua Whatmough: *The Dialects of Ancient Gaul*, p. 990, cites an inscription "Maponus Apollo" found in the north of England; also the one-time place names in France: *Fons Maboni* and *Locus Maponi*. The element *(a)grain/grin* is not satisfactorily explained. Erec's adventure represents ultimately a mortal hero's battle against the sun god; compare his defeat of "King Death in person," p. 80 above.

MAHAUTE—42,1; 126,4 (*-aude*); 127,2 (*-aude*). L has *-aute* in all three cases.

Mother of Schionatulander and sister of Ehkunat *phalenzgrâven* of Berbester, 42, 126; *talfinette* 126,3; mourned her husband, the *talfîn* Gurzgri, 127, whose jousting she had witnessed in many lands.

2 x in P (178,16 and 24): "With (Gurzgri) rode Mahaute in her beauty, whom her haughty brother Ehkunat had given him for a wife," and, from Gurzgri's death "Mahaute lost her beauty."

Germanic *Mahtilt*, Latinized as Mat(h)ilda, yielded OF nicknames *Mahaut/Mahoudte* and English "Maud(e)." Kolb, p. 11, notes the troubadour form *Maeut* and Poitevin *Matheode*.

Saint Matilda, d. 968, was the wife of German King Henry I, "the Fowler," (the King in Wagner's *Lohengrin*).

Flutre lists *Mahault/-haut* and *Mehaut* for three romances each. Langlois lists *Mahaut* for two late *chansons de geste*.

We believe that Wolfram's Mahaute represents the historical Countess Matilda of Albon who died *circa* 1144; see pp. 108–113 above; her title of *talfinette* seems to be "Wolfram's Old French" for *Dauphine*.

The very frequent name "Matilda/Maud(e)" was especially favored by the royal Normans. It was the name of William the Conqueror's (1) great aunt, who died in 1015; (2) step-niece (by the Conqueror's half brother Roger Montgomery); (3) daughter, the first abbess of Holy Trinity Abbey in Caen, Normandy, who died in 1113;

(4) the Conqueror's wife, Tarasia of Flanders, who assumed the name Matilda upon marriage to William in 1054; crowned Queen of England (separately from William) on May 11, 1068; d. 1083; (5) Princess Eagdyth (Edith) of Scotland likewise assumed the name Matilda at her marriage on November 11, 1100, to the Conqueror's son, King Henry I of England (1100–1135), allegedly because her Norman subjects could not pronounce her baptismal name.

Three daughters of Henry I were all named Matilda: one (6) married Rotrou II, Count of Perche; another (7) married Conan III, *le Gros*, Duke of Brittany; and (8) the eldest of the three married German Emperor Henry V, whence she was commonly known as "the Empress Maude;" see page 125 above for a sketch of her biography.

(9) The wife of (Norman) King Stephen I of England was Matilda, daughter of Count Eustache of Boulogne.

To these Norman Matildas may be added three Angevin Matildas: (10) a sister of Geoffrey V, "Plantagenet," married William, one of the nearly twenty illegitimate half brothers of the Empress Maude; (11) Matilda Plantagenet (1156–1189), daughter of Henry II of England and of Eleanor of Aquitaine; in 1168 she married Henry the Lion, Duke of Saxony, to whom she bore (12) a daughter Matilda,—as well as a son who became German Emperor Otto IV, during whose nominal reign, 1208 to 1218, much of Wolfram's poetic work was realized; see footnote 13 on page 154 above.

MANFILOT (*-ôt*)—23,1. Duke Manfilot, of unspecified territory, from sympathy for the bereavement of his brother Kiot of Katelangen, followed Kiot in renouncing knighthood.

2 x in P as *Manpfilyôt*,—In P 186 (passage quoted under "Kiot" above) Condwiramurs, as the maiden queen of Brobarz, is attended by her two uncles, Kyot of Katelangen and Manpfilyot, "dukes both," who live as hermits in a wild mountain glen (190) not far from Pelrapeire, capital city and port of the kingdom of Brobarz; they make equal contributions of food for the starving population of the besieged city.

After P 190 Manpfilyot is never mentioned again, neither in P 477 where Trevrizent tells Parzival about Kyot, nor in the "family reunion," P 797–805.

Surely connected, in name, with the *Malivliôt von Katelange* listed as a knight of Arthur's in Hartman's *Erec* 1679, but not, in our opinion, borrowed from that source. Tradition somehow associated the name with "Katelangen," as Hartman's *Erec* shows, but we have discovered no such name among the Catalonians of history. For a possible historical counterpart we look to one of the three brothers who were successive Kings of Aragon; see page 139 above. The name Manfilot itself is unexplained.

MUNTSALVATSCH (*-âtsch*)—12,4 (*M—vaesche*); 26,2; 27,4 (*-vâtsche*); 44,4 (*-vâtsche*). L has MUNSALVÂSCHE in all four cases.

"Upon Muntsalvaesche Frimutel worthily possessed the Grail," 12; King Kastis wooed Herzeloyde at Muntsalvatsch, 26; Herzeloyde was sent forth from Muntsalvatsch (to Waleis and Norgals), 27; "Sigune was also of that same seed which was strewn abroad in the world from Muntsalvatsch . . . ," 44.

38 x in P as *Munsalvaesche*; once, in 340,1, as *Muntsalvâsche*. In

P 445,28 "the knights of M." = *diu Munsalvaescher schar*. In P 261,28 the form *Salvâsche ah muntâne* is not satisfactorily explained, though *ah* may = *à*.

First mentioned (250–1) by Sigune as a *castle (burc)* with dense forest "for thirty miles around;" we take "thirty" to mean "many, many."

> "Rich is it in all earthly perfection. He who diligently *seeks* it will not find it, . . . He who shall see the castle must chance upon it unawares. . . . Munsalvaesche is its name, and the kingdom of the lord of the castle is called Terre de Salvaesche. . . . Anfortas is (its) present Lord. . . ."

In 286 King Arthur, at the River Plimizoel, says:

> "We are nearing the host of Anfortas which rides out from Munsalvaesche to defend the forest in combat. Since we do not know where the castle lies, things might well go hard for us."

In 426 Liddamus says: ". . . never was a house so well defended." The defenders are "templars," but not "Templars," as we explain under "'Templars' and 'templars,'" p. 203 below.

The *Terre de Salvaesche* (P 251, 792, 797) is dense forest, with Munsalvaesche, both hill and castle, at the center. Yet within the forest are located: 1 Trevrizent's hermitage at *Fontâne la salvâtsche* 452, 456); 2 Sigune's hermitage (435); 3 the lake of *Brumbâne* (225 unnamed, 261, 340, 473, 491). In 446–450 Good Friday pilgrims know their way into the forest as far as Trevrizent's hermitage (448).

Nineteenth-century scholars took *Mun(t)salvaesche* as Latin *mons salvationis*, "Salvation Mount." Martin says: from French *Mont sauvage*, from a Latin *mons silvaticus**, "Wild Hill." Kolb, pp. 129–133, says: *mont salvage/salvaige*, from a Latin *montem salvagium**, "Mount Salvage," i.e. a *purgatorium* where nearly perfected souls wait for heaven. *Terre de salvaesche* is, parallelwise, a "Land of Salvage." But *Fontâne la salvâtsche*, from a Latin *fontem silvaticum**, is simply "Wild Spring."

NORGALS (-*âls*)—82,1 From Norgals—specifically from its capital city of Kingrivals (79,1; L 78,1)—Gahmuret, with Schionatulander, sets out on his second expedition to Baldac.

5 x in P.—King Castis bequeathed Waleis and Norgals to Herzeloyde (494); in Gahmuret's absence Herzeloyde ruled Waleis and Anjou, "and she wore the crown of Norgals in her capital of Kingrivals" (103). After Gahmuret's death Lehelin seized Waleis and

Norgals (no mention of Anjou) (128). Signune prophesies (140) Parzival's future kingship of Norgals. In 803 Parzival proclaims his small son Kardeiz-2 as King of Waleis and Norgals—after he will have regained them—and of Anjou.

In P there is a tendency to name Waleis first and Norgals second, and Parzival is 13 x termed "a Waleis" but never "a Norgallois."

Norgals is OF for North Wales. Flutre lists *Norgal(l)es* for 17 romances, with variants *Norcgalles, Northguales;* in Wace's *Roman de Brut* as *Norwallia;* and defines it as *"la partie septentrionale du Pays de Galles." Not* named in Chrétien's "Perceval."

Geographically, "North Wales" = the northern half of Wales; *politically,* it normally stood for the Kingdom of Gwynedd, of fluctuating borders, primarily the NW quadrant of the country but at times including the NE quadrant as well, where it often vied with the Kingdom of Powys.

PARZIVAL—78,4. Parzival beheld an example of love "in Sigune at the linden tree."

88 x in P, (all in -*âl*).—"Anticipated" in 39,26; *not* named at his birth (112,5 ff.): he first learns his name from Sigune (140).

W 271 alludes to the scene in P 121-4, where the boy Parzival first encounters knights. W 4 alludes to the *poem* of *Parzival* (as completed and variously judged).

In Chrétien's "Perceval" 3573–6 (Roach ed.) the Sigune-character *inquires* the hero's name, and then *Chrétien* adds:

> And he who did not know his name/ guesses and said that his name was/ Perceval the Welshman, (*Devine et dist que il avoit/ Perchevax li Galois a non*)/ nor does he know whether he said rightly or wrongly.

Perchevax/Percheval le Galois also in lines 4562 and 4604.

Hartman's *Erec* 1684 lists *Machmerit Parceval von Glois,* "Perceval of Wales,"—the *Machmerit* is unexplained. The list in Chrétien's *Erec* has no parallel to line 1684.

"Parzival" and Hartman's "Parceval" are German pronunciation-variants of OF *Perceval,* which passed into English as "Percival;" later development "Percy." Sigune (140) interprets, presumably from OF, as *mitten durch,* "through the middle," though Chrétien's poem offers no etymology at all. OF *perce aval* might = "Pierce downslope!", parallel to heroes *Perceforest,* "Pierce-forest!" and *Percehaie,* "Pierce-hedge!" from the OF verb *percier/parcer;* (but the *Persagué-s* of *Aliscans* 4392, 5844, and 7324, from *perce à gué* (?), "Pierce-ford!", became, in

Willehalm 32, 98, and 288, *Passigweiz*, "Pass-ford!" rather than "Pierce-ford!"). Schröder, p. 96, however, understands *Per-ce-val* as "Through-the-valley!", taking *per* as *par*, and cites *Diu Crône* 6390–3; that poem recalls Wolfram's hero in lines 6377–93 and speaks of his superintendence of his mother's farming and land-clearing, "as his name signifies, for *parce* means 'through,' *val* a 'valley' or a 'furrow:' such is the meaning of his name in our language." (6390) *Wan p a r c e sprichet durch,* (6391) *V a l ein tal oder ein vurch.* This amateurish speculation, and on false premises, is useless: the poet of *Diu Crône* knew no more about the matter than the rest of us.

The titular hero of the corresponding Welsh prose romance of *Per-edur* (pronounce: Per-AY-dur) offers no clue. Brownwich, in *The Welsh Triads,* pp. 488–492, cites a seemingly historical Peredur of the late 500s, who *may* = Geoffrey of Monmouth's *Perdurus dux Venedotorum* in the *Vita Merlini*, also in III,18, but connection with the romance-hero is dubious. One possible etymology (p. 489) is "Steel Spear," (*par*, "spear," + *dûr*, "hard"), as suggested by *Y Seint Greal*, the Welsh version of *Perlesvaus*.

In short, the meaning of "Perceval"/"Parzival" remains mysterious.

PELRAPEIRE—22,2. Tampunteire "was known as the King of Pelrapeire."

25 x in P.—Parzival, riding through mountain and forest wastes, came to a loud, swift stream, which he followed down to the city of Pelrapeire (180). In a nearby mountain glen (190) live Dukes Kyot and Manfilot. The castle overlooks a harbor (200), where ships arrive with food supplies for the besieged city.

In Chrétien's "Perceval" 2386, 2406, 2687, 3123 (Roach ed.) the city is *Biaurepaire*, located on the sea, and ships arrive with food supplies "before the castle." No other topographical details are given and all characters are nameless except *Blancheflor*, who = Condwiramurs.

Flutre lists *Beau-/Biaurepaire* for Perceval romances, *Bel-* forms in the "Perceval Continuations." *Diu Crône* 605 and 783 mention a knight *Von Belrapeire Joranz* in a tournament.

OF *repairier* (from Late Latin *repatriare*), "*séjourner*," yielded English "to repair (to)" before disappearing from French. The English sense is "Fair Retreat." Martin claims *Beaurepaire* is "not rare" as a French place name, but he cites only the one in Dauphiné.

POMPEIUS (-*êjus*)—73,2 Pompeius (and Ipomidon) attacked Baldac.

2 x in P.—Gahmuret's first tour of service to the Baruch of Baldac was to fight against "two brothers of Babylon, Pompeius and Ipomidon," from whom the Baruch had taken their city of Nineveh (14);

his second tour of service (101–2) was against the same two brothers, who were now attacking the Baruch in his own city of Baldac. Of Pompeius 102,2–3 specifies: "He was not the one who fled Rome before Julius."

P 102,4–13 says further that these two Babylonian brothers were maternal nephews of Nabuchodonosor (Nebuchadnezzar) and descendants of Ninus, who founded Nineveh before Baldac even existed.

This last "historical" detail echoes the opening words of the *Seven Books of History against the Pagans,* which Paulus Orosius undertook at the behest of Saint Augustine and published in 418 A.D.: "Nearly all writers of history . . . have commenced their histories with Ninus, the son of Belus and king of the Assyrians;" Orosius makes Ninus a contemporary of Abraham, 3,184 years after Adam. From Orosius comes the cluster of names in P 101–2: Babylon/Babylonian, Ninus, Nabuchodonosor, and Pompeius; also *der künec Zarôastêr* of P 770,19; all from the first two Books of that Christian book of geography-and-history. Citing from the I. W. Raymond translation, Columbia University Press, 1936, we find:

—p. 49 that Ninus made war against King Zoroaster of the Bactrians and slew him;

—p. 73 that Ninus's widow Semiramis "restored Babylon;"

—p. 74 that Nabuchodonosor and his successors down to Cyrus were Chaldeans though they were reckoned Babylonians;

—p. 53 (and elsewhere) that Orosius cites "the historian Pompeius," i.e., Pompeius Trogus, who, under Augustus, wrote a history of Macedon: *Historiae Philippicae.*

We infer that the Pompeius of P 14 and 101–2 *is* this historian, reduced to a bare name in those name-collections that Wolfram had an amanuensis maintain for his use in literary composition, hence the qualifying remark that he was not the Pompeius Magnus who fled from Rome in 49 B.C. as Julius Caesar approached the city.

(In *Willehalm* 338–9 Terramer traces his claim to "the Roman crown" from his ancestor Pompey the Great. This pseudo-historical concept is traced to a passage in the *Annolied* by Joachim Bumke: *Wolframs 'Willehalm,'* p. 133, fn 107.)

Note that, of the five Orosius-names, "Ninus," "Zoroaster," and "Pompeius" do not occur in the Bible; that "Babylon" often meant either "Cairo" or "Egypt" to medievals; and that "Nineveh," which *is* Biblical, was the common Crusader term for the city of Mosul,—as explained under "Baldac" above.

Flutre lists *Pompee* for nine OF romances, always referring to Pompey the Great.

REPANSE DE SCHOYE—See "Urrepanse de Schoyen" below.

SALVÂSCH FLÔRÎE—151,1 The dukedom of *le duc* Ehkunat. See under "Ehkunat" above.

There is a linguistic problem in taking the noun *Salvâsch* as a form of the OF adjective *sauvage* (from Latin *silvaticus*); see under "Muntsalvatsch" above. There is an esthetic problem in the close juxtaposition of *Florie* as a place name with the personal name of Clauditte's deceased sister Florie. We offer no suggestions in either case.

SARACEN (*Sarazîne;* L *Sarr-*)—93,2 (and note 34) The medieval sense was often: "all living persons who were neither Christians nor Jews."

5 x in P.—42 x in W, corresponding to OF *Sarasin* (more than 100 x in *Aliscans*).

NOT "Easterner(s)," from Arabic *sharq,* "east," as often claimed, but an extension of the *Sarakēnoi,* a tribal name from NW Arabia, already mentioned in Ptolemy and in Isidore of Seville, who died in 636 A.D.: so states Dr. Paul Kunitzsch: *Die Arabica im 'Parzival Wolframs von Eschenbach,* in *Wolfram-Studien II,* 1974; p. 14, fn 22.

SCHIONATULANDER (*Schîo-*)—18 x. 39,4 "He will be the lord of this adventure" (*er wirt dirre âventiure hêrre*), i.e., the hero of the poem called *Titurel,*—which implies that Titurel is NOT the hero.

He is "the young (ruling) prince (*fürst*) from Graswaldan," 83,2; 4 x called *talfîn* (see under *"Talfîn"* below); a *Grâharzoys,* 131,4; a *Grâhardeiz,* 136,4.

A Schionatulander Chronology

FAMILY—His ancestry is narrated second, after Sigune's, because hers was the more distinguished family, 43. His grandfather was Gurnemanz of Graharz, 41; his father was Gurzgri, who died "for Schoydelacurte," 41; his mother was Mahaute, 42, sister of Ehkunat, the Count Palatine known as "from strong Berbester," 42.

CHILDHOOD—Entrusted to the French Queen Anphlise, 39, he was reared by her "from the time he was weaned," 124, and "loaned" by her to Gahmuret (as a squire) at the latter's knighting, 39. First named in 42,3.

At age 11–12 (we think) he accompanied Gahmuret on the first expedition to the Baruch of Baldac, "and Gahmuret brought him back again to Waleis," 40 and footnote 11.

WOOING—While "still short of maturity," 47—age 13–14 (we think)—he fell in love with Sigune while they were both living in the household of Gahmuret and Herzeloyde; he was steadfast in love, 52. From having carried secret messages in his boyhood between Anphlise and Gahmuret, 54, and from observing how Gahmuret spoke of love, 55, he knew something about proper love-procedures. His love plea to Sigune, 57–58; their stylized love dialogue, 59–72; their parting, 75–77.

At age 14–15 (we think) he accompanied Gahmuret on the second expedition to the Baruch, 79–82, at first concealing his love pangs for Sigune, 88. Description of him, 89, at about age 15. On the outward journey Gahmuret counsels him, 92–107; at home in Kanvoleiz Sigune yearns for him, 114–121.

In the *Second Fragment* he is aged 16 (we think), certainly no more than 17. He is the swiftest of runners save for Trevrezent, 133. He captures the runaway dog, 134, which escapes while he is fishing in the stream, 154, 159, and vainly pursues it a second time, 159–161. His colloquy with Sigune, 164–169, leads to his rash vow to regain the dog and its leash on condition that Sigune grant him her love.

None of this information is contained in *Parzival*.

4 x in P, (138, 435, 440, 804, all as Schiâ-).—He first appears—and is first mentioned—in 138, as the just-slain corpse lying across the lap of grief-distraught Sigune. The place is *zem fôrest in Brizljân*, 253,2–3. In 141 Sigune makes three statements about him: 1 he was slain in the defense of Parzival's lands; 2 he was slain by Orilus in a joust, not in war but in chance encounter; and 3 "It was a hound's leash that brought him mortal pain," (141,16).

In 249 he is the embalmed corpse clasped in Sigune's arms as she sits *in* a linden tree. Some years later Parzival finds Sigune in her hermitage at prayer beside Schionatulander's grave: ". . . in the sight of God he is my husband," (435). In 804 Parzival finds Sigune dead in the hermitage, and when the stone is lifted, in order to bury her beside her beloved, "there, uncorrupted, shone Schiantulander, embalmed in all his beauty."

The two Parzival-Sigune encounters, P 138–141 and 249–255, reflect a single encounter in Chrétien's "Perceval" 3422–3690 (Roach ed.), which occupies the position of P 249–255 but contains elements of both. That single encounter is described on pp. 78–79 above. After line 3690 the French poem never again mentions the grief-stricken *pucele* or her slain *ami*.

"Schio-/Schianatulander" doubtless = the *Ganatulander* of Hartman's *Erec* 1691, which has no equivalent in Chrétien's *Erec*, but Wolfram's form of the name would require "*Giana*tulander." We assume a lost French source for Hartman *and* Wolfram. Neither Flutre nor

West lists any name resembling either form. On p. 85 above we discuss Bartsch's alternate explanations of the name: *Li joenet de la lande,* "the youth from the moor," and *li joenet ù l'alant,* "the youth with the (hunting) dog." OF *alan/allan,* of unknown etymology, meant a large dog used for hunting bears and wolves. Wolfram's word is *der bracke,* English "brach," meaning "a sleuthhound." Archaic English has the word "alaunt."

Schoette (*Schô-*)—126,4. Schionatulander inherited "many excellences" from his father, from his mother, "and from his aunt, Queen Schoette."

Thus Queen Schoette and the *talfinette* Mahaute must have been sisters, making their sons Gahmuret and Schionatulander first cousins, 55 and note 16; 75,3; 88,3; 95 entire; and 126,2–4. No such kinship is mentioned anywhere in *Parzival.*

In P 10,13 to 11,30 Schoette appears, but without a name; in 92 we learn that she died of grief from the deaths of her husband Gandin and her son Galoes and from the prolonged absence of Gahmuret from Anjou.

Bartsch: from Provençal *Gaudeta,* pronounced "Jaudeta," (parallel to *Schoysîane,* from Provençal *Gauziana,* pronounced "Jautsiana;" see under "Schoysiane" below). Bartsch further connects the name with French *gaude,* = German *Reseda,* "mignonette." There is some botanical confusion here; modern French *la gaude,* from Germanic *walda,* includes two varieties of a dye-weed, either blue or yellow. *Some* floral interpretation of "Schoette" would suit well with her husband's name, "Gandin," *if* "Gandin" were rightly "Gaudin," from Germanic *wald-,* meaning "a copse, a small stand of trees." See under "Gandin" above.

Martin suggests *Joetha,* "presumably from Latin *Juditha,*" in documents relating to Dauphiné; our genealogy of the house of Albon, p. 114 above, shows no such name.

Schoydelacurte (L *Schoidelakurte*)—41,4. Gurzgri "died for (*umbe*) 'Schoydelacurte.'"

3 x in P.—Gurzgri "rode to Schoydelakurt, where . . . Mabonagrin slew him," (178); Gurzgri "lost his life for (*durch*) Schoydelakurt," (429); 583 recalls how Erec won Schoydelakurt away from Mabonagrin." All allusions in T and P imply that "Schoydelacurte" was the name of the orchard—Hartman: *boumgarten,* Chrétien: *vergier*—that Mabonagrin "owned," whereas both of these poets (Chrétien 5416–7; Hartman 8001–2 and 8006) explicitly state that "The Joy of the

Court" was the name of Erec's final triumphant *adventure*. In the Welsh prose *Gereint ab Erbin* the adventure has no name. See also under "Mabonagrin" above.

SCHOYSIANE (*-îâne*)—10,1; 13,3; 14,1; 19,1; 20,3; 24,4; (dubious stanza 33,4); 37,2; 104,1 and 3; 105,2; 108,3; 111,2.

Named first, presumably as the eldest, of Frimutel's three daughters, 10; wooed by "many kings from many lands," 13, but married Kiot of Katelangen, 14; died in giving birth to Sigune, 19.

"She by whom the Grail first permitted itself to be carried, that was Schoysiane," 24.

5 x in P.—Trevrizent's sister Schoysiane, wife of Duke Kyot of Katelangen, died in giving birth to Sigune, 477,2 and 9. In 800 it is implied that the couple lived at Munsalvaesche until Schoysiane's death in childbirth. Recalled in 823.

P 805 contradicts both P 477 and T 25 by saying that Schoysiane brought up Condwiramurs.

Bartsch: from Provençal *Gauziana* (pronounced Jauziana), "Joy-spreader." (Provençal *gauzir* = French *jouir*.) Compare the parallel case of "Schoette" above.

Martin compares *Tschoysîâne* with *Josiane*, wife of the hero in *Bueves de Hastone*, but gives no etymology. Flutre lists neither name.

SEVILLE (*Sibilje*)—82,1. "From Norgals to Spain and on to Seville" Gahmuret (with Schionatulander) traveled on his second expedition to the East.

5 x in P, (54; 58; 496,19 and 25; 497).—Gahmuret's ship captain (*marnaere*, 55,3) was born "in the city of Seville" (54) and "he was not like a Moor in color" (55); he had brought Gahmuret to Patelamunt, in the kingdom of Zazamanc, presumably from Baldac, and he effected Gahmuret's clandestine departure from Patelamunt (54). "I was told that the sea brought (Gahmuret) to a harbor, and from there he made his way (*kêrter*) to Seville," where he paid the captain handsomely and took leave of him, (58,20–26).

We take this to mean that the ship captain was a Spanish Christian from Seville and that he had transported Gahmuret, on the first expedition to the East, from Seville to Baldac and back again, via Patelamunt, to Seville.

Trevrizent's remarks in P 496–8, however, must refer to Gahmuret's outward journey on his *second* expedition to the East: Gahmuret had taken lodgings in Seville and, upon Trevrizent's subsequent arrival there, recognized him by his resemblance to Herzeloyde. From

Seville, Gahmuret "went to Baldac, where, in a joust, he died," (496); "We went our separate ways. (498) He returned to the Baruch, and I rode to the Rohas" (in what is now Yugoslavia).

(Remarks continued under the next item, "Spain.")

Seville (classical *Hispalis*, Arabic *Ishbiliyah*, Spanish *Sevilla*) was a city of importance under the Romans, under the Vandals, and, from 710 until 1248, under Moslem rule. In art, science, and commerce it rivaled Córdoba, the chief Moslem center. In *La Chanson de Roland* 955 *Sebilie* is a pagan "land," parallel to *Sibilia* in the *Rolandslied* 2677, and probably also in *Willehalm* 221, where *Sibilje* is claimed by "heathen" King Tibalt in inheritance from his "heathen" uncle Marsilje. (The name does not occur in *Aliscans*.)

SIGUNE (*-ûne*)—29 x. The heroine of the poem: "*Duchesse* from Katelangen" (*Ducisse ûz K.*), 109,1; *herzogin*, 144,1; "the (ruling) princess (*fürstin*) from Katelangen," 111,2.

A Sigune Chronology

FAMILY—Her ancestry is narrated first, 43, before Schionatulander's, because she is of the Grail family, which surpasses all others in nobility. Her great-grandfather was Titurel, her grandfather was Frimutel, 1–12; her father was Duke Kiot of Katelangen and her mother was Schoysiane, the first Grail bearer, 24, who died in giving her birth.

CHILDHOOD—Her paternal uncle, King Tampunteire of Brubarz, then "took the little Sigune with him to his daughter Kondwiramurs" in his capital city of Pelrapeire, 25,—Kondwiramurs being then also "an infant at the breast." Five years later, after King Tampunteire and his son Kardeiz-1 had died in close succession, Sigune was removed to the care of her maternal aunt Herzeloyde, Queen of Waleis, presumably to the capital city of Kanvoleiz, 29. There Herzeloyde brought her up, 32,—as P 477 confirms, but P 805,3–10 says in contradiction that *Schoysiane* brought *Condwiramurs* up.

WOOING—Once Gahmuret has married Herzeloyde (P 100), their respective wards, Schionatulander and Sigune, live in the same household (in Kanvoleiz), and there these two "children" fall in love, 47, 52, 57. Their love dialogue, 58–72. Schionatulander's grief at parting and Sigune's grief at his departure, 75. In Kanvoleiz, Herzeloyde counsels Sigune in her love-sorrows, 111–131.

In the SECOND FRAGMENT Schionatulander brings the runaway dog to Sigune in their forest tent, 193. Sigune reads the jeweled inscription on the dog's collar, 144, and has begun to read the continuation on the jeweled leash, 143–153, when the dog escapes, 154–158. She must have dog and leash back, 163–165, and, if Schionatulander will get them for her, she promises him "Favor, and all that a girl should do for her fair and noble friend," 168.

Her excessive demand and Schionatulander's over-trusting vow of compliance are the twin causes of the tragedy which will ensue.

14 x in P.—Like Schianatulander, Sigune first appears in P 138 as young Parzival discovers her in frantic grief over the just-slain corpse of Schianatulander, which she is holding across her lap; the scene is in the forest of *Brizljân,* (P 253,2), i.e., the forest of Broceliande, ca. 50 km/30 m SW of Rennes in E-central Brittany. Sigune informs Parzival of his own name and lineage, identifying herself as his cousin and as the former ward of his mother.

In P 249–255, Parzival, riding away from the Grail Castle, finds Sigune sitting "in a linden tree" (*ûf einer linden,* 249,14) and clasping Schianatulander's embalmed corpse in her embrace. She "speaks prophecy" of utmost fame for Parzival, until he admits having failed to ask any questions at the Grail Castle, whereupon she declares him "dead to happiness" and refuses further speech with him.

In P 435–442, some years later, Parzival finds her in her hermitage in Grail territory and living in perpetual prayer beside Schianatulander's grave inside the cell: "I am a maid, and unmarried, yet in the sight of God he is my husband."

In P 804–5 Parzival finds her dead in the cell and buries her in the same coffin with Schianatulander.

See pages 78–79 above for the parallels and non-parallels with Chrétien's "Perceval."

Bartsch (p. 141): a Germanic name comparable to *Sigiwin/Sigwin.* Martin: reminiscent of *Signy,* faithful consort of the god Loki.

"Now," says Schionatulander, 98,4, "I must speak the name of Sigune: she has been victorious over my heart" (. . . *Sigûnen . . . diu hât ane gesiget mînem herzen*). Wolfram himself "hails her," 105,4, as "Sigune the victorious on the battlefield where maidens chaste and sweet are chosen!",—more literally: ". . . where chasteness and sweetness of maidens are chosen!" (*Sigûne diu sigehafte ûf   dem wal dâ man welt magede kiusche unt süeze!*) Even to the old-fashioned word *wal,* "battlefield," the metaphor alludes to the pre-Christian "shield-maidens" of Odin/Wotan, those *Valkyries* (Old Norse for "choosers of the slain"), who on battlefields marked those destined to die and conducted them to Odin's hall, whence they came to live and fight and die anew each day.—Surely, then, Wolfram understood the name as akin to MHG *sîc/sîge*, modern *Sieg*, "victory."

Since 1903, however, there has been a tendency, based on "Perceval" and *Parzival* but disregarding *Titurel*, to take "Sigune" as an anagram of *cousine*. In "Perceval" 3600–1 (Roach ed.) the "maiden" says: *Je sui ta germaine cousine/Et tu iez mes cousins germains*; in 3612 Perceval calls her *cousine*, in 3664 *Bele cousine*. Wolfram does not use this word. Parzival addresses Sigune as *niftel* in 141,25; as *liebiu niftel mîn* in 255,21; as *niftel Sigûn* in 441,15; and Wolfram refers to her in 804,26 as *die niftel sîn*. And Sigune addresses Parzival in 141,14 as *lieber neve guoter*, referring in 140,22 to Herzeloyde as *mîn muome*, ("maternal aunt"). *Neve* = "sister's son" or "maternal uncle;" *niftel* = "sister's daughter; niece" or "maternal aunt;" yet the story clearly makes Sigune and Parzival first cousins, their mothers having been sisters. Moreover, a perfect anagram would require an original *gusine*, though this may be quibbling.

With any anagrammed name the reader's question is naturally *Cui bono?*, and we bear this question in mind in the section next following here.

A Note on Anagrammed Names

Loomis stresses not only "Sigune" as an anagram of *cousine/cusine*, but also Wolfram's "Arnive," the name of King Arthur's mother, as an anagram of *Iverne*, (more commonly *Igerne*), and "Îblis," the Sicilian Queen in P 656 and 668, as an anagram of *Sibyl*. (See Loomis: *Morgan la Fée in Oral Tradition* in *Romania* LXXX (1959), pp. 337–367, or the same reprinted in *Studies in Medieval Literature*, New York, 1970; pp. 3–33; pp. 21–22.)

Best known of anagrams in medieval German literature is Tristan's reversal of his own name as "Tantris" for his second journey, incognito, to Ireland. Wagner's opera libretto recalls this device. (Note also that Gotfried's *Tristan* uses acrostics.)

We reject the notion of "Sigune" as an anagram, and we wonder whether "Arnive" is not a mere garble of *Iverne*, but "Îblis" is indeed an anagram of *Sibyl*.

Loomis's note 128 to the K. G. T. Webster translation of Ulrich's *Lanzelet* says that *Yblis/Iblis/Ibelis* is "almost certain" to be "an anagram, coined by Ulrich, for *Sibil(e)*,"—for reasons occupying four printed pages in note 128, but especially in allusion to the temptress-goddess Sibyl who lured knights to her voluptuous valley (or cavern) "of no return." The father of the *Lanzelet* Yblis is Iweret, and note 128 adds: "Wolfram seems to have taken over Yblis and Iweret, changed the latter name to Ibert to rime with 'wert,' and altered the relationship from filial to conjugal."—We disagree.

P 656–7 report that "Sicily had a noble king called Ibert, and Iblis was his wife," and that "in the famous castle of Kalot enbolot" Ibert surprised Queen Iblis in the arms of her lover Clinschor, for which he castrated Clinschor. Jessie Weston (Vol. II, p. 212) correctly identified the "famous" (*vest erkant*) castle but not the lady,—misled perhaps by Bartsch's association of "Iblis" with the Sicilian mountain of Hybla, famed for its honey (Vergil: *Eclogue* VII, 37).

"Iblis" is indeed an anagram for the very real *Sibyl* d'Acerra, Queen of Sicily, 1190–94. Recently widowed, this Queen fled, in November of 1194, to the Norman stronghold at Caltabellota, Arabic *Qal'at al-balluṭ*, "Fortress of the Cork-oaks," Wolfram's *Kalot enbolot*, taking with her her three maiden daughters, her small son, her faithful nobles, and the Norman crown, to preserve all these from German Emperor Henry VI, whose conquering army was sweeping toward Palermo. From "Kalot enbolot" the fugitives were lured back to the capital—bringing the coveted crown, only to be arrested on December 29, 1194, for high treason and sent to various punishments. Italian historians down to 1844 repeated the claim that the little "William III of Sicily" was blinded and castrated; actually he perished at Hohen Ems prison in Austria at an unknown date and amid circumstances wholly unknown. The last known date for Queen Sibyl is 1198, when, Henry VI being dead, she was freed from her Alsatian convent-prison at the order of Pope Innocent III. She was then of grandmotherly age. Of her character we know only what her enemies reported. Possibly the news of her death prompted the allusion to her in P 656–7; if so, Wolfram's harsh jest grates on modern sensibilities.

We are inclined to believe, however, that the harsh jest was Wolfram's only at second hand and that he borrowed the whole scurrilous anecdote (as related by Queen Arnive to Gawan) *en bloc*, with French names and French anagrams included, from the "Virgil of Naples" tales, using the anecdote for comic effect in the comic sequence of Gawan adventures in *Parzival*. We refer to those off-color jokes told, many of them in French, about the prankster "Virgil of Naples" as described by Domenico Comparetti in *Virgilio nel medio evo*, 1896; (English translation by E. F. M. Benecke, London, 1895, from the Italian proofsheets). The prankster-magician "Virgil of Naples" was an imaginary figure in numerous anecdotes of the late 1100s, originating in the Naples area and taking his name from the poet Vergil who spent much of his life in Naples and was buried there.

In P 656 Wolfram makes Clinschor, the seducer of Queen Iblis, a "nephew" (*neve*) of *von Nâpels Virgilîus* and, like his uncle, a comic character and a magician, but also with a streak of malice in him. His "land" is the *Terre de Lâbûr* (656,14), i.e., the district of the *Terra di lavoro* N of Naples and around Capua and Caserta, (though Plutarch's Life of Cicero, ca. 100 A.D., equates it with Campania). His capital is *Câps*, i.e., Capua, the city long famed for luxury (in both senses) and in Wolfram's time deemed more important than Naples. The rich area of Capua-Caserta-Naples formed the northern bulwark of the Norman Kingdom (of Sicily) of which Queen Sibyl d'Acerra was the claimant in 1194. The French forms of these names led Jessie Weston to suggest a French source for P 656–7. We agree; and furthermore the same deciphering system that produces "Iblis" from "Sibyl" turns "Ibert" into "Tibre," a French form of the River Tiber.

1	2	3	4	5		5	1	2	4	3	
I	B	L	Y	S		S	I	B	Y	L	
I	B	E	R	T		T	I	B	R	E	

We suggest that our hypothetical French original of Wolfram's anecdote was both comic in nature and pro-Papacy political, most likely after Emperor Henry VI's death in 1197, and that the French-language anagrams served to disguise the political features of the story. We wonder, for instance, whether Clinschor may reflect Henry VI's deputy in Capua, 1191–4, Konrad von Lutzelinhart, whom the Italians called "Conrad Bee-in-his-Bonnet" (*Corrado Mosca-in-cervello*)?, the same who, at Henry's order in 1195, razed the walls of both Capua and Naples.

In P 658 Clinschor is said to have taken a certain mountain height (where he erected the Castle of Wonders) from a King *Irot*, whose name *could* be an anagram of *Troi*, not classical Troy but S-Italian Troia, where, in December of 1194, Henry installed Bishop Walther of Troia as chancellor of the newly conquered Norman kingdom.

On the other hand, the simple cryptographic device of "running down the columns" *could* connect the name "Clinschor" with the name "Irot":

```
C L I  N S C H O R
d mj  o t d i  p s
e n k  p u e j q t
f o l  q v f k r u
```

g p m r q g l s v
h q n s x h m t w
I R O T y i n u x

Or again, "Clinschor" may be a "semi-anagram" of OF *roche (a)clin*, "subjected crag;" or it may have to do with OF *clinche*, "latch;" or it may be of some other origin. In any case, the Hungarian minstrel *Klingsor* of *Der Wartburgkrieg*, before 1241, seems to represent a wholly new understanding of the name,—for all that he is said to be Wolfram's Clinschor, and Novalis, Hoffmann, and Wagner all had their own reasons for taking the name as *Klingsohr*; perhaps they took it as a form of *klingesaere*, "minstrel," or perhaps they liked the suggestion of "ring-in-the-ear."

The present writer is half serious, half ironic, in extending these anagramming possibilities. The primary question to be asked about any anagrammed name in literature is, after all, *cui bono*?

SPAIN (*Spange;* L *Spâne*)—82,1. "From Norgals to Spain and on to Seville . . ."

3 x in P, (48, 58, 400).—Gahmuret's cousin Kaylet (termed *der Spânôl* in 39 and 91) is the ruler of "Spain," with capital at Toledo (*Dôlet*), 48, and Gahmuret travels (58) from Seville to visit him there.

Toledo (classical *Toletum*, Arabic *Ṭulayṭulah*, OF *Toulete*; Wolfram's *Dôlet*), located just S of the geographical center of the Iberian peninsula, was captured from the Moslems on May 25, 1085, by Alfonso VI, King of Leon (since 1065) and of Castile (since 1072), and Christian-held from 1085 on.

To Wolfram, "Spain" meant *Christian* Spain, more specifically Leon-Castile, with capital at Toledo, and distinct from Catalonia, Aragon, and Navarre. If, along with other *chansons de geste, Aliscans* considers *Espaigne* a "pagan" land in some 20 occurrences, that is because of the historical setting in the era of Charlemagne and Louis the Pious. Significantly, Wolfram does not mention "Spain" in *Willehalm*.

Assuming that both P and T respect the political realities of their time, we take T 82,1: "From Norgals to Spain and on to Seville" to mean an overland journey to Christian Toledo, where the Christian ruler arranged safe-conduct for an armed knight and his attendants through Moslem-held, southern Spain as far as Seville. At Seville sea-transport might be arranged through Moslem authorities.

Seville, some 80 km/50 m up the Guadalquivir River, was itself probably not the port of embarcation, as P 58,20–26 suggests: ". . . the sea brought Gahmuret to a harbor, and from there he made his way to Seville;" the actual port was doubtless Cadiz, an easy overland journey from Seville. From Cadiz on the Atlantic the voyage passed through *az-zuqaq*, Arabic for "The Strait (of Gibraltar)" and, in our opinion, the origin of the "kingdom" of Azagouc, and thence to Baldac. (In LT, H-2524 ff., Schionatulander sails from Marseille, not from Seville (as the text emphasizes), but the poem has the ships driven off-course in order to bring them to Azagouc; from there the voyage is resumed *eastwards* (H-2628,2).

Talfîn—Schionatulander's title in 92,2; 94,2; 126,1; 135,2. Gurzgri's title in 127,2. In 126,3 *talfînette* is Mahaute's title. These titles are nowhere used in *Parzival*.

Supplementary to pp. 105–108 above:—The word is from Greek *delphís, -phînos*, by way of Latin *delphinus*, meaning "dolphin," the marine mammal of the whale family.

The Delphinos of mythology was an emissary of sea god Poseidon in his wooing of the sea nymph Amphitrite. As reward for his success on this mission he was transformed into the small constellation "Delphinus," just below the Northern Cross. "Jupiter," says Ovid (*Fasti*, II, 117–8), "received the dolphin among the constellations and bade him have nine stars."

Ancient Christian gravestones attest a "Delfinus" and a "Delfina." Compare the given names *lupus*, "wolf," as in Saint Loup, Bishop of Troyes, d. 479, and *ursus*, "bear."

A Saint Delphinus, Bishop of Bordeaux, died ca. 400. A Bishop Aunemundus of Lyon has for centuries been venerated under the name of Saint Chamond, but, from 655 to 658, Wilfrid, Bishop of York and "apostle of Northumbria," studied *apud Dalfinum archiepiscopum Galliarum Lugduni*, who was surely this same Aunemundus/Chamond. Why Wilfrid called him "Dalfinus" is unknown, but from him probably came the widespread use of "Dolfin" as a baptismal name in northern England and southern Scotland. Bede's history of the Anglo-Saxon church mentions this Bishop Dalfinus, and only from Bede could Rhone-valley folk around 1100 have learned that their Saint Chamond was *also* known as Dalfinus.

Besides the baptismal name "Dolfin," Middle English has the common nouns *delfyn* and *daulphin*. Shakespeare's *Henry V* refers to the future Charles VII of France as "the Dolphin."

Once the name Dalfinus came to be felt as a title, "the Dauphin,"—after 1184 and before 1222, it is paralleled only by the evolution of the Latin *cognomen* "Caesar" into a title meaning "emperor,"—*Caesar* in Latin itself after 70 A.D., German *Kaiser,* and Russian *Tsar',*—and by the development of *Karl,* Charlemagne's name, into a common noun in Slavic, e.g., Russian *korol',* "king."

TAMPUNTEIRE—15,2; 22,1; 25,1; 28,1. King of Brubarz (capital city Pelrapeire); brother and overlord of Duke Kiot of Katelangen and of Duke Manfilot; father of Kondwiramurs and of Kardeiz-1.

Tampunteire came (from Brubarz) to Katelangen for the wedding of Duke Kiot and Schoysiane, 15. Upon Schoysiane's death Duke Kiot begged Tampunteire to bestow the fief of Katelangen upon Kiot's infant daughter Sigune so that he (Kiot) and his other brother, Duke Manfilot, might renounce knighthood, 22–23. Tampunteire took the infant Sigune to Pelrapeire as a companion for his own infant daughter Kondwiramurs, 25. About five years later Tampunteire died, 28, and at about the same time his son, Kardeiz-1, also died,—slain in love service to an unnamed lady.

7 x in P, (all as Tampen-). The father of Condwiramurs, (211, 425, 808), to whom he bequeathed the city of Pelrapeire (180); "My father Tampenteire left me as a poor orphan in frightful straits," (194). *Kardeiz(-1) fiz Tampenteire,* (293). In P 222 Parzival's "father-in-law Tampenteire had left him bright jewels and red gold in Pelrapeire."

Bartsch (p. 144): from Provençal *tamp-en-taire,* "Cloak in silence!", from *tampir,* "to enclose." (Compare his explanation of "Tampanis," [Gahmuret's chief squire, P 105,1 and, without name, P 59,30] as *tampa-nis,* "Close the nest!") Martin suggests the initial *T* = a French *d',* but proposes no proper noun to follow the *d'.* (Note W *Tandarnas* and *Todjerne,* which definitely represent the *d'Andernas* and *d'Odierne* of *Aliscans.*)

We now suggest a *d'Ampunteire*,* representing *d'Ampun terre*,* "from Ampurias," the port town in the extreme NE of Catalonia, Greek-founded as *Empórion* but called *Emporiae* by the Romans: "Market (Town)." Or, possibly, from the River *El Ampurdán* in the district of *Ampurdán* in the same general area.

Either explanation connects King Tampunteire with "Katelangen," of which he is said to be the overlord. We think his historical prototype was one of the three brother-kings of Aragon.

"Templars" and "templars."—11,2 (and note 1): Many a templar (*templeis*) grieved at Titurel's abdication.

Several times in P, first in 444,23, where "templars" guard Munsalvaesche. Lexer's MHG Dictionary calls it an OF term, from Medieval Latin *templensis.* We take Wolfram's Grail-defenders as a fictional specialization of the actual Templars: OF *Templiers*, from Medieval Latin *templarii*. Wolfram's OF-derived form suggests an OF *fictional* source.

The Historical Templars

The Knights Templars of history were the *Pauperes Commilitiones Christi templique Salomonis*, "Poor Knights of Christ and of the Temple of Solomon," an order founded by two Frenchmen in 1119 to protect Jerusalem-pilgrims after the First Crusade. The first installation granted to them was at Soure, in W-central Portugal, near Coimbra, in 1128. In 1130 they were given Graneña, in Catalonia, and in 1136 the Count of Foix granted them quarters just N of the Pyrenees, adjoining Aragon. Their official name derived from the headquarters assigned them by Baldwin II, King of Jerusalem, 1118–31, in a section of his palace, which was regarded as the Temple of Solomon. Thus Templar headquarters shared the same roof with the Jerusalem Angevins after 1131.

To the Patriarch of Jerusalem these knights swore an oath to guard roads, forsake worldly chivalry, and obey the Benedictine Rule of "Chastity, Obedience, and Poverty." Originally they wore any old clothes; later they adopted the white robe, the white cape, and the emblem of the four-pointed cross worn on the left shoulder.* Membership might be for a specified term or for life. Three ranks accommodated members of different social levels. Married men might join on condition of willing their property to the Order.

Their numbers, and their wealth and power, grew rapidly. Saint Bernard of Clairvaux lent them his personal support in 1127. The following year the Council of Troyes defined their particular Rule, which is lost. By mid-century they owned their own churches, were exempt from taxes, and took commands only from the Pope in person, being reponsible to no other authority, ecclesiastical or secular. After 1163 they had their own priests, who were called chaplains and who were obliged to belong to the Order. With a network of "temples" extending from Ireland to Armenia, they became international financiers and guardians of treasure, while their land-holdings in country after country grew steadily larger from kings' donations and

---

* Wolfram's insistence, in W 406, on the three-pointed cross instead of the four-pointed one may reflect no more than his awareness that the Templars did not exist in the time of Willehalm.

by terms of the wills of pious persons deceased. As a military élite their fighting record was grimly awesome. To all intents and purposes they were the Pope's private army.

Under Saladin, however, the Moslems recaptured Jerusalem in 1187 and neither Templar prowess nor further Crusades could win it back. Christian-held territory was lost piecemeal down to 1291 and the withdrawal of all Christians from the Holy Land. Thus, after 1291, the Templars were an anachronism.

Around 1305 King Philip IV of France began plotting the annihilation of this church-within-a-church and this state-within-a-state. On October 13, 1307, with Pope Clement V helplessly in his power, Philip arrested Grand Master Jacques de Molay and sixty other Templars in Paris. In 1308 he contrived to discredit the Order internationally by charges of obscene and blasphemous initiation rites, idolatrous worship in secret, and homosexuality, extorting confessions under ferocious tortures. Similar arrests and confiscations of wealth took place in all countries except Portugal. Under duress the Pope issued these commands, and under duress he formally abolished the Order in 1312. In March of 1314 Grand Master Jacques de Molay was burned alive in Paris.

A century earlier, when the Order was the pride of Christendom, Wolfram set "templars"—but not "Templars"—to guard the Grail and its territory.

TITUREL—1,1; 12,1. The first 10 stanzas of T contain Titurel's speech of abdication from the Grail kingship: at his advanced age feats of arms are beyond him, 2; he is past love of women, 3; his "young successors" will maintain his knightly virtues, 4–5; his were the first human hands to receive the Grail; a host of angels brought it to him, and he "found (his) entire Rule inscribed thereon," 6; of his children he reserved Frimutel for the Grail, 7; he lists the five children of Frimutel, 9–10 (parallel to P 823), implying that these five persons' lives delimit the story's scope.

6 x in P, (251 Ty-; 455 Ty-; 474 Ty-; 501, 813, 816).—Bequest of the *Terre de Salvaesche* to Frimutel (= T 1–10), together with his turtledove emblem, (251 and 474). In the much-debated passage, 452,29 to 455,20, "Kyot," Wolfram's alleged informant, read, "in Latin books," either *in* Anjou or *about* Anjou, an account of Gahmuret's ancestors "and further how Titurel and his son Frimutel bequeathed the Grail to Anfortas."

In 501 Parzival asks Trevrizent: "Who was the man lying there before the Grail? He was quite gray, but his skin was bright and fresh." Trevrizent replies:

> "That was Titurel. He is your mother's grandfather. He was the first to be entrusted with the banner of the Grail and the charge of defending it. He has a sickness called podagra, a lameness for which there is no help. Yet he has never lost his fresh color, for he sees the Grail so often that he cannot die. They cherish him, bedridden though he is, for the sake of his counsel. In his youth he crossed many a ford and meadow in search of a joust."

With two small great-great-grandchildren Titurel (813) is still "the aged, crippled, bedridden man," but still alert with counsels. That is the last we hear of him; his ultimate fate is nowhere indicated.

Nowhere does P name Titurel's wife; his daughter Rischoyde (84,10) is the wife of King Kaylet of Spain, but no other children are mentioned except Frimutel.

Hartman's *Erec* 1651 lists *Blîobleherîn und Titurel*; (*Blîobleherîn* = Plihoplîherî in P 134,28 only). The corresponding line in Chrétien's *Erec* (F 1713–14; R 1687–8) has: *Et Tristans qui onques ne rist/Delez Bliobleheris sist*, "And Tristan who never laughed/sat beside Bliobleheris." Kolb, p. 56, sees the name, in both Wolfram and Hartman, as reflecting the name of the hero of the OF *Lai de Tidorel* (or *Tydorel*), of uncertain date and authorship. Martin ruled out that possibility, believing the *lai* to be later than 1200, but scholars disagree on this point; some even attribute it to Marie de France before 1184. Ernst Brugger (in *Festschrift Morf*, p. 94) took the name as Breton, perhaps a variant of *Tudoret*, but Kolk is dubious; trisyllabic names in Breton, he says, do not end in *-el*.

But Kolb thinks both name and character-type derive from the *Lai de Tidorel*:

> A handsome knight rises out of a lake, wins the love of a certain queen ten years childless in marriage, and begets upon her a son named Tidorel, and subsequently a daughter. He forbids all questions about his name and origin, but he proves his connection with the lake by plunging in, in full armor, and returning some hours later. When a vassal of the king's surprises the lovers, the knight disappears forever.
> Tidorel grows to manhood, the king dies, and Tidorel inherits *Bretagne*, rules in peace, and fathers numerous offspring. Ten years later he learns his true paternity from his mother.

Instantly he rides his horse into the lake to seek out his true father—and is never seen again.

Here are motifs which parallel Wolfram's brief account of Loherangrin in P 823–6: mystery, forbidden questions about name and origins, association with water, etc. Kolb, pp. 56–64, raises significant esthetic issues: Titurel, as first King of the Grail, "prefigures" Loherangrin, the fifth and last King of the Grail.

Complicating interpretation further is the popular, 12th-century association of Loherangrin/Lohengrin with Godfrey of Bouillon: born 1060, led the First Crusade to victory in 1096–99, elected "Advocate of the Holy Sepulcher" (rather than "King of Jerusalem") in 1099, died July 18, 1100.

We find Kolb's concept extremely attractive: Titurel emerges out of mystery and Loherangrin is left to recede into mystery, and these two figures make a frame around the central story about the five children of Frimutel and *their* offspring. Admittedly, however, grave problems remain unsolved. We regard the LT accounts of Titurel's origins and ultimate fate as alien to Wolfram's poetic purposes.

TREVREZENT—9,3; 133,3 (M Tref-). "The swift;" younger brother of Anfortas, 9. Schionatulander is fleeter of foot than any, 133, "except Trevrezent the pure (*der reine*), who outran and outjumped all who practiced such knightly sports."

12 x in P, (all as Trevri-). Contrary to Grail vows, Trevrizent, in his youth, rode in love service to an unnamed lady (495) and for her sake jousted in Europe, Asia, and Africa, 496, (see under "Agremuntin" above). In Seville he met Gahmuret, (see under "Seville" above), and there Gahmuret gave him "his kinsman as squire, Ither, the King of Kukumerlant," with whose murder Trevrizent now (498) reproaches Parzival. From Seville he sailed to Aquileia, (498), Cilli, the Rohas, "Gandine," and the "land" of Styria. These places lie between Venice and Vienna and, in our opinion, reflect the overland flight of Richard Lion Heart in December of 1192.

At some point he retired as a hermit to a cave in the wall of a cliff (268), "making atonement for sin," (251). The place is *Fontâne la salvâtsche,* "Wild Spring," in Grail territory, (268 compared with 452), and there the spiritually weary Parzival spends two weeks with him (501,11), learning wisdom that supersedes the wordly wisdom gained from two weeks' stay with Gurnemanz (in 176). With "faith in God since departing from Trevrizent," (741), Parzival reports at Arthur's court "what Trevrizent had said," (786).

In 788 Trevrizent beholds writing on the Grail announcing Parzival's second coming to the Grail Castle. Once Anfortas is cured, Parzival "rode to see Trevrizent," (797), to report that event. In 798 Trevrizent tells Parzival: ". . . you have forced God by defiance to make His infinite Trinity grant your will."

P 433–502 (Book IX; 2,100 lines) = Chrétien's "Perceval" 6216–6515 (Roach ed.), 299 lines. There the unnamed hermit is the hero's maternal uncle (as he is in P); Perceval stays only two days with him and receives religious instruction, but the hermit tells nothing about his autobiography and gives only meager details about the Fisher King (= Anfortas) and about the Grail.

In the Welsh *Peredur* the Trevrizent-character is an unnamed priest who reproaches the hero for bearing arms on Good Friday; their interchange parallels that between Parzival and the pilgrim knight in gray, P 446–450, rather than anything said between Trevrizent and Parzival. Peredur then proceeds on foot until late that same day, when he encounters the same priest at the gate of a towerless castle. (This resembles Parzival's seeing Anfortas first in a boat, fishing, and then—mysteriously—in the Grail Castle hall.) Peredur stays with the priest until the third day, receiving "guidance" of unspecified kind.

Bartsch (p. 140): from Provençal *treu*, "peace," + *rezems* (from *redemptus*), "redeemed," meaning apparently *"by* peace redeemed (from youthful sin-guilt)." Kolb, pp. 31–33, objects that Provençal *treu* (masc.) and the more common *treva* (fem.) = "truce," not "peace," (which would be *patz*). Martin: ? from OF *tref* (now *trève*), + *recevant*, "peace-receiving." Mergell proposed *tref récent*, "recent truce." Fourquet merely lists similar-looking names, e.g., *Traverain* and *Tenebroc* in Chrétien's *Erec*, both place names. Though linguistically problematical, Bartsch's interpretation is the most plausible of all these.

URREPANSE DE SCHOYEN (L . . . *Schoien*)—10,4 Last-named of Frimutel's five children.

MS G, containing *Parzival* and the 164 stanzas of *Titurel*, writes "Urrepanse" throughout; other MSS have "Repanse." Marti, to T 10,4, assumes a handwriting error in the MS from which G was copied. Otherwise the *Ur-* is unexplained.

8 x in P as REPANSE DE SCHOYE.—She is the Grail Bearer, (235), who "tends" (*pfliget*) the Grail, (477), and Parzival's aunt, (807). In 228 her "cloak of flawless Arabian silk" is loaned, via a chamberlain, for Parzival to wear at the Grail ceremony. Feirefiz wins her in marriage,

(810–822 passim), and the two depart for "India," where the son born to them (822) is Prester John.

Her eldest sister, Schoysiane, was the *first* Grail Bearer, (T 24). Wolfram does not say by whom the Grail "permitted itself to be carried" (T 24) during the two generations before Schoysiane came of age. Albrecht says it "hovered."

Bartsch (p. 143): Provençal *repense*, "concept, essence," + *de joie*: "epitome of joy." Martin: ? "Recollection of Joy," from French *repenser*. The final *n* in T 10,4, Martin says, shows that the three-word name was taken as *one* word. French has no noun form of *répandre* (Latin *pandere*), "to shed, spread, strew."

Loomis, pp. 376–9, shows that the Grail Bearer (and her equivalents in various continental stories) is identical with the "Loathly Damsel" whom Wolfram calls *Cundrie la sorcière*: both = the Irish goddess Eriu, a personification of Ireland, beautiful in summer and monstrously ugly in winter. Eriu has other names also: The Sovranty of Ireland, Cathleen ni Houlihan, etc.

WALEIS (*Wâ-*)—40,3 ". . . and Gahmuret brought (Schionatulander) back again to Waleis."

8 x in P as a country; 2 x as a nationality; 13 x as *der Wâleise*, meaning Parzival, who is "the Angevin" only once, ambiguously, in 746; that title is used 16 x for Gahmuret and 16 x for Feirefiz, as Gahmuret's elder son. Chrétien's *li Galois*, 6 x in "Perceval," = *der Wâleis/die Wâleise*, but not always in parallel positions in the two texts.

The two countries, Waleis and Norgals, were bequeathed to Herzeloyde by King Castis, (P 494); she ruled them for an unspecified period until her marriage to Gahmuret and then, while Gahmuret was in the East (for the second time), she ruled them again, and Anjou as well, (P 103). Waleis and Norgals were wrested away in her early widowhood by "the proud, bold Lehelin", (P 128)—no mention of Anjou at that point, but in P 803 Parzival assigns all *three* kingdoms to future rule by his small son Kardeiz-2.

4 x in Chrétien's "Perceval": 501 and 603 (Roach ed.), the crude costume of *Gales*; 2753 *Disnadaron en Gales* (= *Dîanasdrûn*, as a city of Arthur's in P 216, 432, 525, and, we believe, Dinas Bran, a site in NE Wales; see under "Brubarz" above); 4134 *Saint Davi,/Que l'en aore et pric en Gales*, (= Saint David/Dewi, patron saint of Wales).

For the *country* Wales, Flutre lists *Gales/Galles* for more than 40 romances, *Wales* for 3, and 1 each: *Walie, Walis, Wale/Walle*, and *Guales*; (also *Gale/Galle* and *Gaule* for "Gaul"). For the *inhabitants* of Wales,

Flutre lists *Galeis/Galois* for 13 romances, plus variants *Gasois, Hasois*. Note also: *Parcefâl von Glois* in Hartman's *Erec* 1684; the adjective *gâlois* in Gotfried's *Tristan*, and "Galoes" as the name of Gahmuret's older brother.

We list the modern terms, which are themselves sometimes confusing:

	the country	*the inhabitants*	*the language*
English:	Wales	Welshman, Welshwoman Welshmen, Welshwomen the Welsh adjective: Welsh	Welsh
French:	le Pays de Galles (but "Gaul" = la Gaule)	Gallois, Galloise adjective: gallois(e) (but "Gallic" and "Gaulish" are both gaulois(e)	le gallois
German:	Wales (pronounced "Wallis")	Walliser(in) adjective: wallisisch	wallisisch
Welsh:	Cymru	(masc.) Cymro, (pl.) Cymry (fem.) Cymraes adjective: cymreig (English: "Cymric")	Cymraeg

These Welsh forms reflect a native word used after ca. 600 A.D. and known in Latin as *Combroges* (singular *Combrox*), "co-landers." The base-word is represented in Gaulish as *broga*, "country," (cognate with Latin *margo*, Germanic *marca*, and English "march," in the sense of "border district;" this is the word *bro* discussed under "Brubarz" above). Compare the *Allobroges*, (singular *Allobrox*; Horace: Epode 16,6), "other-landers," "exiles," who were the Keltic ancestors of the inhabitants of Savoy and Dauphiné.

From the same native word Medieval Latin formed *Cambria*,

"Wales." The variant *Cumbria* developed separately into "Cumberland," the NW county of England, centered on Carlisle.

English "Wales" developed out of Old English *wealas*, (singular *wealh*), "foreigners;" Anglo-Norman *Guales/Gualles*, Latinized by Geoffrey of Monmouth as *Gualia*; elsewhere *Wallia*. The English adjective "Welsh" comes from Old English *wǣlisc*, "foreign." (Compare German *welsch*, "south-European, of Romance-language origin," and Swiss *Welschschweiz*, "French-speaking Switzerland, *la Suisse romande;*" also *Kauderwelsch*, "jibberish.")

Linguistically, *Norgâls* = "North Wales," and *Wâleis* = "Wales." Both terms are OF and necessarily after 1066, though to Wolfram they were probably *merely* names. He probably did not realize that "Wales" *included* "North Wales," so that it would be futile to constrain *Wâleis* to mean geographical South Wales or the political kingdom of Deheubarth.

Under "Extra Note 1: Valois" at the end of this item we explain why we reject the identification of *Wâleis* with the N-French region of Valois, claimed by Bartsch, Martin, and Marti.

Under "Extra Note 2: Spain" we explain why we reject Jessie Weston's 1894 claim that *Wâleis* and *Norgâls* "are located by Wolfram in Spain."

Geography

An overview of Chrétien's "Perceval" to line 4813 (parallel to Books III–IV–V of P) shows a scenario that could have been appropriately set in in northern Wales in some "earlier" Welsh version of the story "before 1100."

The hero grew up in the region of Mount Snowdon (Loomis, p. 490), the area of Wales least troubled by warfare. He rode his nag to Arthur's court, quite plausibly to be localized at the legend-haunted Roman ruins of Segontium just outside of modern Caernarvon, (Loomis: *From Segontium to Sinadon*, in *Speculum* XXII, 4 (1947), pp. 520–533). Thence he rode eastwards to the broad River Conway, following downstream to Gornemans's castle at the Conway estuary, and thence to another seaside town—"Biaurepaire"—on the north coast of Wales. Leaving that city to revisit his mother, he rode by mistake southeasterly to "the district of Bran," our *Bro Bran** (as explained under "Brubarz" above), north of Llangollen and to the hill

of Dinas Bran (Chrétien's *Disnadaron*, Wolfram's *Dianazdrun*) over-
looking the River Dee; in the hilltop castle there he beheld the food-
and-drink-multiplying talisman of the *graal* as the legendary king
"Bran the Blessèd" sumptuously feasted. The very name of Gah-
muret, as explained under "Gahmuret" above, is traceable to *Gwy-
nedd*, which regularly signified the political kingdom in the northwest
of Wales and which sometimes included the whole of North Wales.

In Breton transmission this original, coherent geography was gar-
bled, and the hero's adventures, once he had left home, were re-set
in and around the Forest of Broceliande SW of Rennes in Brittany,
as evidenced by the *Brizljân* of P 129, 206, 253, and 271. Arthur's
kingdom in P is *Bertâne/Bre-/Bri-* (12 x), and its capital city is Nantes
(12 x). Chrétien's "Perceval" mentions neither the Forest of Broce-
liande, nor Nantes, nor Arthur's kingdom of *Bertâne*, though Arthur's
subjects are *li Breton* in line 4320 (Roach ed.). We therefore postulate
Wolfram's use of a "Perceval" manuscript differing from the fifteen
known to us, or else deliberate intrusion of "Arthurian" place names
from other sources. Arthur's realm also includes *Cardoeil* ("Perceval"
336, 839)/*Karidoel* (4 x in P), which, linguistically, = Carlisle, in the
north of England. Wolfram also makes the Grail territory (our "dis-
trict of Bran") adjacent to *Brizljân/Broceliande*, with the River Plimizoel
to separate them. The river name, as suggested in our *Willehalm*, p.
375, may = *Plim* + Breton *izel*, "lower," i.e., the river called Tamar
which separates Cornwall from Devon and which reaches the English
Channel at "Plym-mouth." Modern Breton *Breiz-Izel* = "Lower Brit-
tany." For the river Tamar/Plim, see C. M. Matthews: *Place Names in
the English-speaking World*; Scribners, New York, 1972; p. 112.

Under "Briton" above we estimated the scope of Wolfram's *Bertâne*.
The total geography of the story, however, was unrealistically gar-
bled *before* Wolfram, and in P Wolfram himself further adjusted the
geography for his own poetic purposes. An original setting is, never-
theless, in northern Wales, with telltale residues still to be discerned.

The Wales of History (to 1283)

Roman Wales

43—47　Roman invasion of Keltic Britain from the SE; frontier forts
　　at Lindum (Lincoln), Uniconium (Wroxeter), and Glevum
　　(Gloucester).
60—61　Frontier fort at Deva (Chester; *castra legionis*); invasion across
　　the N coast of Wales, including the island of Anglesea.
74—78　Governor General Julius Frontius conquered South Wales;

fort at Isca (Caerleon; *castra legionis*); the civilian settlement at Venta Silurum (Caerwent), 9 miles E of Isca, became the principal Roman town in Wales.

78 Julius Agricola conquered central and northern Wales; fort at Segontium, near modern Caernarvon.

78—ca. 380 Direct Roman rule in Wales; little Romanization except around Caerwent. Roads connected the major forts at the four corners of Wales: Segontium (NW), Deva (NE), Isca (SE), and Maridunum (Carmarthen, SW).

410 Roman withdrawal from *Britannia* (Keltic *Prydyn*), leaving local administrators to rule until a promised return; the Romans never returned.

400—616 A tumultuous period, imperfectly documented.

Ninth-century tradition assigned to "400–450" the arrival in North Wales of a leader named Cunedag (modern Cunedda) and his eight sons from S Scotland and their founding of the Kingdom of Gwynedd, centered probably at the Conway estuary on the N coast of Wales. These were the *Cymry,* "co-landers," "compatriots."

Between 410 and 450 English raids on the E and S coasts of Britain; then intensified raids and piecemeal conquests, forcing the semi-Romanized Kelts westwards. Irish raids on the west coast of Wales were followed by Irish settlements in NW and SW Wales. Picts out of Scotland harassed the N border of Roman Britain.

Local Keltic dynasties, sometimes claiming Roman descent, ruled as best they could, while many Kelts migrated across the Channel to Armorica (Brittany).

Even before 400, SW Wales saw a revival of pagan Keltic religion, e.g., a new temple to the god Nodens (= Wolfram's "Noyt"). Christianity probably came to North Wales ca. 500, from Irish "holy men."

516 (or 518) The westward advance of the English was halted at an unidentified "Mount Badon" in the upper Thames valley; the victory was later attributed to "Arthur."

537 Arthur perished in the Battle of (unidentified) Camlann, according to the *Annales Cambriae* of ca. 955.

ca. 550 The English advance resumed, taking all of what is now western England and southern Scotland; capture of Chester, 616, followed by a temporary invasion of North Wales.

616—844

Two North-Welsh kingdoms maintained local rule: Gwynedd (Medieval Latin *Venedotia/Venedocia*) and Powys. South Wales was fragmented under local Welsh chieftains.

844—1066

The male line from Cunedag/Cunedda having died out, Rhodri

Mawr (through his grandmother) inherited Gwynedd, 844; he succeeded his uncle as King of Powys, 855, and his brother-in-law as King of Ceredigion ("Cardigan"), 871; but this near-unification of Wales was undone by his death in 878, when his sons partitioned his territories.

942   Hywel Dda, grandson of Rhodri Mawr, combined his own inherited lands with his wife's South-Welsh territories, then (942) seized Gwynedd. Ca. 950 Gwynedd revolted.

986—999   Maredudd, Hywel's grandson, regained Gwynedd. In 999 Gwynedd revolted.

1018—1023   Llewlyn ap Seisall, Maredudd's son-in-law, usurped Gwynedd. In 1023 Gwynedd revolted.

1039   Gruffydd ap Llewlyn seized Gwynedd, and, ca. 1041, most of Wales.

1062—1063   Harold the Saxon invaded Gwynedd; Gruffydd ap Llewlyn was assassinated.

1066   Harold the Saxon became King of England, January 6, 1066; died October 14, 1066, in the Battle of Hastings against William the Conqueror, who, on Christmas Day 1066, was crowned as King William I of England.

Wales in Norman times: 1066—1154

1066—1087   While William the Conqueror unified England his barons disrupted Wales, carving out vast estates where they ruled like petty kings. In general, they Normanized the plains and valleys of eastern Wales, leaving the hill country as "Welshries."

1087—1100   William II, "Rufus," allowed this process to continue; in 1094 the North-Welsh revolted and reestablished the Kingdom of Gwynedd.

1100—1135   Henry I acquired the first *royal* estates in Wales, around Carmarthen in the SW, whence he granted subsidiary districts to his supporters.

1135—1154   While civil war raged in England between King Stephen I and "the Empress Maude," the Welsh drove the English out of Wales and reestablished the kingdoms of Gwynedd, Powys, and Deheubarth (South Wales). (Pronounce: De-HÜ-barth.)

Wales in Angevin times: 1154—1283

1154—1189   With England reunited, Henry II sought to reestablish royal domains around Carmarthen, but in four separate struggles he was forced to recognize Rhys ap Gruffydd as King of Deheubarth.

1188   Giraldus Cambrensis (Gerald the Welshman) made his tour of Wales; his *Itinerary* is a prime source work for the era.

1189—1199   During the reign of Richard I, the Lion Heart, the sons of "the Lord Rhys" partitioned Deheubarth at their father's death, 1197. In the same decade Llewlyn ap Iorwerth began a successful reunification of Gwynedd, which had been fragmented since the reign of his grandfather, Owain Gwynedd.

Of the various Llewlyns in Welsh history, this Llewlyn ap Iorwerth is the one most likely to be represented in *Parzival* in the name of *Lehelin*.

1199—1216   King John I began his reign by invading Gwynedd and forcing Llewlyn ap Iorwerth to surrender, but troubles in England called his home and, as soon as he was gone, Llewlyn ap Iorwerth returned to power.

By supporting John's rebellious vassals Llewlyn gradually increased his holdings until he had direct or indirect control over almost the whole of Wales.

1216—1272   Under Henry III the prestige of Llewlyn ap Iorwerth and of Wales reached maximum. Officially, Llewlyn became "the Prince of Aberffraw and Lord of Snowdonia;" he was also termed "Llewlyn the Great." But at his death in 1240 his well-intentioned son David was unable to sustain his father's power, with the result that in 1247 Henry III was able to reduce the three Welsh kingdoms to vassal status.

In 1267 Llewlyn ap Gruffydd, grandson of Llewlyn the Great, defied Henry III anew and reestablished Welsh power.

1272—(1307)   Edward I, returning from Crusade in 1274, invaded Wales and defeated Llewlyn ap Gruffydd.

The definitive English conquest of Wales is usually dated to 1283.

After 1272 Edward I built the great castles of Gwynedd: Caernarvon, Harlech, Conway, Beaumaris (on the island of Anglesea), etc. The division into shires dates from the same period.

(The all-Wales revolt of Owain Glyndŵr—the Owen Glendower of Shakespeare's *Henry IV, Part I*—came in 1400–1403 and gradually died out 1404–1409.)

Extra Note 1: Valois

Bartsch, p. 117, simply states that, where Chrétien understood *Gales* to be Wales, Wolfram's *Wâleis* signifies Valois. A footnote remarks that *Diu Crône* 2208 ff. distinguishes between *Gâlois* and *Wâlois*. No evidence is offered.

Martin tended to agree that *Wâleis* = Valois. Marti's Names Index unqualifiedly defines *Wâleis* as Valois, and the notes to P 59,23, 103,7, and 121,5 strive to defend this interpretation.

Special pleading marks the note to 103,7: *Wâleys* means "Valois" though it is "blended" (*verquickt*) with "Wales."

The distinction made by *Diu Crône* needs to be examined. The first episode (466–3131) of that poem depicts King Arthur's Christmas festival at Tintaguel, to which a supernatural knight out of the sea has come, bringing a huge drinking cup: only those loyal in love can drink from it without spilling. In a series of comic mishaps "Parzival the *Gâlois* took the cup next after the *Wâlois* and drank" (*Parzival der Gâlois/ Der nam nâch dem Wâlois/ Den kopf unde tranc*; 2208–10). Again the wine spills

> because of the poor Fisher (*Vischaere*) whom (Parzival) left in great distress when from courtesy he left him without asking any question, as the maiden later told him . . . as he left the tree where he found her sitting and as she recognized the power of the sword that his uncle had given him as he was about to ride home (*dô er wolde rîten heim*). (2214–2221)

Compare P 249, 255, 253–4, and 239, in that order.

"The *Wâlois*" is *Calocrêant* (Hartman's *Iwein* 92 *Kâlogrêant*; Chrétien's *Yvain* 57 *Calogrenant*). Loomis, p. 275, explains: *Cailo-grenant*, "Kay the Grumbler," from the verb *grenir*; in other words, a "doublet" of Kay. The Welsh *Cei* was Arthur's "knight" from earliest times, (Bromwich: *The Welsh Triads*, pp. 393–7), and tradition located his castle near Lake Bala in Gwynedd. There was nothing "Valois" about him or about his "doublet." The present *Calocrêant* appears only in this passage; no one else is called a *Wâlois* in the poem; in our opinion, *Gâlois* and *Wâlois* were two decorative adjectives in Heinrich von dem Türlin's "Arthurian" vocabulary, he opposed them in a single facile rhyme-pair, and understood nothing geographical whatsoever about them. Heinrich's home province is unknown, though he concludes his poem with a remark hostile to Swabians; Lachmann thought he might have lived in the Tyrol, the Alpine region of western Austria.

Diu Crône 332–5 lists eight countries of Arthur's: *Britanje, Gâl, Normandîe, Rinâl, Scote, Îrlant, Wâlois,* and *Engellant,* of which the last four "summarize" the British Isles; *Gâl* is likely to be "Gaul;" *Rinâl* is unidentified. Six nationalities in 623–5 are: *Briton, Norman, Mande* (?), *Wâloise, Engloise,* and *Franzoise.* We believe the two cases represent "Wales" and "Welsh" respectively, with no hint of "Valois" about either of them. In short, the alleged opposition of *Gâlois* and *Wâlois* in 2208–9 amounts to nothing more than a freakish rhyme.

Valois itself, moreover, knew no particular distinction until after 1328.

> As a region ca. 50 miles NE of Paris, it constituted the Merovingian and early Carolingian administrative district of the *pagus Vadensis,* chief town Vez. Annexed to Vermandois after 1077, it became a comté which was annexed to the royal domain in 1214; in 1406 it was elevated into a duchy. It now comprises, approximately, the *départements* of Aisne and Oise; chief town Crépy-en-Valois, population ca. 6,500. The name became well known only with the line of French kings of the House of Valois, 1328–1589.

Nor is there any reason whatsoever for identifying *Wâleis* with the Swiss canton of *Valais,* though—almost inevitably—that claim has now been made in *Holy Blood, Holy Grail,* by Baigent, Leigh, and Lincoln; Delacorte Press, New York, 1982.

> Canton *Valais* (German *Wallis,* Italian *Valese*) in SW Switzerland consists essentially of the upper Rhone valley, between very high Alps; capital *Sion* (German *Sitten*); cantonal population 148,000. The name has nothing to do with that Germanic term for "foreigners" mentioned above, but represents Latin *vallis,* "valley," translating prehistoric Keltic *Nantos* of the same meaning.

Extra Note 2: Spain

Nor is Wagner's last opera, *Parsifal* (text by 1887; première 1883) set "in the mountains of northern Spain," though program

notes to that work and editors' forewords to its libretto regularly
so affirm. The text of *Parsifal* does not mention Spain; the text
of *Lohengrin* (1845; première 1851) does not mention Spain; Wag-
ner himself, in his non-creative writings, never said anything
of the sort.

Musical program notes are commonly mines of misinforma-
tion, but even a fine scholar like Jessie L. Weston, in a note to
P 59,23 (p. 304, Vol. I, of her 1894 *Parzival* translation), says that

> . . . the two kingdoms of Queen Herzel*e*ide are located by
> Wolfram in Spain, but they are undoubtedly Wales and North
> Wales (the North galis of Malory), the Northern border-land.

The spelling "Herzel*e*ide" reflects Miss Weston's deliberate
choice, in her enthusiasm for Wagner's opera, but her false and
curiously hedged geographical claim reflects a notion *about* that
opera which may well have been Wagner's own.

Wagner's own misconception derives from the 78-page Intro-
duction to Joseph Görres's 1813 edition of the 13th-century poem
of *Lohengrin*—see p. 35 above—which Wagner read in the sum-
mer of 1845. In those 78 pages of reckless pseudo-scholarly fan-
tasy Görres devoted half the space, not to the 13th-century poem
of *Lohengrin,* but to "The Later Titurel," and on page XI we
read:

> The temple of *Montsalvaez* is located in *Salvatierra,* not, as has
> been thought, in distant *Galicia,* but in *Aragon* at the entry-
> point of Spain, close by the valley of *Ronceval* and the great
> highroad that leads from France toward *Galicia* and *Compos-
> tello.*

Görres cites no basis for this claim in "The Later Titurel," for
the simple reason that "The Later Titurel" says nothing of the
sort. In southern Spain, between Toledo and Córdoba, there
was indeed a Castle Salvatierra, captured from the Moors in the

1160s, lost again, and recaptured in 1212, and it was associated with the military-religious Order of Calatrava, founded in 1158. The location is nowhere near the point described by Görres, and the point alleged by him is in Navarre, not in Aragon. The spelling "Montsalvaez" appears to be Görres's own pseudo-Spanish. Whence Görres in his turn derived this misinformation is not known to the present writer. The 1858 edition of the 13th-century poem of *Lohengrin* (1970 photographic reprint) by Heinrich Rückert finds Görres's poem-text "unusable in every respect," but it passes in silence over the sea of errors in Görres's Introduction.

Wolfram's Grail *castle* (*burc*) of Munsalvaesche is located "somewhere" in the fabulous land of *Bertâne.* So too, doubtless, is "the Fisher King's" castle, of no name, in Chrétien's "Perceval." In Welsh tradition the counterpart was some structure, real or imaginary, on top of the high hill of Dinas Bran north of Llangollen in NE Wales.

In "The Later Titurel," however, Albrecht half-committed himself to a location on lands donated by "France," "Anjou," and "Cornwall" (H-265). But if "Anjou" and "France" (in the sense of the royal domain) are contiguous with each other, neither is contiguous with Cornwall (*kornuale,* H-265 and H-103),— whether Albrecht understood the Cornwall of SW Britain or the Cornouaille now contained within the *département* of Finisterre at the western extremity of Brittany.

To us, Albrecht's location suggests either a garbled or a deliberately adapted description of the famous Benedictine establishment of Mont Saint-Michel, at high tide on an island off the SW corner of Normandy but accessible at low tide to foot-goers from the mainland. After war-damage in 1203 Philip II, Augustus, of France sponsored important construction there; and in 1256—when "The Later Titurel" is likely to have been in composition—Saint King Louis IX made a pilgrimage to Mont Saint-Michel and generously contributed to further construction, including systematic fortifications. The architecture is Norman Gothic. The establishment was also renowned in the twelfth and thirteenth centuries as a seat of learning.

So much for Albrecht's imagined *site*. His grandiose Grail *temple* is more difficult to account for. Reports of splendid new constructions at Mont Saint-Michel may have set his imagination soaring, and he may have combined those impressions with reports of Hagia Sophia in Constantinople or of the Dome of the Rock in Jerusalem,—or even with reports (through channels hard to conceive) of the world-omphalos of the Zoroastrians at Shiz. We tend, in any case, to see the Grail temple of "The Later Titurel" as an imaginary structure.